Library of Congress Cataloging-in-Publication Data:

Names: Vincent, Nishani, author. | Igou, Amy, author.
Title: Emerging technologies for business professionals : a nontechnical
    guide to the governance and management of disruptive technologies /
    Nishani Vincent & Ms Amy Igou.
Description: Hoboken, New Jersey : Wiley, [2023] | Includes index.
Identifiers: LCCN 2023020824 (print) | LCCN 2023020825 (ebook) | ISBN
    9781119987369 (cloth) | ISBN 9781119987383 (adobe pdf) | ISBN
    9781119987376 (epub)
Subjects: LCSH: Business enterprises—Technological innovations. |
    Artificial intelligence. | Blockchains (Databases) | Computer security.
Classification: LCC HD45 .V563 2023 (print) | LCC HD45 (ebook) | DDC
    658.5/14—dc23/eng/20230719
LC record available at https://lccn.loc.gov/2023020824
LC ebook record available at https://lccn.loc.gov/2023020825

Cover Design: Wiley
Cover Image: © Galeanu Mihai/Getty Images
Author Photos: Nishani Vincent - © University of Tennesee at Chattanooga;
Amy Igou - © Sean O'Neal

SKY10052794_080823

EMERGING TECHNOLOGIES FOR BUSINESS PROFESSIONALS

A NONTECHNICAL GUIDE TO THE GOVERNANCE AND MANAGEMENT OF DISRUPTIVE TECHNOLOGIES

Nishani Vincent and Amy Igou

WILEY

CONTENTS

ACKNOWLEDGMENTS   V

CHAPTER 1 Introduction to Emerging Technologies   1

CHAPTER 2 Information Technology and Ethics   15

CHAPTER 3 Introduction to Data Analytics   27

CHAPTER 4 Data Analytics Governance and Management   51

CHAPTER 5 Introduction to Artificial Intelligence   71

CHAPTER 6 Artificial Intelligence Implementation and Management   87

CHAPTER 7 Cryptocurrency and Blockchain   107

CHAPTER 8 Blockchain Developments and Governance   127

CHAPTER 9 The Metaverse and Non-Fungible Tokens   147

CHAPTER 10 Introduction to Robotic Process Automation   163

CHAPTER 11 Robotic Process Automation Implementation and Management   179

CHAPTER 12 Quantum and Edge Computing   201

CHAPTER 13 Augmented Reality   219

CHAPTER 14 Introduction to Cybersecurity   233

CHAPTER 15 Cybersecurity Management   249

APPENDIX: GOVERNANCE FRAMEWORKS 265

ABOUT THE AUTHORS 281

ABOUT THE WEBSITE 283

INDEX 285

ACKNOWLEDGMENTS

A special thanks to our accounting department colleagues, in particular, our department chairs, Rebecca Shortridge and Joseph Ugrin, for their support and encouragement. Thank you to our graduate assistants, Reedhi Bamnelkar, James Cooper, and Derek LaBarge, for their assistance in compiling material for the book. We also appreciate the love and support from our families, especially our husbands, Vinod Vincent and Patrick Igou, for their patience during this project.

CHAPTER 1

Introduction to Emerging Technologies

Netflix versus Blockbuster – The Original Disruption

Blockbuster, in its prime, had a stronghold on the U.S. video rental industry. It had brick-and-mortar stores in 2,800 locations worldwide in 1992 and 9,000 stores at its peak. Two years later, Viacom purchased Blockbuster for $84 million. During the 1990s, a Blockbuster store offered the latest releases and classic movie hits for the entire family in most neighborhoods. Besides revenue from rentals, Blockbuster also made significant income from late fees.

When Netflix arrived on the scene with a subscription-based DVD rental business in 1997, Blockbuster did not see it as a worthy competitor. Netflix, known today for its streaming service, started renting out DVDs. For a monthly fee, subscribers entered a wish list of movies they wished to view, and Netflix sent the customer their first two DVDs. When the customer finished with the video, they sent the DVD back to Netflix, which would, in turn, send a different DVD from the subscriber's wish list. A subscriber could keep any DVD for as long as they wanted, thus eliminating the pressure to return a movie on time to avoid costly late fees.

Netflix infiltrated this market by utilizing technology to provide what the customer wanted – reasonably priced, convenient entertainment. Their model also eliminated late fees, which were the customers' least favorite feature of Blockbuster. As of January 2021, Netflix was worth over $230 billion, whereas in 2022, Blockbuster had one remaining store, in Bend, Oregon.

(Continued)

(*Continued*)

> Netflix is considered to be one of the first companies to use the internet to reach customers and completely change the entertainment business. While the concept may seem relatively simple today, the change in the home entertainment business was revolutionary and started a new trend of digital disruption by changing an entire industry.
>
> Blockbuster CEO Jim Keyes stated in an interview in 2008, "Neither Redbox nor Netflix is even on the radar screen in terms of competition."[1] Looking back, maybe they should have been.

Impact of Emerging Technology

The past decade has seen significant technical advances leading to a flurry of new technologies. Technology implementation and management traditionally required technical skills possessed by information technology (IT) professionals. Historically, automating a process required heavy coding and the specialized technical skills of an IT professional. However, today, the addition of new end-user tools, combined with better processing speeds, has put technology in the hands of the end-user. For example, robotic process automation (RPA) software enables nontechnical users to automate basic processes without significant technical knowledge. Consequently, the developments in software and hardware tools have made it easy for nontechnical users in all areas of the organization to be active participants in using technology. The increased dependence on technology, not only for communication, collaboration, record-keeping, and decision-making but also for improving efficiency, increasing profitability, creating a competitive advantage, and innovating new products and services, makes understanding emerging technologies critical for all business professionals.

The proliferation of emerging technologies is disrupting organizations and industries more than ever. A period of rapid technological change generally disrupts how businesses operate and what services and products they offer. For many, the term *disruption* has a negative connotation. However, disruption can bring new opportunities for those who anticipate and embrace the change. Gartner defines digital disruption as "the effect that changes the fundamental expectations and behaviors in a culture, market, industry or process through digital capabilities."[2] Digital disruption often leads to new products and services and possibly new industries. An existing business that does not adapt and take advantage of new developments can be left behind and become the Blockbuster of the current generation. With a strategic mindset, companies can create a competitive advantage, even with minor technological changes. Early examples of disruption included cars replacing horses, telephones replacing telegraphs, and online reference sites replacing traditional encyclopedias. Recent advances in technology have already transformed several industries. Consider these examples:

- One of the largest taxi companies does not own any vehicles (Uber).
- One of the largest accommodation providers does not own any real estate (Airbnb).
- One of the largest retailers does not hold any inventory (Alibaba).

When managers think about increasing productivity, exploring new revenue models, moving into untapped markets, or cutting the cost of operations, they revert to technological solutions. Often, people think that technology can solve the problems they face in a company. Today's managers are more likely to embrace technology because they are familiar with and dependent on smart devices, such as smartphones, watches, TVs, and virtual assistant technologies. However, using technology will not always solve the problems facing a company but will always increase the risks to the company if not properly managed. For example, during an English professional football game, the automated technology did not notify match officials to award a goal. Players and the goalpost blocked all goal line cameras, preventing unobstructed tracking of the ball into the goal. The lack of a clear view by the cameras cost one team a point and determined the outcome of the championship match.[3] Even though this technology worked properly in 9,000 previous games, one failure was detrimental to one team. Therefore, organizations must consider these isolated risks as they weigh new technology options.

Many organizations chase the latest technology without considering the long-term implications, functionality, risks, and threats, thus picking the wrong solution for the wrong task in the short and long terms. Therefore, when adopting, implementing, and using technology, managers must do their due diligence to understand which technologies would help their organization thrive in changing markets while minimizing threats.

When selecting technology, organizations must keep the users in mind. Individuals will only use the technology if they find it easy to use and valuable. For example, a customer service manager may consider using chatbots to support customer service inquiries, focusing on the benefit of cost savings while increasing productivity. However, if the chatbot is not implemented correctly, it may frustrate customers and increase customer dissatisfaction. It will also increase the costs of resolving issues and complicate maintaining the company's image and reputation.

Technologies, such as artificial intelligence, in manufacturing, procurement, and sales generation, can increase companies' productivity. However, using artificial intelligence can also increase risks to the company if management ignores ethical issues. This technology may also increase vulnerability to cyberattacks and other security risks.

Marketing professionals use advanced analytics techniques by gathering data from new sources to gain insights into their customers. However, not understanding the process and tools may lead to bias and inaccurate interpretation of data, leading to bad decisions. Consequently, a better understanding of technological advances will help managers determine the right solution for the right task and manage the associated risks.

Business managers and external stakeholders, such as auditors and regulators, need a broad understanding of technologies and how they are used in organizations to provide insights into financial information. To provide assurance of financial statements, auditors must understand whether the client organization accurately captured, processed, analyzed, and reported the data. Suppose data is collected and analyzed using emerging technologies. In that case, auditors need to understand how technology influences the processing of data when collecting evidence. They also need to evaluate critically the outputs generated using technology. Further, regulators need to know how emerging technologies, such as blockchain, may impact the capital market and provide oversight and guidance over organizations to protect the investors and maintain fair, orderly, and efficient markets.

This book is designed to help nontechnical business professionals navigate the complex and changing world of new technologies. All business professionals will benefit from foundational knowledge of many of the disruptive technologies available today. By understanding each technology's functionality, risks, and benefits, professionals can help make better-informed decisions when selecting and managing technologies. In this book, you will find:

- A single source of information for a variety of emerging technologies.
- A nontechnical explanation of the functionality of a given emerging technology.
- Examples and use cases to help relate technical topics to a specific business context.
- A discussion on challenges, issues, and concerns related to the management and governance of a particular technology.
- Discussions on how disruptive technologies will impact business operations.

This book will help professionals understand the complexity involved in making decisions on technology adoption, implementation, management, governance, compliance, and reporting, and hence, be active and informed technology participants in their organizations.

IT Governance

Knight Capital Americas LLC was a financial services firm with its primary operations on the execution of market trades. Before Knight's collapse, it was the largest trader of U.S. equities. However, that abruptly stopped in 2012, when a system failure caused the firm to incur $440 million in trading losses in 45 minutes. Within two days, its market capitalization fell by approximately 80%.[4]

Since Knight was engaged in high-volume stock trades, it relied heavily on technology to process the transactions. Two months before the incident, Knight's CEO, Thomas Joyce, commented, "Our data centers are some of the largest and most reliable in the industry. We spend tens of millions of dollars every year making our technology platform better, faster, and more reliable."[5]

On August 12, 2012, an error in one of the eight trading servers allowed the continued generation of trade orders without tracking which orders were completed. In short, the system created multiple trade orders when it should have only created one. The system sent 97 messages to employees, signaling an error in the trading system. However, the employees ignored the messages for over an hour. When a team responded to examine the situation, they operated without documentation on how to proceed. During this time, the server continued to generate trade orders en masse. A large number of trades affected stock prices, leading the New York Stock Exchange to stop trading affected stocks.

After the incident, the Securities and Exchange Commission (SEC) showed that Knight did not have proper risk management controls or supervision in place. The lack of controls led to both system failure and delayed detection. The company did not have adequate systems for testing and review. In 2013 the SEC fined Knight $12 million for not having controls in place for deployment and inadequate guidelines for how to respond.[4]

The story about Knight Capital Americas LLC exemplifies how system issues can negatively impact not only an organization's operations and financial performance but also the capital markets. Therefore, business managers, auditors, and regulators must consider whether proper oversight and controls have been established around technology to prevent, detect, and correct mistakes.

Governance in a corporation includes overseeing the business operations and the mechanisms used to control and hold the organization and its people accountable. Information technology governance is one component of corporate governance. However, because of the dependence on IT for business operations today, this single component has become not only the most significant subset of corporate governance but also the most complex.

The COBIT (Control Objectives for Information and Related Technologies) framework defines enterprise governance of information technology as the process by which

the board that oversees the definition and implementation of processes, structures and relational mechanisms in the organization that enable both business and IT people to execute their responsibilities in support of business/IT alignment and the creation of business value from I&T-enabled business investments.[6]

Information technology enables organizations to create value for their stakeholders, increase productivity and efficiency in operations, innovate new products and services, and serve new and niche markets, which leads to improved financial performance. As a result, managers are increasingly interested in adopting emerging technologies.

However, proper governance and management of IT risks and resources are particularly crucial when considering emerging technologies because of the uncertainties surrounding them and the novelty of the technologies. An organization takes risks each time it introduces a new system, but the risk is greater if the technology is unfamiliar to IT management and those in the company. Therefore, organizations must provide oversight over IT and be proactive in their IT management to ensure long-term success. These practices can help ensure that the organization can fulfill its mission and achieve its strategic goals.

Several governance frameworks and guidelines are available for managers to ensure that the systems and IT processes keep the company's assets safe and secure and minimize interruptions to business operations. The Appendix provides brief descriptions of several governance and assurance frameworks available. Good governance practices enable organizations to prioritize IT spending through budgetary controls and to align spending to support their strategic objectives. Governance practices help manage IT applications, infrastructure, and architecture and mitigate and control potential threats. These practices also help organizations to comply with regulations, manage and control third-party IT services, and support and maintain IT assets and resources. Governance and management of the entire information technology will create a competitive advantage for the organization by aligning IT with the business strategy. We look at several aspects of IT risks next.

IT Risks

Every business activity has some form of risk associated with it. Risk, by definition, is uncertainty. Risks can lead to negative or positive outcomes. Potential adverse outcomes are considered threats or events that may jeopardize an organization from achieving its objectives. In an organization, we want to mitigate adverse outcomes while increasing the positive effects. For example, when an organization decides to implement a new enterprise resource planning (ERP) system, the company is taking a risk. However, this decision can also lead to increased productivity, making it worthwhile to take the risk.

On the other hand, the centralized nature of the system can also increase cybersecurity vulnerability, which is a negative outcome. IT risks can stem from external sources, such as cybercriminals and third-party vendors, and internal sources, such as employees and various IT components. Every IT component at every level of the organization can increase IT threats. Table 1.1 shows some typical IT risks and an example of a negative consequence

Table 1.1   Potential IT Risks

IT Component	Potential Risks	Negative Consequence
Architecture	The planned or current architecture does not meet the needs of the stakeholders	Loss of competitive advantage and customer satisfaction
Infrastructure	Network crashes	Lost business and productivity
Information security	Unauthorized use of data, loss of data, system outages	Damage to the company's reputation. Potential for increased fines. Lost business and productivity
Hardware	Hardware malfunction	Loss of data, disruption to business operations
Software applications	Not having proper patch management controls	Disruptions to business operations, system malfunctions
IT development	Insufficient understanding of user requirements, development using incompatible technology, inadequate testing	Users not accepting the system, wasted resources, inaccurate system processing
People	Lack of IT skills, employee turnover, lack of IT security awareness	Not using the system for daily work. Increased security vulnerabilities
Change management	Incorporating unauthorized changes, inadequate testing	Fraudulent processes and business activities
Project management	Missing the target dates, cost overruns, inadequate resources	User dissatisfaction, increased costs, not meeting the target

associated with different IT components. Management should take extra care to mitigate these risks, especially when considering emerging technologies. In subsequent chapters, we discuss risks specific to a particular technology. Keeping these risks in mind can help organizations select the appropriate governance practices to optimize (reduce threats and create value) the risk to the organization.

When considering adopting, implementing, and using any technology, organizations should evaluate potential risks and develop a risk response to mitigate any dire negative consequences. All IT projects have uncertainties associated with them. Failure to mitigate these risks while planning and implementing a project can frequently lead to loss.

Why IT Projects Fail

Even with a skilled project team, good project management, and a plan, a new technology implementation may not be completed as expected. Experience shows that many system projects fail, that is, the project outcomes are never delivered, are significantly over budget, or, at minimum, do not meet the stakeholders' expectations.

Some well-documented project failures include:

- The U.S. government spent approximately $840 million to release the healthcare.gov online insurance site. In the first week, the system failed as millions of users attempted to use the system. Users became frustrated when they were unable to get their applications sent. The website was taken offline and rebuilt for a new deployment months later.[7]
- Lidl, a German grocery store chain, implemented a new inventory management system for 500 million euros, only to scrap the project three years later.[8]
- In 1999, Hershey's could not deliver its Halloween candy to the U.S. market due to an issue in the supply chain application of its newly installed ERP system.[9]

No matter the type of technology, several overarching factors can cause IT project failure. When using new technology, the risks can be even more significant. Managers should consider some of the following factors when adopting, implementing, and using emerging technologies.

- **Not understanding the technology selected.** Before adding new technology into the organization, managers should be sure that they understand its functionality, advantages, appropriateness for a given business context, and potential risks. Each technology offers different benefits that should be maximized and threats that need to be mitigated.

- **Not understanding the needs of the business.** Business managers need to work closely with their IT partners to understand the business requirements and how business processes affect the underlying financial performance of the organization. Managers can assign business team members to IT project teams to increase and enhance communication between business and IT.

- **Expecting a silver bullet.** Most often, end-users and nontechnical business managers assume that new technology will solve all problems. Implementing a new technology on top of existing flawed processes will not fix the root problem. Expecting the system to fix everything will only lead to disappointment. Therefore, managers should do their due diligence to understand the new features of the latest technology and how it will create value for the organization before deciding to adopt and implement it.

- **Not defining the scope of the project.** A clear definition of the system's boundary (i.e., where the project starts and ends) is necessary to implement any technology successfully. Scope definition begins with a clear understanding of what processes will be implemented and, more importantly, what will not be included. Otherwise, if the project scope keeps changing, the project deadline will be delayed, leading to frustration among stakeholders.

- **Not getting buy-in.** All stakeholders must agree that the project and the end objectives are needed. Buy-in is required for enterprise-wide implementations from the top down to the individual users. For implementations not acquiring buy-in from employees, there is a risk of nonacceptance by the users that will lead to finding ways to bypass the system.

- **Implementing the wrong technology for the issue.** Business and IT partners must best assess what technology solution will work for the desired task. When deciding which technology to implement, managers should consider the availability of resources, whether the solution matches the organization's needs and current industry standards, and how it affects its overall business strategy, mission, and vision.

These are just a few of the common causes of project failure. By understanding the reasons for potential failures of IT projects, managers can consider how to manage the risks of a given implementation. Additional risks of specific emerging technologies are discussed in subsequent chapters.

Managers can use the frameworks listed in the Appendix to help develop appropriate controls to reduce the overall negative outcomes and increase the positive outcomes of adopting emerging technologies.

Introduction to Technologies

This section provides a short synopsis of the technologies addressed in subsequent chapters.

Data Analytics

Analytics itself is not a new technology. However, today's analysis methods are much more advanced than those of 10 years ago. Some advanced analytical techniques are available through end-user software rather than tools that require significant coding. In addition, the types of data that can be analyzed are more varied than in decades past. Further, data analytics may need to navigate newer database models, such as graph databases, rather than relational databases.

Artificial Intelligence

Artificial intelligence, also known as AI, simulates human intelligence through a computer. Although advanced AI models can provide some degree of intelligence, these programs still lack consciousness and emotion. There are many uses of artificial intelligence, ranging from learning how to win a game, such as chess, to developing business forecasting models and understanding speech. You use AI in many daily tasks, such as asking Alexa or Siri questions, navigating to a new location, or choosing from many recommendations on your favorite streaming service.

Blockchain

Blockchain is the underlying technology used in many cryptocurrencies, such as Bitcoin. A blockchain stores data in a decentralized and distributed ledger, in contrast to a single instance of a traditional database. There are several applications of blockchain besides cryptocurrencies. Recent developments in smart contracts, the metaverse, non-fungible tokens (NFTs), and Oracles use blockchain development. Blockchain can be used in almost every industry, including financial services, logistics and supply management, real estate, and healthcare.

Robotic Process Automation

Robotic process automation, known as RPA, is a simplified form of artificial intelligence. This technology mimics human actions without learning or acting intelligently. RPA works similarly to an Excel macro but can work with various applications, including e-mail, ERP, and other systems. The automation between these systems is created without complex programming. The software is usually user-friendly so knowledgeable business end-users can build a bot to automate a task without coding.

The Metaverse and Non-Fungible Tokens

The metaverse has been depicted throughout science fiction novels and video games, but now it is a reality and has many implications for businesses. The metaverse is made up of connected virtual worlds in which individuals can interact, purchase virtual goods, and immerse themselves in different environments. New markets for virtual goods and entertainment will be available for businesses, as well as new ways to market goods and meet with others. Non-fungible tokens will play a larger part in the metaverse as they are digital assets that can be traded, bought, and sold online.

Advanced Computing

One of the major recent advances in computing is quantum computing. This revolutionary method of computing uses many of the principles of quantum theory to calculate and process data faster. These computers are best used for extensive data analyses or conducting simulations. Advanced computing can help expand other fields, such as artificial intelligence, machine learning, and blockchain.

Edge computing is a newer framework that also provides faster data processing by moving the computation and storage of data closer to the data sources. Data processing may occur on an Internet of Things (IoT) device or distributed servers enabling immediate data processing.

Augmented Reality and Virtual Reality

Augmented reality (AR) and virtual reality (VR) simulate an environment so the user can experience them through a device, such as an Oculus. Virtual reality is used frequently in gaming as it is a fictional environment where users can immerse themselves. Augmented reality is an environment that is overlaid with the real world. Businesses use these technologies to enhance training, facilitate employees' onboarding experience, prototype new products, and enhance the customer shopping experience, for example.

Cybersecurity

Incorporating emerging technologies in the organization's architecture and infrastructure increases a company's information technology risk exposure. Therefore, business professionals need to understand how information technology risks increase, how to protect their existing systems from insider and outsider attacks, assess the risk exposure and create appropriate risk responses, and audit and disclose appropriate information to the relevant stakeholder.

Final Thoughts

Selecting the appropriate technology can be a daunting task for managers. The first focus should be on what problem needs to be solved. Losing focus on this can lead an organization down the wrong path. Once managers have a general idea of the technical solution, many organizations benefit from following a system development methodology to help keep them on track and ensure proper controls throughout the process.

Notes

1. Satell, G. (2014). A Look Back at Why Blockbuster Really Failed and Why It Didn't Have To. *Forbes* (5 September). https://www.forbes.com/sites/gregsatell/2014/09/05/a-look-back-at-why-blockbuster-really-failed-and-why-it-didnt-have-to/?sh=760df3ec1d64.
2. Gartner. (n.d.). Gartner Glossary: Digital Disruption. https://www.gartner.com/en/information-technology/glossary/digital-disruption.
3. Ranson, J. and Gardner, J. (2022). Another Refereeing Nightmare! *MailOnline* (5 September). https://www.dailymail.co.uk/sport/football/article-11181079/EFL-confirm-hawk-eye-goal-line-technology-failure-major-error-Championship-clash.html.
4. Austin, R., and Meister, D. (2015). Knight Capital Americas LLC. Ivey Publishing. Available at https://hbsp.harvard.edu/product/W15077-PDF-ENG.
5. United States House of Representatives. (2012). Testimony of Mr. Thomas M. Joyce to the Committee on Financial Services Subcommittee on Capital Markets and Government Sponsored Enterprises (20 June). https://financialservices.house.gov/uploaded-files/hhrg-112-ba16-wstate-tjoyce-20120620.pdf.
6. ISACA. (2019). COBIT 2019 Framework. Introduction and Methodology.
7. Government Accountability Office. (2014). Healthcare.gov Ineffective Planning and Oversight Practices Underscore the Need for Improved Contract Management (July). https://www.gao.gov/assets/gao-14-694.pdf.
8. Grill, Gooman, J. (2018). Lidl Suffers €500 Million Euro Supply Chain Failure. *RIS-News* (1 October). https://risnews.com/lidl-suffers-eu500-million-supply-chain-failure.
9. Stedman, Craig. (1999). Failed ERP Gamble Haunts Hershey; Candy Maker Bites Off More Than It Can Chew and "Kisses" Big Halloween Sales Goodbye. *Computerworld* (1 November): 1.

CHAPTER 2

Information Technology and Ethics

The development of technology brings forth additional ethical questions. The following are some recent events that highlight some of the questions companies need to consider.

On January 13, 2021, the *Australian Financial Review* reported that Google had removed some Australian news content from its search results for some local users. A Google spokesperson told *The Conversation* that the experiment did not prevent users in the trial group from accessing a news story. Rather, they would not discover the story through the search function and would have to access it another way, such as directly on a publisher's website.[1]

"A Cambridge report published in October 2022 claims the United Kingdom police's use of facial recognition technology (FRT) has breached numerous ethical and human rights obligations. The report audited the use of facial recognition technology by the Metropolitan Police and the South Wales Police. The report outlined three key issues: privacy, discrimination, and accountability."[2]

Ethics

Technology can enhance many aspects of business operations and human conditions. However, as the two opening stories indicate, some uses of technology add complications when trying to maximize profit at the expense of others. Therefore, when introducing new technology, managers should consider how technology would impact society and individuals. In this chapter, we explain information technology ethics and discuss managerial considerations of IT ethics.

Ethics, Morals, and Law

What is ethical behavior? The Merriam-Webster dictionary defines ethics as the "discipline dealing with what is good and bad and with moral duty and obligation."[3] Even though many use ethics and morals synonymously, these terms have slightly different connotations today.

Morals are one's personal beliefs about right and wrong. These beliefs are generally influenced by religion, culture, social status, and upbringing, whereas ethics "deals with the justification of moral principles (or with the impossibility of such a justification) and must take into account the variations in moral systems."[4] Ethics recognizes that there are common features that are universally valid regardless of one's feelings, beliefs, culture, or religion.

On the other hand, the law attempts to make what is unethical illegal. Good legal practices allow similar freedom of activity for all people. However, the law generally lags behind developments in society. Laws, such as the apartheid law in South Africa,[5] are unethical; therefore, the law cannot be equated with ethics. Moreover, not every unethical action can be made illegal because ethics can be broad and allow for degrees or context.

In summary, ethics is not a religion, even though religion can set high ethical standards. It is also not the same as being lawful, and it is not the same as doing what society in general accepts. Next, we attempt to address why ethics is an important consideration in the use of information technology.

Information technology ethics is defined as the study of ethical issues related to the development and use of technology. Information technology has become ubiquitous in the lives of individuals and business operations. We use technology to operate business processes, analyze data, and communicate with internal and external stakeholders. Technology plays an important underlying role in the decision-making process. However, sometimes, the influence of technology and its unintended impacts are not at the forefront of decision-makers' considerations. Therefore, people often make decisions without understanding the complexity of the long-term implications and tend not to take responsibility for the outcomes of these decisions.

The following are several interrelated themes about why people avoid taking responsibility for their decisions and the corresponding outcomes.

- **The myth of amoral computing and information technology.**[5] The myth of amoral computing and information technology suggests that computers cannot use moral judgment. Therefore, it is improper to apply moral language to computers and their actions. This myth disregards the responsibility humans have when they purchase, design, develop, and use computers. People often ignore this responsibility because they do not understand the technology or its impact on others. Since technology can be complex, they pass on the blame to the technology. They perceive that what the computer does is not real and cannot affect others. Consequently, most people do not take responsibility for their decisions, how they design the system, and how it impacts others. However, as managers responsible for making technology-related decisions, you need to be aware of this myth and recognize that the outcome is a consequence of people's decisions, design, development, and use of the technology.

- **The lure of the technological imperative.**[5] Technology has advanced tremendously during the past few decades and has proliferated in organizations. To some extent, the use of the latest technology can be associated with achieving a higher status. For example, when an organization announces the adoption of new innovative technology, the market perceives this as a positive trend. Today, when faced with a business challenge, most managers believe that the latest technology would solve the problem. This pursuit of technological development without considering the immediate and long-term effects and consequences on society in general, employees, and other stakeholders can be dangerous. As managers, you need to be aware of how technology may lure you to the latest development. Therefore, it is important to do your due diligence when considering technology investments.
- **The danger of hidden structures.**[5] How the technology works and how it is developed is often hidden from the users. When a technology firm releases an update, what is being updated, how it might impact user behavior, and what other files are being accessed and shared may not be transparent to the user. As managers who make decisions about technology that impact the firm's customers, employees, and other stakeholders, you need to be aware when making technology-related decisions that there are hidden structures in the technology. Managers should encourage others to do their due diligence to understand the hidden design and the implications of the changes on business processes and various stakeholders and evaluate the impact of the use of the technology on people in the short and long terms.
- **The acceptance of technological inertia.**[5] All of us understand that technology has developed and that these developments have, in some ways, enhanced various aspects of our lives. However, most of us fail to accept that some elements may not be beneficial or ethical, despite the improvements to us. As managers, we should be willing to acknowledge the negative consequences and change the way the technology is developed or used in cases where it is not ethical.

- **Modularizing.**[6] Today, a single company does not produce all the parts necessary for the product it sells. In a competitive market, companies strive to produce small components to be assembled later by a different company. This disaggregation of development responsibility makes it difficult to know who is responsible for the ethical outcomes of the final product. Another related issue with modularization is that companies have no control over how another organization could use the simple component manufactured by your company in a complex, disruptive product. Therefore, it is important for managers to understand the inner workings of simple components and their impact on the larger, complex system/product to avoid unintended negative consequences.

Given these complexities and behavioral elements, managers need to be aware of their own biases and tendencies if they want to make ethical decisions about technology. Greater globalization leads to complex work environments and uncertain economic climates creating pressure to increase productivity and profit margins. When faced with such pressures today, managers turn to various technologies as a solution, often without considering the consequences of the decisions. However, considering ethics in technology-related decision-making can have several benefits, such as:

- Protecting the firm and its employees from legal actions.
- Complying with regulations.
- Creating a reputation of being an ethical and socially responsible company.
- Increasing productivity while improving processes.
- Retaining top talent by creating an ethical business environment.
- Reducing unnecessary risk by creating a fair business culture.

Reasons for IT Ethical Issues

Today, people want access to information and to obtain information using easy-to-use applications. They also expect to receive this information inexpensively or, preferably, for free. At the same time, users also want their information to be secure, reliable, and stable. Providing more security over information comes at a cost, conflicting with the ability to provide low-cost output. Further, lowering the costs of producing information may also impact the quality of information. These conflicting interests create the moral paradox of information technology. Therefore, program designers/developers have to make uncomfortable compromises when designing information systems.

When deciding on conflicting interests, several factors may influence decision-making concerning information technology and lead to ethical issues. The factors can be divided into data, system, and people categories.

Data-Related Factors

Data is central to decision-making; however, how we use data can have ethical implications. When making decisions, managers should consider whether the following practices would lead to intentional or unintentional harm to others.

- **The sources of data.** Organizations collect data at various points using various applications, devices, and systems. Technology makes it easy for organizations to collect, analyze, and use data. However, individuals may not have consented to or be aware that their data is being collected.
- **The increased volume of data.** Given the ease of obtaining data using technology, organizations collect massive amounts of data. Internet of Things devices collect more personal data than traditional sources do. Cell phones track movements and behavior to establish behavioral patterns that can be stored and misused. Much of the data collected by these devices is personal data about specific individuals.
- **Complex analytics.** Technology enables organizations to combine data from various sources to create a profile of an individual. As an individual, you may not be able to dictate whether the profile created for you is accurate. This profile can limit the type of services and products you see and the opportunities available to an individual.
- **Inconsistency in data.** Inadequate updating, incomplete data, erroneous data, and other data issues may lead to incorrect analyses creating false positives or negatives.
- **Fake data.** An increased amount of fake data and information makes it very difficult to identify which data is false and which data is not. Cleaning and separating fake from real data requires a lot of time and effort. Therefore, many users of data may not take the time to distinguish which data is reliable, leading to incorrect inferences.
- **Easy reproduction.** Digital data can be easily copied and distributed without the owner's knowledge. This dilemma leads to new concerns about data ownership and when it is ethical to use data without permission. Unlike physical assets, one may say that the data owner does not lose the original copy. However, the data may be proprietary and essential for an organization's ability to make a profit.

Systems-Related Factors

Decisions made during systems development can change how an application functions, possibly leading to ethical concerns. Management should consider these factors when developing new systems.

- **Complex systems.** Systems can be complex because of integration with other systems, modularity, and interactions between components. Many also have complex algorithms. The algorithm's decisions are not always visible to the users, especially when using neural networks or machine learning. The outputs produced by complex systems can influence management decision-making.
- **Large teams.** Large teams subdivided into small groups develop small components that make up integrated and complex systems. Lack of proper oversight and inadequate accountability can impact the final output of the system. Further, when using open-source software, where various users can make modifications, managers might lose control over design considerations, leading to unintended consequences.
- **Integration.** Most systems used in organizations are integrated with other systems. Not taking the time to evaluate whether integrated systems have the same level of controls, design considerations, and blind dependence on different system outputs can lead to ethical issues for the company.
- **Service providers.** Many organizations use a variety of software services provided by third parties. If managers do not understand where the third party is storing or using the data, it can lead to ethical concerns for the company. Not understanding the complex terms by third parties can also lead to ethical issues.

People-Related Factors

The final decisions are made by individuals, each having downstream ethical implications. It is important for managers to understand what motivates them throughout the decision-making process.

- **Black-box effect.** People blindly using outputs from various systems without fully understanding how the output was created may lead to ethical issues.
- **Impersonal interactions.** Automation is increasing remote work, changing how work is done and how people interact. This lack of interaction creates an impersonal environment, leading to more indifferent and distant relationships.

- **Line of command.** In the systems development process, the line of command from the decision-maker to the programmer can be very long. Therefore, people may blindly follow their immediate supervisor without questioning whether the choices have long- or short-term negative consequences for others. The long chain of command may blur the responsibility people have toward others.
- **Information overload.** A person cannot thoroughly analyze all available information given the increased volume of data. This causes a person to only focus on a subset of the data, which can lead to ethical issues.

Ethical Issues Related to Information Technology

Managers should consider the following to ensure ethical decision-making about technology. The oldest theoretical model discussing ethical issues in information and communication technologies identifies four main areas, namely privacy, accuracy, property, and accessibility.[7]

Privacy suggests that information systems should not invade someone's private space. Accuracy implies that the information collected is accurate and without errors or omissions. Property proposes the protection of intellectual property and the flow of information. Accessibility indicates that information systems should be accessible to all.

Below we discuss these issues in detail.

- **Privacy.** Today, for many businesses, the organization's most costly and valuable asset is data. Data can originate internally or externally and contain private or personal information about individuals, such as Social Security numbers, addresses, first and last names, and other personal details. Organizations are responsible for ensuring that this data is not misused and that specific identities of individuals are protected when appropriate. Recently, laws such as the California Privacy Act and the European Union's General Data Protection Regulation (GDPR) were passed to protect consumers' right to data privacy. Managers should consider the following when making decisions about the privacy of data.
    - Collecting, recording, and storing information. Technology enables companies to collect massive amounts of data about individuals. Using various devices and programs such as smartphones and apps, organizations can monitor various individuals, such as customers and employees, and collect data about their behavior. However,

managers should determine whether every data item collected and stored about individuals is necessary. Further consideration should be given to how these data are stored and whether the data at rest and in transit are secure to protect the privacy of the individuals.

- Communicating information. Managers should be aware of how the information collected about individuals is communicated and who receives that information. Also, managers should evaluate whether employees with access to personal information follow protocols set by the organization to protect the privacy of the individuals.

- **Accuracy.** Data flows from various sources in massive volumes. When collecting data from various sources and using them for analysis, managers should be aware of the state of the data and eliminate any inaccurate and incomplete data. Including erroneous data can skew the results of the analysis conducted and can lead to ineffective decisions. Managers should encourage and educate employees to do their due diligence in identifying and eliminating fake data and verifying the accuracy of data received from various sources to increase the quality of the information.

- **Property.** One of the major challenges of protecting intellectual property stems from its distinguishing feature that intellectual property can be infinitely shared. For example, an idea I have can be shared with others. When shared with others, it does not diminish, as I still hold the idea. Further, most ideas build on prior knowledge that may or may not belong to the same person. There are two ethical justifications for intellectual property rights protection. First, a utilitarian justification states that if society wishes to encourage the production of such ideas, then the producers should benefit financially. Another justification, based on fairness, states that those who spend their effort, time, and money deserve compensation. Given that technology develops over time using the knowledge of various researchers from different fields, managers should be aware of the challenges of considering the ethical issues of property rights.

- **Accessibility.** Organizations' IT architectures today use many different third-party applications to collect data from customers, employees, and other stakeholders. Even though accessibility says that everyone should have access to all the data collected about themselves, in today's environment, this is not possible. The information we receive on social media and search engine sites is determined by algorithms or artificial intelligence models based on our past selections and information consumption. Organizations can tweak these algorithms to show only the items they believe will get the most clicks or interactions. Restricting the information a user sees limits the content they can view. The user may not see information other than what they have clicked on previously.

This limitation provides the user less control over the content they can view and use. Even though many third-party applications are used, managers making decisions about technology adoption should consider how these third parties use the data collected from individuals, where they store the data, whether the individuals have access to their personal data, and whether they can opt out or opt in to various programs.

In the subsequent chapters, we discuss specific ethical issues related to a particular technology.

Ethical Framework for Information Technology Decision-Making

The general ethical framework for managers to address situations in business operations has four steps: identify, consider, act, and reflect. This framework can also be applied to decision-making for emerging technologies as well.

1. **Identify.** When making a decision, managers should first consider which ethical principles are at stake, who will be directly or indirectly affected by the decision, whether there is a conflict of interest, and the facts about the technology.
2. **Consider.** Managers should take time to assess the alternatives and evaluate the possible outcomes of the decision. Here managers should be aware of how information overload may influence their evaluation.
3. **Act.** When carrying out the chosen alternative, managers should assign responsibility and ensure that every employee is aware of their responsibilities.
4. **Reflect.** Evaluate the implemented processes and outcomes to identify any ethical issues.

Actions managers can take when implementing technology to evaluate various situations from an ethical standpoint are to:

- Involve an ethics specialist in the design phase of the technology. Since most processes are automated, managers should consider ethical issues early during development. Therefore, consider including an ethics specialist in the technology development team.
- Create an ethical culture by leading by example. Manage employee expectations and responsibilities so that they are not enticed to cut corners to meet unrealistic deadlines.

- Assign accountability by involving people in the decision-making process.
- Create clear policies about the treatment of data at rest and in transit.
- Evaluate and understand what can go wrong.
- Document the design process and provide transparency for the algorithms used for decision-making, data processing, and analyzing data.
- Educate employees on how they may unintentionally include personal bias in code development and how to mitigate such situations. Managers can create diverse teams with different educational backgrounds, experiences, perspectives, and so forth to mitigate bias in the development process.
- Educate employees on how to identify and reduce biases.
  - Measurement bias. The data collected does not measure the correct variable.
  - Data bias. Over- or underemphasizing certain elements in a data set.
  - Stereotype bias. An oversimplified opinion, prejudiced attitude, or uncritical judgment toward certain groups.
- Take an ethical standpoint when auditing and evaluating an information system.

Notes

1. Karp, P. (2021). Google Admits to Running "Experiments" Which Remove Some Media Sites from Its Search Results. *The Guardian* (13 January). https://www.theguardian .com/technology/2021/jan/13/google-admits-to-running-experiments-which-remove-some-media-sites-from-its-search-results.
2. Radiya-Dixit, E. (2022). *A Sociotechnical Audit: Assessing Police Use of Facial Recognition.* Cambridge, UK: Minderoo Centre for Technology and Democracy. https://www .repository.cam.ac.uk/handle/1810/342533.
3. Merriam-Webster. (n.d.). Definition of ethic. *Merriam-Webster Online dictionary.* https://www.merriam-webster.com/dictionary/ethic.
4. Brittanica. (n.d.). Anthropology and ethics. *Brittanica.* https://www.britannica.com/ topic/ethics-philosophy/Anthropology-and-ethics.
5. De George, R. (2003). *The Ethics of Information Technology and Business.* Malden, MA: Blackwell Publishing.
6. Wessel, M., and N. Helmer. (2020). A Crisis of Ethics in Technology Innovation. *MIT Sloan Management Review* 61 (3, Spring): 71–76.
7. Mason, R. O. (1986). Four Ethical Issues of the Information Age. *MIS Quarterly* 10 (1): 4–12.

CHAPTER 3

Introduction
to Data Analytics

The following excerpt from Inc. *demonstrates how analytics is changing all types of businesses, including sports.*

This Map of NBA Fandom Is Also a Data-Driven Viral Marketing Strategy

In the heart of Alaska, there's a solid fanbase for the Miami Heat. That's just one of the many fascinating takeaways from a map offering a window into where fans of pro-basketball teams cluster across the United States – and an intriguing marketing strategy for data-savvy companies.

An analysis of ticket sales from the NBA's 2018–2019 regular season surfaces such quirks as the Los Angeles Lakers' stranglehold on much of California, despite the Golden State Warriors' three recent NBA Finals wins. There's also the Utah Jazz's dominance across not just Utah, but also Nevada, Idaho, and parts of Montana and Wyoming. It's a county-by-county look at where team allegiances lie across the country from Vivid Seats, a Chicago-based ticket marketplace.

"We want to use our data to tell great stories that are representative of the fanbase, that give some insight into what is actually happening, and where consumers are passionate about events," says Vivid Seats CEO Stan Chia.

Vivid Seats is counting on basketball fans to keep coming back for a second and third look, even if they aren't in the market to buy tickets at that very moment. The strategy combines a customer-obsessed, data-driven focus with low-cost and quick-turnaround tactics.

Using its data to reflect back its customers' own interests and obsessions is part of the company's larger strategy. "Consumers have ever-changing habits and desires, and it's our responsibility to not only keep up with them but to stay in front of that," says Chia.

(Continued)

(Continued)

> The company turned a corner in terms of using data to tell stories in 2018, according to Stephen Spiewak, the company's digital content marketing manager. Maps, the company found, had more appeal than standard stories about ticketing around the highest and lowest price points, which mostly interested only fans who were already planning to attend an event.[1]

Data Analytics

Data analytics is not a new concept in business. What is different now is the abundance of data. New technology enables organizations to gather and analyze vast amounts of data to create useful information for decision-making. Today, organizations do not depend solely on data recorded in their information systems. Data options are moving beyond financial and enterprise resource planning (ERP) data to using a vast array of input from sensors, multimedia, social media, or email. Therefore, businesses can combine internally generated data with an array of publicly available or purchased data sources to create insights into market trends.

The technology available today can process large amounts of data faster than before. Technology advancements in data analytics have not only improved processing speeds but have also improved the ease of use of analytic tools. Analytic software tools created for end-users require less programming or technical knowledge, thus has enabled employees throughout the organization to take advantage of data to solve business problems facing the organization. With more data and analytic tools, organizations can improve decision-making through data analysis as well as discover growing market trends. This chapter focuses on business analytics, a branch of data analytics that provides information for business decision-making.

Organizations must continuously improve and adapt to changing customer needs in today's competitive market. Senior advisor at Microsoft, Craig Mundie, stated that big data is the "raw material of business activities,"[2] while Geoffrey Moore, author of *Crossing the Chasm*, asserted, "without big data analytics, companies are blind and deaf, wandering out onto the web like a deer on a freeway."[2] Both experts show how vital analytics is to organizations' survival in the 2020s.

At the center of analytics is the collection and storage of data. However, data analytics aims to transform the collected and stored data into

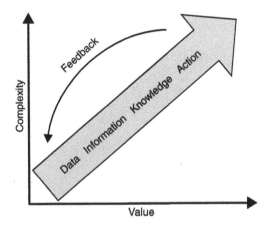

Figure 3.1 Data to Knowledge Conversion Process
Source: D. Bumblauskas, H. Nold, P. Bumblauskas, and A. Igou, "Big Analytics: Transforming Data to
Action," *Business Process Management Journal* 23, no. 3 (2017): 703–720. https://doi.org/10.1108/
BPMJ-03-2016-0056.

valuable information. Valuable information can help provide insights into
the organization, including what has happened and why, and help predict
future actions. Thus, good information creates knowledge that helps managers determine effective actions. As Figure 3.1 indicates, once the actions
have been evaluated, the feedback loop enables continuous improvement by
collecting more data.

Analytics Concepts

Big Data

The first mention of big data occurred as early as 1997 to denote a volume of
data that did not fit into local memory.[3] Even though this is one of the first
occurrences of the term, it wasn't until a decade later that it became more
commonplace within business realms. Big data is considered a volume of data
that cannot be processed with traditional software applications due to its size
or complexity.

Big data evolved as computer processor speeds increased and storage of
large quantities of data became less costly. Experts traditionally distinguish
big data from conventional data using the 5 V's shown in Figure 3.2.

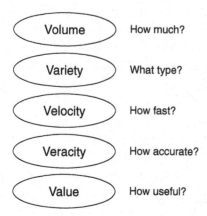

Figure 3.2 Big Data Characteristics – The 5 V's

The characteristics of big data include[4]:

- **Volume.** The size of the relevant dataset. Typically, these datasets are a petabyte or more. Larger datasets may include data for an extended period, additional variables, or additional files/tables/records.
- **Variety.** The different types of data. Data included for analysis can be from various sources and contains structured and unstructured data:
  - **Structured data** has a predefined format, making it easy to search and filter. This data is typically stored in a tabular form, such as a spreadsheet or a database. Each column contains a specified field of data that is the same for each record. Transactional data generated from a traditional ERP system generally contains structured data.
  - **Unstructured data**, such as those in social media files, images, or audio files, are not in a predefined format and are stored using different file types. Therefore, it can be challenging to search, filter, and analyze.
  - **Semi-structured data** contains both structured and unstructured data, such as data from e-mails and CSV files.
- **Velocity.** The speed at which the data is generated. Today, technology enables various devices to monitor and collect data continuously in real time. These sources include location data collected by your cell phones, temperature monitored using sensors, and behavior monitored using keystrokes or cameras.
- **Veracity.** The accuracy and reliability of the data. Since big data combines data from various sources, there may be discrepancies or missing or incomplete data. The analyses may lead to inaccurate inferences if the data has low veracity.

- **Value.** The usefulness of the data for decision-making. Even though an organization may have access to various data sources, managers must consider whether the data is relevant to the decision and whether it adds value to the organization. Simply put, the data creates value when the benefit is greater than the cost to collect and process the information. Data creates value when it helps managers make decisions about operational effectiveness and efficiency, controls, financial performance, or customer satisfaction. Data adds the most value when acquired at a reasonable cost. Value increases if the data source is stable, can be legally used without restrictions, or can be used to train an artificial intelligence model.

Recently, other characteristics of big data have emerged.[5] They are:

- **Validity.** The correctness of the data used for analysis. Managers should ask whether they are using the right data for the right analysis. If the data does not reflect the characteristics we wish to analyze, the inferences will be incorrect.
- **Variability.** The dynamic, evolving nature of the data. The constant updating of data impacts data analytic outcomes. For example, if the same data is requested at different times, the results will be different as the data is constantly updated.
- **Venue.** Data that is derived from multiple platforms, such as public and private clouds and personal systems. Obtaining data from a variety of sources increases the complexity of data cleansing.
- **Vocabulary.** Data models and semantics that describe the data. Managers should pay attention to the variable names because different data sources may use similar names to refer to different attributes.
- **Vagueness.** The confusion over the meaning or uncertainty about what the data might convey. For example, a column just labeled as a date could mean several things, such as the date paid or the date received. Without a concise meaning, the data is not useful.
- **Visualization.** How the data is presented in a graphical form. Given the volume of data, visualizations have become an important tool used to communicate insights from analysis to a nontechnical audience. Visualizations include charts, maps, and graphs. Visualizations help summarize the data and enable users to conduct what-if analysis, understand, and interpret the data easily.

Data does not have to fit the criteria of big data to have value within the organization. Smaller but complete datasets can provide many insights for the organization. However, if your analysis expands into modeling and prediction using artificial intelligence, the amount of data will extend into the big data realm.

Data Storage

Analytics relies on a large volume of data. Understanding how the data is stored is an essential first step to undertaking a large analytics project. Both structured and unstructured data need to be stored. Most of us are familiar with how structured data is stored.

Flat Files

Flat files are the most straightforward form of data storage, as all related data is stored in a single file of columns and rows. Flat files store simple, structured data. This format makes accessing the data user-friendly and easy to import into another analytics application. We can imagine most flat files as a spreadsheet, at least logically. The data for each record has the fields separated by a delimiter, such as a comma or a tab. The file may also store the data in a fixed-length format with the same number of characters reserved for each field. Figure 3.3 shows an example of a flat file for purchase orders.

Even though flat files are easy to use, they have several downsides. The most apparent is data redundancy, as shown in Figure 3.3. The vendor's name is repeated for each purchase order. This redundancy not only takes up additional storage space but also increases the chance of data errors or at least inconsistencies. For example, changing the vendor's name from Southern Garden Wholesale to Southern Garden Wholesale, LLC would be challenging because every field in many rows needs to be updated.

Flat files are typically accessed by only one person or application at a time. Flat files are more challenging to merge with other datasets because they require cleaning and formatting for duplicates. Further, flat files do not enable complex querying of the data. A flat file typically does not store enough data to be considered big data because of storage limitations on flat files. Although some applications still use flat files, most use a relational database.

PO No	PO Date	Vendor ID	Vendor Name	PO State	Item ID	Line Description	Qty Ordered	Qty Received	Qty Remaining
10201	2/1/19	SOGARDEN	Southern Garden Wholesale	Open	TOOL-35300	Catalog #W564330: Wheelbarrow-Metal 6 cubic feet	6.00	0.00	6.00
10201	2/1/19	SOGARDEN	Southern Garden Wholesale	Open	TOOL-35260	Catalog #W570020: Scoop Shovel	12.00	0.00	12.00
10201	2/1/19	SOGARDEN	Southern Garden Wholesale	Open	TOOL-38510	Catalog #S100325: Flower Shears	10.00	0.00	10.00
10202	2/10/19	DEJULIA	DeJulia Wholesale Suppliers	Open	SEGR-32100	Catalog #: 101130: Kentucky Bluegrass Seeds	12.00	0.00	12.00
10202	2/10/19	DEJULIA	DeJulia Wholesale Suppliers	Open	SEGR-32110	Catalog #: 101140: Fine Fescue Seeds	12.00	0.00	12.00
10202	2/10/19	DEJULIA	DeJulia Wholesale Suppliers	Open	SEGR-32120	Catalog #: 101150: Tall Fescue Seeds	12.00	0.00	12.00
10300	3/1/19	DEJULIA	DeJulia Wholesale Suppliers	Open	BOOK-11010	ISBN: 0004455565445 BGS Gardening Handbook	6.00	0.00	6.00
10300	3/1/19	DEJULIA	DeJulia Wholesale Suppliers	Open	BOOK-11030	ISBN:0007860565445 BGS Vegetable Garden Primer	12.00	0.00	12.00
10300	3/1/19	DEJULIA	DeJulia Wholesale Suppliers	Open	POTS-30210	Catalog # P70320: Clay Flower Pot - 8 in.	12.00	0.00	12.00
10300	3/1/19	DEJULIA	DeJulia Wholesale Suppliers	Open	SEFL-31100	Catalog #: 101020: Carnation Seeds (Mix)	12.00	0.00	12.00
10300	3/1/19	DEJULIA	DeJulia Wholesale Suppliers	Open	SEFL-31140	Catalog #: 101024: Marigold Seeds (Mix)	12.00	0.00	12.00
10300	3/1/19	DEJULIA	DeJulia Wholesale Suppliers	Open	SEVG-33100	Catalog #:103000: Bean - Bush Seeds	12.00	12.00	0.00
10302	3/3/19	SOGARDEN	Southern Garden Wholesale	Open	EQLW-14120	Catalog #LM40090: Reel Mower	6.00	0.00	6.00
10302	3/3/19	SOGARDEN	Southern Garden Wholesale	Open	EQLW-14110	Catalog # GA44564: Gas-Powered Leaf Blower/Vacuum	6.00	0.00	6.00
10302	3/3/19	SOGARDEN	Southern Garden Wholesale	Open	EQWT-15180	Catalog # WT1005290: Sprinkler - Impulse	12.00	0.00	12.00

Figure 3.3   Example of a Flat File

Relational Database

Relational databases are the most common form for storing structural data. A relational database consists of related tables linked together by specialized fields in the tables called keys. See Figure 3.4 for a diagram of a relational database for purchase orders.

Each table has one field designated as the primary key, a unique identifier for that record. In Figure 3.4, PONumber, SupplierNo, and InvCode are all primary keys. When a primary key is referenced in another table, it is called a foreign key. For example, the SupplierNo field in the TPurchase Order table is considered a foreign key. The SupplierNo, as a foreign key, links the two tables together. The linking of the tables makes combining data from multiple tables easy to query.

The advantages of relational databases are numerous. First, relational databases enable the separation of data entry from data storage. Database rules ensure that the data is accurate and complete before storing new data in the database. Some of the possible database rules include the following:

- **Field check.** The type of data you can enter in a field, such as text or numerical.
- **Size check.** The number of characters you can enter into a field.
- **Completeness check.** Ensures that all fields are complete.

Second, the use of a relational database eliminates the redundancy of data. In the purchase order example, the supplier's name and address are maintained in only one location (TSupplier) and not repeated with individual purchase orders.

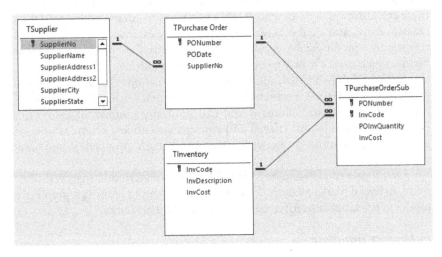

Figure 3.4 Example of Relational Database Tables

Relational databases have various controls, such as concurrent user access and write-protection mechanisms, to allow multiple individuals or applications to access and update the data simultaneously. These controls allow only one individual to change the data at a time, making databases more secure than flat files. The final advantage is that relational databases can enforce business rules through referential integrity. For a foreign key to be entered into a table, it must be a primary key in another table. For example, a purchase order cannot be created for a supplier that is not already in the supplier table.

Data stored in relational databases is well-organized, but, similar to flat files, the data is stored on some form of disk media. This storage slows down the time required to retrieve the data. For many applications, the time to retrieve the data is negligible, but for massive computational applications, this may add considerable processing time.

Graph Database

Business decisions require managers to understand dynamic relationships between data and how they are connected. Interpreting the data and recognizing the value of the data requires that we understand how different data elements are connected. Rather than tables, rows, and fields, a graph data model represents entities as nodes and the way the entities are related as relationships.

A graph database management system "is an online database management system with create, read, update, and delete methods that explore a graph model."[6] Graphs enable us to model all kinds of scenarios, like how these entities are related in the real world. Even though relational databases can store and navigate the relationships depicted in graph databases, querying these relationships is done with JOIN operations to connect database tables, cross-lookups, and rigid schemas that can be very expensive in terms of processing. In a graph database, relationships are stored alongside the data elements, which makes it easy to move through data quickly.

Information in a graph model is organized as nodes, relationships, and properties. Nodes are entities that can be tagged with labels representing different roles in a domain and can hold any number of properties. Relationships can be directional and connect two nodes. There can be any number of relationships between two nodes with properties associated with them.

Graph data models can be used to identify money laundering, credit card fraud, or social media analysis. Figure 3.5 is an example of using a graph data model to track funds transferred between different accounts.

In-Memory Database

An in-memory database stores data in the main computer memory, such as the random-access memory (RAM), rather than hard disks or solid-state drives.

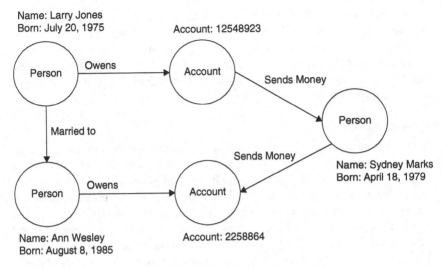

Figure 3.5   Graph Data Model: Fund Transferred Between Accounts

This storage allows for significantly faster processing time as the computer does not access a hard disk to find the appropriate data. Due to how the data is accessed, the number of steps is reduced to access the data, causing fewer CPU instructions.

Although the processing time for many applications is faster than hard disk storage, there are a few downsides to using an in-memory database. First is the expense. RAM is more expensive than solid-state disks or other types of permanent storage media. The cost of RAM is about 80 times higher than traditional hard disks, requiring strategic use of this technology.[7] The main risk with using an in-memory database is the volatility of the memory. If a power disruption or any other crash occurs, all data is lost, making a backup system for data storage necessary. However, if an application for data analytics requires faster processing or immediate access to data, this may be a preferred storage method. In most cases, data stored in an in-memory database usually has a backup with a traditional disk to reduce the potential of data loss. However, restoring from a disk to an in-memory database takes time.

Applications that use in-memory data storage must be modified and, in some cases, completely rewritten, if data storage is converted from a traditional relational database to an in-memory. When applications use relational databases, programs are written to reduce the number of times data is read from the database to increase performance. However, since this latency is not a factor with in-memory databases, different algorithms and methods can be used in application development. Despite the risks of data loss, it makes sense to use faster data storage and processing for some applications.

In-memory data storage can be used for a portion of the data processing and storage in an application. Traditional storage can be used for data that does not require immediate processing and access. For example, many e-commerce applications use in-memory storage for the shopping cart and checkout processes. However, the more extensive catalog of products is stored on a disk for retrieval.

Data Warehouse

A data warehouse contains an organization's structured data in a single location. Data warehouses are needed to store and integrate data within the organization because of the vast amount of data generated daily using various systems. In a data warehouse, data from multiple systems, such as the enterprise resource planning system, external partner systems, or internal applications, are combined into a single source for the primary reporting and information source. Generally, the data in a data warehouse has been cleansed and then stored in a format that makes it readily available for further analysis.

Before loading data in a data warehouse, an analyst reviews it to ensure that it meets naming standards and the defined data schema.[8] It will take longer to load data into a warehouse due to this review, but this step is necessary to maintain the integrity of the data in the warehouse. A data warehouse generally has a central database that integrates and stores an organization's data, ETL (extract, transform, load) tools, metadata (including business and technical) providing context for the business user, and access tools that enable users to interact with the data in the data warehouse. These components typically fall into the three tiers of the data warehouse architecture.[9] The tiers are shown in Figure 3.6.

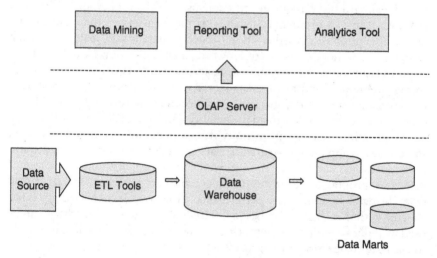

Figure 3.6 Three-Tier Architecture of Data Warehouse

1. **Top tier.** Contains a user interface enabling the user to analyze data. This tier is known as the application server.
2. **Middle tier.** Allows fast query processing using an online analytical processing (OLAP) server. This tier is the database server.
3. **Bottom tier.** Contains the data warehouse server and ETL tools. The data is stored in this tier.

There are several types of data warehouses. Each provides different benefits for your organization. Examples of the types of warehouses include:

- Cloud data warehouses – managed service
- On-premised or licensed data warehouses – more expensive but provide more control to the organization
- Data warehouse appliances – a pre-integrated bundle of software and hardware that can be connected to the organization's network.[9]

A large, central data storage provides greater access to data for more complex or real-time analyses. It is particularly useful for a wide range of ad-hoc queries, custom reporting, and data mining. Because the data from different systems is now in a single data structure, there are greater possibilities for cross-functional analyses. Since the data has been structured and standardized to help define many predefined questions for analysis, business users within the organization can use the data for analysis, leading to consistent and accurate reporting across various departments. The query tools frequently integrated with a data warehouse make accessing information easy for a non-programmer.

Data Lakes

A data lake contains all of the organization's data, including unstructured data. The structured data from individual applications is stored along with non-structured data, such as social media extracts and data from sensors or mobile apps. When loading data into a data lake, the data does not require cleansing or integration into the database structure. Since the data does not go through a preparation step and is stored in its raw format, it can be available for analysis much faster than in a data warehouse.

Because of the unstructured nature of the data, a data lake is used more by technical staff and data scientists than by end-users. For this reason, data lakes can be more conducive to predictive analytics, data discovery, and more exploratory methods. Because of the lack of a formal schema in the data, the query time is slower with a data lake. However, the overall costs for storage are lower for a data lake than for a data warehouse.

Even though a data lake does not have a consistent schema for defining the data, data analysts still need to define a data catalog to ensure that data can be located when needed. Adding consistent metadata to ensure accessibility and search capabilities for the data can keep the data lake from becoming a data swamp. A data lake can quickly evolve into a data swamp, making the data inaccessible.

Data Marts

Sometimes, the amount of data in an entire data warehouse is too large or too cumbersome to analyze. A data mart is a subset of data typically extracted from a data warehouse. With a data mart, a smaller, more focused portion of the data is available to specific users.[9] For example, a global corporation could create separate data marts for each geographic region. Individuals in that region could only query and analyze data within their regional data mart. Other organizations may align their data marts with the business functions such as sales, finance, or operations. Since data marts are designed to meet the specific needs of a user group, the smaller focused design enables end-users to set up a data mart faster and at a lower cost, simplify data access and data maintenance, and increase the speed at which data is analyzed.

Data marts can be categorized into three categories based on their relationship to the data warehouse.[10] A dependent data mart is a data mart that is a partitioned segment within an enterprise data warehouse. In contrast, an independent data mart does not rely on a data warehouse. Organizations may decide to have a hybrid data mart where data is combined from an existing data warehouse and other sources.

Table 3.1 summarizes the differences between a data warehouse, data lake, and data mart.

Table 3.1   Data Storage Comparisons

	Data Lake	Data Warehouse	Data Mart
Data scope	Broad, raw data	Cleaned data, general	Cleaned data, focused
Data types	Structured and unstructured	Structured	Structured
Ease of navigation	Difficult	Moderate	Easy
Data scheme	Defined after storage	Defined before storage	Defined before storage
Users	Data scientists	Business professionals	Business professionals in a specific function
Storage	Low-cost	High-cost	High-cost
Agility	Most agile	Less agile	Less agile

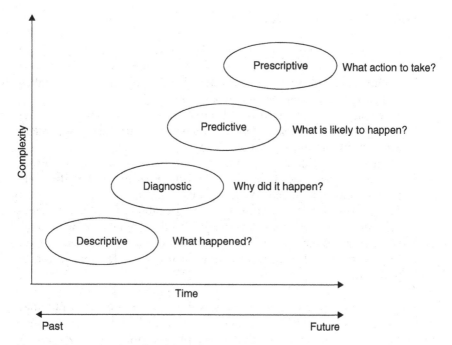

Figure 3.7 Types of Analytics Based on Two Dimensions

Types of Analytics

Analytics can be divided into different categories based on two dimensions:

1. Whether the analysis is forward-looking to the future or backward-looking to the past
2. The complexity of the question addressed

The following sections explain the types of analytics shown in Figure 3.7 based on these two dimensions.

Descriptive Analytics

Descriptive techniques focus on what happened in the past. Most employees are familiar with this type of analysis, making it the easiest to implement using readily available tools. Most analytics projects start with descriptive techniques, as it provides analysts with an overview of the data. Descriptive analytics is used daily to convey information about various business activities. The analyses can answer questions such as how much the company earned this month, how many items were sold this month, who were the top 10 customers based on sales, or how many machine failures occurred this quarter.

Descriptive analytics generally use the following techniques:

- **Data queries.** The simplest technique is retrieving and organizing data into useful information using a query language, such as SQL. For example, a simple query could extract all of the purchases in December of a particular product from database tables.
- **Summary statistics.** Statistical calculations to describe the data. Some examples include mean, median, average, standard deviation, range, variance, minimum, and maximum.
- **Distributions.** Summarize data by each subcategory, such as sales by customer age or sales by region. You can visualize the data distributions for easier analysis with histograms.
- **Filtering or data reductions.** Extracting a subset of the data to examine only specific categories of data or periods. Having less data to analyze can increase the focus of the analysis. For example, extracting data for a particular sales region can allow the user to understand customer preferences in a specific region.

In most cases, descriptive analytics is used as a starting point. It provides the foundation for all other types of advanced analytics. Descriptive techniques are easy to understand, require little training or expertise, and usually offer a quick and easy return on investment. A preliminary descriptive analysis may show that the average warranty costs increased during this period compared to last year. To provide further context and usefulness, you would continue by using diagnostic techniques to assess the possible reasoning for an increase.

Diagnostic Analytics

Diagnostic analytics also focus on events in the past but provide more insight into why things happened. Diagnostic analytics can help a user go deeper into the data to find more details, identify anomalies, or discover relationships or patterns between variables in the data. These techniques take the insights gained in the descriptive analysis and attempt to put additional meaning in the data. This type of analytics helps companies understand their customers better, improve operations, and potentially increase overall efficiency. In the warranty example above, you would drill down into the data using diagnostic techniques to see whether a specific item caused the increase.

Types of diagnostic techniques include the following:

- **Compare descriptive statistics.** Simple diagnostics analysis can compare the descriptive statistics to established benchmarks, such as comparing descriptive statistics with historical or industry-wide statistics.
- **Drill-down.** Drilling down into the data involves focusing on a particular aspect, such as a particular product or customers from a specific region.

- **Outliers.** Detecting outliers to determine what data points significantly differ from others in the dataset. This technique determines the typical traits of a population and then finds items or individuals that significantly differ from the norm.
- **Clustering.** This technique helps find groups of individuals or objects most similar. This analysis groups all objects into groups based on their similarities in the given variables. The analysis is considered unsupervised, as predefined attributes are not provided in the data. Clustering can answer questions such as what are the characteristics of the customers that spend the most at this location?
- **Co-occurrence groups.** This technique identifies links between individuals and particular events. For example, if a person watches this movie, they will likely enjoy it. Many retail sites use this function to suggest additional goods to purchase.

Data visualizations and dashboards provide an easier way to interpret and quickly understand diagnostic analysis. Dashboards can provide a quick visual overview of the data, allowing the user to focus on more specific areas for analysis. Users can create dashboards using various tools, such as PowerBI or Tableau. Visualizations using dashboards can often have drill-down functionality to retrieve the underlying data for further analysis. Figure 3.8 shows an example of a dashboard analyzing the results of a sales team.

Figure 3.8 Example of a Dashboard

Diagnostic analytics are still relatively easy to understand and implement. Many end-user tools are designed to handle most diagnostic techniques. Even though diagnostic analytics is a bit more advanced than descriptive, diagnostic analytics offer a good return on the investment by providing more insights for decision-making.

Predictive Analytics

As the name implies, predictive analytics predicts what will happen by building a model using historical data from several sources. Frequently, this is done by analyzing relationships between variables within the data. For example, a grocery store may predict which groceries to stock on shelves based on past and current points of sales data. Combining external information, such as predictions of an incoming blizzard, could determine the volume of groceries needed for the few days preceding the storm. Companies using predictive analytics can improve performance and increase efficiency throughout the organization.

Some of the common types of predictive analytics include:

- **Decision trees.** This is the simplest predictive analytics model because it is easy to understand. Decision trees place data into different scenarios based on other variables. Branches indicate the different choices available, from which you can determine the alternative that will be selected.
- **Regression.** Regression evaluates several input variables to determine the possible effect on or the association with a dependent variable. For example, we may want to determine the likelihood of a customer making a purchase in our store. The likelihood of a purchase is the dependent variable. Based on various characteristics such as past customer behavior, day of the week, current discounts offered, age, gender, or economic status, we can predict the probability of a new customer purchasing a product at this location.
- **Classification.** Classification uses labeled data to build a model to determine if an observation will be in a particular group. For example, based on the characteristics of a travel and expense report, classification determines the likelihood of it being a suspicious transaction. Another example is using historical data of loan recipients to determine which individuals will most likely repay a loan.
- **Time series modeling.** This specific predictive analytics relies on time to identify patterns, seasonality, and trends. Time series models can help organizations identify when sales will peak or whether there is a high volume of returns.

Predictive analytics is the fastest-growing market for technical analytics investment. These tools can provide greater insights into business operations and help managers make informed data-driven decisions. For more information on advanced predictive techniques, see Chapter 5 on artificial intelligence.

Prescriptive Analytics

Prescriptive analytics advance predictive analytics by determining the best action under specific conditions or circumstances. These models typically require artificial intelligence or machine learning techniques to build optimal data models. These techniques allow flexibility for the model to make decisions automatically. For example, self-driving cars use several prescriptive analytics models to gather real-time data and to be able to react quickly to the current conditions.

This type of analytics can help companies predict what actions to take by combining internal data with economic forecasts, sensor data from machines, social media text, and various other data sources. Prescriptive analytics aims to help streamline decision-making by providing different scenarios from which management can select. Ultimately, problem-solving should be quicker and more accurate with these tools.

- **Decision support systems (DSSs).** A DSS aids management decision-making using complex rules developed by data and human expertise over time. These systems will adapt over time and typically use a series of IF and THEN statements to help guide a manager to the right decision.
- **Optimization models.** These systems build a model to help determine the best scenario using several input variables. For example, an optimization model can select the best mix of investment holdings to maximize earnings under various conditions.
- **Artificial intelligence and machine learning.** Many techniques in this category use a form of artificial intelligence to recommend options. See Chapters 5 and 6 for more information on this topic.

The primary goal of prescriptive analytics is to help streamline management's decision-making. Some day-to-day decisions can be made using prescriptive techniques; however, these models may not be perfect. Therefore, management should closely monitor and review the models and verify that no data quality issues are affecting the model. A benefit of automated decision-making is that it removes repetitive decisions to allow management more time to focus on the big picture.

Analytics Tools

Given the breadth of analytics and techniques, companies can use several tools and platforms to perform analytics. Most firms will adopt a combination of tools to execute their analytics plans. The following list of tools is divided into the categories of end-user tools and data management tools.

End-User Analytics Tools

Many applications allow end-users to perform analytics without coding knowledge. These tools put the power of analytics into the hands of the end-user. These applications are easy to use and generally have a point-and-click user interface.

Tableau

Tableau is a market-leading data visualization software with desktop and online versions. The application provides various tools for visualizations and data preparation. Tableau can connect to multiple data formats relatively easily. The interface is drag and drop, making the software easy to use. Tableau can interface with Python or R to perform more complex calculations. The software creates professional-looking visualizations. Even though data-cleansing capabilities within Tableau are minimal, it offers Prep Builder software that can perform many data preparation tasks.

Microsoft Power BI

Power BI is a leading tool in the business intelligence market. It is still strong in visualizations but performs other analytics and trend analysis. Since Power BI is part of the Microsoft suite, it integrates well with Microsoft products but will also connect with other data sources. However, Power BI is not available for Mac computers. Power BI is easy to learn, especially for someone familiar with the Microsoft suite of products, has good visualizations, and can connect to various data sources. Power BI uses a proprietary expression language for formulas called DAX, which is not as user-friendly as other tools.

Qlik Sense

Qlik Sense is a visualization tool that integrates artificial intelligence for deeper data analytics. It is available as a software, service, and hybrid solution. Qlik can perform extensive calculations quickly and connect to more data sources than some of the competitors. Qlik has integrated AI and machine learning functionality into the platform. However, using the software does not require extensive data science skills.

Alteryx

Alteryx is a data analytics software specializing in the ETL process. Users can build a workflow to enable a repeatable process to prepare data for extraction, cleansing, analyses, and output generation. Alteryx can also generate other analyses, including predictive and spatial analysis. In addition, some modeling and intelligence modules are available within the application. Alteryx can be used as standalone software or on a server. Alteryx uses a point-and-click interface to assemble the tools into a streamlined workflow.

SAS

Statistical Analysis System, more commonly called SAS, is a statistical software suite of programs that has been available in various formats since the 1960s. Its strengths are statistical analysis, including data mining and predictive modeling. The primary market for SAS software is larger firms. Even though some end-user functions are in SAS, some advanced functions are only available with coding. SAS is primarily used for business applications. The data visualization functions in SAS are limited and do not produce as professional-looking graphs as other visualization tools.

Microsoft Excel

Excel is a starter application for analytics. The use of formulas and pivot tables enabled many business professionals to start analyzing data without really thinking about the work of analytics. This tried-and-true software package is very effective in analyzing smaller datasets. However, Excel has some limitations. First, with larger datasets, the processing speed is slower. In addition, datasets over 1 million lines cannot be opened in Excel without the PowerQuery add-in. Despite these shortcomings, many users still rely on Excel for analyses.

Coding-Required Tools

These tools, although end-users can use them, require more coding and usually some technical expertise. Business professionals should understand these tools to help with the software acquisition decision-making process.

Python

Python is an open-source programming language that is useful for a variety of applications, but in particular, for analyzing data. Even though it is a programming language, it is relatively easy to learn and is widely used in business applications. Python relies on several libraries that contain various predefined functions that can be used together for data analytics. The libraries NumPy and pandas are useful for statistical analysis and data manipulation. Other libraries, such as Scrapy, can be used for data mining. The library Matplotlib is used for data visualization. The drawback of Python is that it is slower than some other languages and can require more memory to execute the code.

R

R is another open-source programming language that can also perform many statistical analyses, data visualization, and data mining. Similar to Python libraries, several software packages are available for coding. It is best for heavy computational tasks. A significant benefit is that programmers can integrate code from other programming languages into an R program. Programmers can use the Rstudio environment to develop their programs. Although R and Python are similar in their overall functionality, many see R as more complex to learn with complex syntax.

Data Management Platforms

Hadoop

Hadoop, developed by the Apache Foundation, is an open-source software platform allowing data processing across several servers. The most significant advantage of this type of software is it is highly scalable to run from one or two servers to hundreds of them. The specialty of Hadoop is performing many complex computations against a large volume of data. Hadoop utilizes a program library called MapReduce, which contains code for processing data across servers. There are many more utilities available in the Hadoop Common library for programmers.

A large part of the Hadoop structure contains the Hadoop Distributed File System (HDFS), which breaks larger files into smaller components and distributes them across the network of servers for faster data processing. Also, part of the Hadoop tools is a job or task scheduler.

Several software companies distribute Hadoop, such as Cloudera, Hortonworks, and MapR. Each of these companies provides the base Hadoop system from Apache Foundation but adds unique proprietary functions that work within Hadoop for easy implementation.

Apache Spark

Apache Spark, also developed by the Apache Foundation, is an open-source database that processes data across multiple computers. Unlike Hadoop, it uses random-access memory (RAM) to process the data rather than traditional file storage, allowing Spark to process data many times faster. However, this makes using Spark more expensive. Spark can be used for real-time processing and analyzing unstructured data streams. Spark is used more often than Hadoop for machine learning algorithms or more complex calculations and data analysis. Typically, Spark is considered easier to use.

Use Cases

Accounting

Tax calculations. Organizations can perform data analytics on transactional and nontransactional data to evaluate and plan direct and indirect taxes and manage intercompany margins.

Audit risk. Audit teams can use analytics to determine areas of risk in a client firm. Auditors can combine accounting data with external data, such as economic or market analysis, and create visualizations to identify anomalies, outliers, and trends when performing analytical procedures.

Accounts receivable management. Visualizations can show how quickly each customer is paying and alert management for customers behind in payments. Additional charts can show which customers are taking discounts to pay earlier. Management can conduct predictive analysis to plan and budget cash flow.

Marketing

Customer analysis. Retail operations can group customers into subsets by various characteristics using clustering algorithms. For example, a large department store can group customers by shopping characteristics, demographics, and purchased products. This analysis will help stores determine which products to stock, new products to introduce, or other environmental changes.

Personalized marketing. Gathering data about each customer from social media interactions, rewards cards, or other sources of information can help organizations create customer profiles to provide a personalized marketing campaign that closely meets the customer's interests and purchasing patterns.

Operations

Predictive maintenance. Many pieces of factory equipment come with sensors that collect operational data and log entries from the machine. This data can be combined with other structured data about the equipment, such as its type, age, and recent maintenance records, to predict the equipment that is likely to fail. Management can proactively plan maintenance and help determine if replacement is required by using this analysis.

Production optimization. Analyzing the movement of items through a factory production line can pinpoint areas of inefficiency and determine whether particular processes are causing delays. Manufacturing engineers can use the data to change processes, update machines, or take other steps to improve efficiency.

Service operations. One of the complicated aspects of any service industry, such as retail, food service, or hospitality, is effectively managing staffing levels. Predictive analytics techniques can help determine days or time slots for additional staffing based on historical trends, upcoming events, or weather patterns.

Human Resources

Talent management. Analytics can help management understand the skills and expertise of employees to ensure that the workforce has sufficient skills in the future. Training and professional growth opportunities can be identified for each employee to strengthen the talent portfolio of the employees. The results can also help with succession planning for critical positions or functions within the company.

Employee turnover. Past employment records can identify areas of high employee turnover and predict future employment needs. Analytics can also identify departments or functions with high turnover to help management determine whether changes are required to reduce further attrition.

Notes

1. Devlin, N. (2019). This Map of NBA Fandom Is Also a Data-Driven Viral Marketing Strategy. *Inc.* (29 October). https://www.inc.com/nick-devlin/nba-fan-map-vivid-seats-marketing-strategy.html.

2. Adediwura, P. (n.d.). Big Data – The Raw Material for 4.0 Business. Interlogica. https://www.interlogica.it/en/insight-en/without-big-data-analytics-companies-are-blind-and-deaf-wandering-out-onto-the-web-like-deer-freeway-geoffrey-moore/.

3. Press, G. (2013). A Very Short History of Big Data. *Forbes* (9 May). https://www.forbes.com/sites/gilpress/2013/05/09/a-very-short-history-of-big-data/?sh=7fe4ba8965a1.

4. Demchenko, Y., Grosso, P., De Laat, C., et al. (2013). Addressing Big Data Issues in Scientific Data Infrastructure. *2013 International Conference on Collaboration Technologies and Systems*, San Diego, CA (20–24 May 2013), pp. 48–55.

5. G. Kapil, Agrawal, A., and Khan, R. A. (2016). A Study of Big Data Characteristics. *2016 International Conference on Communication and Electronics Systems (ICCES)*, Coimbatore, India (21–22 October 2016), pp. 1–4. doi: 10.1109/CESYS.2016.7889917.

6. Robinson, I., Webber, J., and E. Eifrem. (2015). *Graph Databases: New Opportunities for Connected Data*. Sebastopol, CA: O'Reilly.

7. MongoDB. (n.d.). In-Memory Databases Explained. https://www.mongodb.com/databases/in-memory-database.

8. IBM. (n.d.). What Is a Data Warehouse? https://www.ibm.com/topics/data-warehouse.

9. Chaudhary, S., Murala, D. P., and Srivastav, V. K. (2011). A Critical Review of Data Warehouse. *Global Journal of Business Management and Information Technology* 1 (2): 95–103.

10. Oracle. (n.d.). Data Warehousing Guide. Available at: https://docs.oracle.com/cd/A81042_01/DOC/server.816/a76994/marts.htm#.

CHAPTER 4

Data Analytics Governance and Management

An excerpt of Mathew Chacko's, Coca-Cola's director of enterprise architecture, interview with Sam Ransbotham, an associate professor of information systems at the Carroll School of Management at Boston College and the MIT Sloan Management Review *guest editor for the Data and Analytics Big Idea Initiative is given below.*

Coke is the world's largest beverage company, with more than 500 brands and 3,500 products sold worldwide. In 2013, the company had $46.9 billion in net operating revenues, and a net income of $8.6 billion. It has about 250 bottling partners with 900 bottling plants, and employs over 700,000 system associates worldwide.

Can you talk a little bit about the challenges of marrying all these external datasets from your bottlers? That seems like a particular challenge at Coke, where there's this huge infrastructure of "data middlemen," for lack of a better term.

Chacko: Well, point-of-sale data, scan data, is actually very big. Our commercial department really wants to have good information about that from one set of customers so that they can take that information and go to other customers and say, "Hey, we have this other customer that did these kinds of campaigns with this kind of strategy, and they were able to see this lift."

Our team wants to go to our customers with real numbers. It's important for us when we go to our customers to be able to give them fact-based information. We also want to take in things like event data and social media data and provide these value services back to our customers. That's a big thing for us.

(Continued)

(Continued)

> In some areas we have to have flexibility, and in other areas we can standardize. Currently our bottlers run their own system, and so they send us data in all sorts of different formats. We have to be flexible in being able to inject data. But when we transform that data, we need to transform into those standardized taxonomies or hierarchies.
>
> We also have the reverse problem because we need to transform information back into the bottler's view – we have to give them back their information in formats they can read. We aspire to provide data as a service, both to our customers and to our bottlers.[1]

Data Analytics Projects

Implementing an enterprise-wide data analytic project with many data sources can be challenging. However, the following best practice guidelines may help data analytics projects go as smoothly as possible.

- **Have a clear objective.** Determine what the overall goal for undertaking an analytics project is. Align the project goals with the business strategy.
- **Know your stakeholder needs.** The objective of analytics is to provide useful information for decision-making. Therefore, it is imperative that you understand the competing interests of different stakeholders. Once stakeholder needs have been identified, data analytic projects can focus on creating value while balancing these competing needs.
- **Know your technology.** Adopting the right technology tools is very important to get various datasets that are in silos connected.
- **Train your employees.** Hiring competent staff in data science is important. However, managers should also consider training their team on the functionality of the selected technology tools and business operations. Encourage your data scientists to work with messy data and trawl through the data until they find insights.
- **Ensure that action is possible.** Is it viable to take action on the findings of the analytics? According to a study by Gartner, only 20% of insights from data analytics will result in an action taken.[2] The remainder of the analyses will go unused. Without any possible action, the organization will not gain value.
- **Be flexible.** Generally, data analytics projects work better with an agile approach than a more rigorous development approach. Most of the time, the process will be more iterative and lead to the organization discovering additional use cases.

- **Take time to improve data quality.** Data quality issues can cause various problems, from inaccurate results to delayed projects. Taking time up-front to review and cleanse data will save significant time in the future and lead to better quality decisions.
- **Plan for the future.** Unlike other types of technical development, a business intelligence environment will continually change due to more data, changes in the business environment, and new information requirements for decision-making. It is better to have a plan in advance to manage changes.

Implementing Analytics

Even though analytics projects may be more iterative than other technical development projects, every analytic project may follow the software development lifecycle. A larger analytics project can encompass developing tools, such as a data warehouse, affecting data analytics projects throughout the organization. The goal is to ensure data consistency while providing flexibility to explore the data with minimal constraints.

Planning

Even though you may be beginning an enterprise analytics project, other departments may have done some analytics work already. If that is the case, it would be helpful to start the new project by identifying any work that has been done previously in the various departments. Some of these may be scripts developed using end-user software tools. But getting a better understanding of what already exists will help centralize knowledge within the organization and streamline analytic projects in the future.

Next, determine the questions to answer with analytics. Prioritize which analyses to tackle first. Ask if the organization can take action due to this analysis or if it is informational only. The actionable analyses should be of higher priority as they will provide the most significant value to the organization. Therefore, create a process to communicate the results to the appropriate stakeholder and evaluate and monitor the outcomes of the analysis. The type of analyses conducted will help to decide the breadth of team members needed for the project. Be sure to include employees from each functional area who understand their department's data.

Develop an overall strategy for the organization's analytical needs for the next few years. Even though you may only focus on a few projects in the immediate future, many decisions that are made with the first vital projects will affect future projects. Consider whether data analytics will be centralized or decentralized, as this will determine the required controls and governance processes. The types of applications, oversight responsibilities, and reporting process will be determined by whether the organization uses a centralized, decentralized, or hybrid approach. Determine if the organization will select standardized tools to be used by all functions or if there will be some decentralized choices. If analytics is decentralized, establish a policy of which types of analysis end-users can perform and what will require oversight by analytics experts. Many organizations can use a combination of centralized and decentralized tools. For example, the organization can use a standard data lake and warehouse administration application for most of its central data storage. However, individual departments can choose an end-user analytics tool, such as Powerbase, Tableau, or others.

Analysis

Based on the questions generated in the planning phase, this phase determines what data is needed to perform the analyses. Evaluate whether the data exist internally or externally. Some data will likely exist internally, but it will probably reside in different systems and formats. Therefore, take the time to understand various internal data sources, where the data resides, the types of data formats, and who the data owners are.

Further, consider what external data is needed or would help to extend the analyses. Determine whether the data is accessible or if alternatives are available. Based on the list of data sources, determine what types of data storage are needed to allow the appropriate individuals to access the data. Evaluate if the amount of data requires a more extensive data solution, such as a data warehouse or a data lake.

If using a data warehouse, determine how much data cleansing will be required to make the data useable across the organization by various users. Develop a process to ensure that the data loaded into the data warehouse is valid and in the proper format.

Design

A significant part of the design will be modeling the data, especially if using a larger storage capacity, such as a data warehouse. The data model will provide a roadmap of all the data components for the warehouse, such as the databases, tables, and indexes. To complete this part of the project, you will need experts on data warehouse management with experience in data modeling and business experts with an understanding of the conceptual relationships between the data.

At this point, the analysts should design and implement the controls to manage the data. Design and implement formal processes to address questions such as the following:

- What data will be loaded into the data warehouse? How often?
- How will a new data source be approved?
- What types of end-user analysis tools will be available? Who will have access to those tools?
- What data can the end-users have access to?

In the future, the organization will most likely obtain new data sources, require additional analyses, or change business operations. Therefore, consider whether the system is scalable when designing your data warehouses or lakes. Looking ahead will reduce the probability that the system will need a major overhaul in a few years.

Implementation

In this step, you will implement the plan by loading the data and preparing the way for analysis work. Using the list of data requirements from the design and analysis phases, obtain the data to load into the data warehouse.

Next, clean and format the data to load into the data warehouse. Allow more time than expected for data preparation, as it will reduce issues in the future. Budget additional time for each new data source. Several items to consider when preparing the data are:

1. **Dates.** Are all dates in a consistent format and a form usable for calculations?
2. **Consistency.** Are the data in a specific field consistent throughout? For example, states can be consistently spelled out or abbreviated. Having a combination will affect data analysis and give inconsistent results or eliminate data if the analysis is based on the abbreviation, for example, rather than the full name of the state.
3. **Units of measure.** Do all data in a specific field have a consistent unit of measure? For example, are length measurements all in meters?
4. **Blank fields.** Is there missing data? Determine whether the rest of the record should remain or be removed.
5. **Irrelevant fields or records.** Data that will not be used can be removed from the dataset.
6. **Duplicate data.** After merging data from various sources, are there duplicate records to remove?

These are just a few examples of items to clean before using or loading the data into a data warehouse. After the initial data cleansing, perform some fundamental descriptive analysis on the data, such as central tendency statistics, a histogram, or an overall data profile, to verify the accuracy of the data. These simple analyses will help determine if your data is adequately cleaned and whether there are outliers.

Besides loading data, create user-specific dashboards, queries, or other reports during this phase to help end-users with specific analyses based on the planning stage.

Maintenance

Use the long-term strategy developed in the earlier phases to continue to improve and maintain the data storage, such as the data warehouse/data lake, data analytics applications, and the communication, reporting, and oversight processes. Appoint a team consisting of various functional disciplines to periodically evaluate changing business needs, the adequacy of data analytics to meet current requirements, and the effectiveness of the communication processes and report the findings to the steering committee.

Data Analytic Process

When beginning an individual analytics project, it is helpful to break it into several tasks. The public accounting firm, EY, developed a four-step methodology to approach an analytics problem and create an analytics mindset. Even though there are other analytics processes available, they all follow similar steps, as listed below.[3]

The four steps a user can take when starting data analysis are:

1. Ask the right questions.
2. Extract, transform, and load the data.
3. Apply the appropriate data analytics techniques.
4. Interpret and share the results.

The process provides a roadmap for users to perform accurate analysis and ensure that the information generated is precise and reliable. These steps are further explained next.

Ask the Right Questions

Data analytics starts with determining what questions you are trying to answer. Users who attempt to skip this step often find themselves wandering in an attempt to find an answer. This step requires more thought than just jotting down some questions.

First, you need an understanding of the stakeholders/audience. Who will be the recipients of the data? What decisions are they trying to make? Understanding how the information will be used will help better define the scope of the questions required for the analysis.

Next, the analyst needs to understand the business environment well. Some analyses rely on industry knowledge to put the data into context. For example, you should understand the typical key performance indicators in the industry or any other norms to help compare the data. Besides understanding the industry, users must understand the business processes that generated the data. A deeper understanding of the context will generate better questions before the analysis.

Finally, determine how the analysis will be used.

- Can the organization take action or make a specific decision with this data?
- Will it be useful and provide value?
- Is the analysis required for external reporting purposes?

If the answer to these questions is no, reevaluate the purpose of the analysis.

Extract, Transform, and Load Data

The next step is to obtain and prepare the data for analysis. During this step, select which data analytic software applications you will use for the analysis. You may need one application to cleanse the data, another to perform the analysis, and another to visualize the data. The order in which data is extracted, transformed, and loaded will depend on the data analytics application(s) used.

Based on the questions generated in the previous step, you need to determine what data types are needed. The following is a short list of things to ask about each dataset.

- Where is the data stored?
- What date range of the data is needed?
- Is there a subset of data? For example, are all vendors needed for the analysis?
- Can I retrieve the data, or do I need to contact IT?

The answers to these questions may differ for each dataset. If this is an analysis that needs to be done regularly, establish a standard process or, if possible, automate the data collection, possibly with robotic process automation (RPA).

If the organization uses a data warehouse or data lake, then the data may already be transformed and loaded into a central repository. If this is the case, you will still need to determine which data tables must be accessed and understand the relationships between the data fields.

Once you determine the appropriate datasets, be sure you understand the data. Review the data dictionary to understand what each field in the dataset represents. Are any of the fields coded or linked to a master table that contains detailed information? For example, if the dataset has a column with a customer number, you may need a list of customers to provide the customer's name for the corresponding number.

Before starting your analysis, make sure the data has been cleaned. First, eliminate any data fields that are not required for the analysis. Next, review the data for data quality issues, such as inconsistencies in the data. The clean dataset reduces processing time later and allows you to focus only on the needed items. Once the data has been cleaned, it can be loaded into the data analytics tool.

Apply the Appropriate Analytics Technique

Applying the appropriate analytics technique can be an iterative process. Based on the questions in the first step and the data available, select the appropriate method for analysis. A high-level review of the basic techniques is in Chapter 3.

When analyzing new data, analysts often start with the most basic form of analytics – descriptive. Descriptive analytics provides an overview of the data to confirm further plans for analysis. This analysis also determines if any additional data quality issues were missed in the previous step or if any outliers need to be examined.

Then additional analyses would progress through diagnostic and predictive methods, stopping when the question has been answered. Sometimes, the initial analysis choice does not provide the insights you wanted. Evaluate and determine if there is a more appropriate methodology, whether more data is needed, or whether the analysis is not possible now.

After the initial analyses, take a minute to review the results to ensure that they make sense within the context of the organization. Reviewing the findings before moving forward with an action plan ensures that the analysis is complete and accurate. Using your knowledge and a bit of skepticism, examine the results to determine whether they appear reasonable and explainable. With complex analysis, many things can alter the results, so performing a final review can be a good backup.

Interpret and Share the Results

This last step may be the most essential. You can perform complex analyses, but if you do not take the time to interpret and communicate the results properly, the time and effort spent on analyses will be wasted. The first part of this step is interpreting the results or visualizations. What does the result of the analysis mean to this organization? Can we better understand what happened in the past or forecast the future?

With interpretation, the analyst uses the intuition and knowledge of the industry, company, and environment to put the output of the analysis into context. Blind acceptance of the output can be dangerous, especially if the analysts have rushed through prior steps. Combine critical thinking, intuition, and human knowledge and experience with the findings of the analyses when using data analytics for decision-making.

Next, since most analysts work with various stakeholders, the results should be in a format that users easily understand. Therefore, analysts should understand their audience well, such as their statistical knowledge or business acumen, when communicating the results to the appropriate stakeholders. The communication to users can be in the form of visualizations, a narrative, a report, or a combination. When creating visualizations, keep them simple, reduce clutter, and follow best practices in graphing so that they are easy to understand and not misleading. All narratives should be written clearly, concisely, and understood by someone who is not as well-versed in analytics. These guidelines will help make the analysis useful to the organization.

Having a plan helps an analyst see the process and have a roadmap for how to solve a new problem. Following this approach for data analytics can help generate results that can be used in decision-making.

Data Quality

"Garbage in, garbage out." The quality of the output from data analytics will significantly depend on the quality of the input data. If input data is not of high quality, the ability to rely on the output is questionable. Before using the output data for decision-making, you need to consider the quality of the data used for the analysis.

For example, do you have a good understanding of the following?

- **Data source.** For example, did the data come from an internal source such as an ERP system, or was the data extracted from social media data about your firm?
- **Age of data.** How old is the data? Is the data updated frequently? Are these changes reflected in the current analysis?
- **Input controls.** What type of controls are in place for the data capture process? Did the data source have data integrity controls when capturing the data?

Data is a unique asset. Some factors that make data unique are:[4]

- **Non-fungible.** Different units of data can be used differently by the same company.
- **Non-exclusive in its use.** Two companies can use the same data at the same time.
- **Becomes obsolete rapidly.** Data changes, sometimes in an hour; therefore, newer data is more valuable.
- **Larger volumes generate more value.** Larger datasets are more valuable for data analytics.
- **Not created in isolation.** Data can be created when two or more instances of users interact.
- **Individuals have rights over their raw data.** Sharing personal data is illegal.

Given these unique characteristics, managers should consider the quality of the data used in an analysis. The Financial Accounting Standards Board (FASB) outlined several characteristics for useful financial information.[5] Although the guidance was explicitly written for financial data, the characteristics can apply to any type of data, financial or not, that is being used for decision-making. Consider the characteristics listed in Table 4.1 when collecting data for analysis.

Table 4.1 Characteristics of Quality Data

Fundamental Characteristics		
Relevance – Data is able to aid in making a decision	Predictive value	Applies to future events
	Confirmatory value	Can help confirm a decision or change
	Materiality	Significant enough to influence decision
Faithful Representation – Data must be unbiased and accurate	Complete	Data is not missing from the dataset
	Neutral	Unbiased information to not sway a decision
	Error free	Is as accurate as possible
Enhancing Characteristics	Comparability	Is consistent in how data is presented
	Verifiability	Independent individuals reach the same conclusions
	Understandability	Information is presented clearly, making it easy to understand
	Timeliness	Data is available before decisions are required. Information is up to date

When adding a new data source to the data warehouse or using additional data in an analysis, use these characteristics to determine whether you store and use quality data. When using data, evaluate whether the available data can add value to a decision without providing inaccurate results. For example, will older data suffice if the most current data is unavailable? If incomplete data is used, what is the impact of the end result, will it skew the results, and are we aware of the skewed results? As a manager, the most critical point is that you are aware of the limitations of the data used and understand how these limitations affect the results produced by data analytics.

Data Governance

Organizations today are collecting and using more data than ever before. Data is an important asset to firms today because it enables us to understand trends in customer perceptions and behavior, the effectiveness of business operations, and firm performance. If used well, data enables organizations to create value and competitive advantage. The increased reliance on data makes this resource more valuable; hence, safeguarding data like other physical assets is critical. If key data is lost or falls into the wrong hands, it can harm the organization. For this reason, most companies establish data governance policies and processes to ensure that the data stays secure and data integrity is maintained.

The Data Governance Institute defines data governance as "a system of decision rights and accountabilities for information-related processes, executed according to agreed-upon models which describe who can take what actions with what information, and when, under what circumstances, using what methods."[6] In short, data governance helps ensure that the data can be trusted.

Good data governance policies throughout the data lifecycle will enable organizations to safeguard their data and ensure that the integrity of the data is maintained. The policies should address data collection through storage, use, and final disposal of data. The goal of good data governance is to secure data, making sure it is private. In addition, governance includes policies to ensure that the data is accurate, available when needed, and usable by the appropriate individuals.

The Data Governance Institute lists seven goals of any governance program. These goals will help most organizations establish better policies to achieve their goal. These universal goals are as follows:

1. Enable better decision-making.
2. Reduce operational friction.

3. Protect the needs of data stakeholders.
4. Train management and staff to adopt common approaches to data issues.
5. Build standard, repeatable processes.
6. Reduce costs and increase effectiveness through coordination of efforts.
7. Ensure transparency of processes.

There are several benefits to establishing good data governance policies:

- **Compliance.** With increasing laws and regulations regarding protecting an individual's data, ensuring that data is safe is a necessity. Failure to comply with such rules as the General Data Protection Regulation (GDPR) can have severe reputational consequences and hefty financial fines. Most privacy laws require assurance that data is being protected and used only for the reasons provided in the privacy notice.
- **Trust.** Establishing good data processes will help to gain the trust of customers and other business partners. If these individuals know their data is protected, they are more apt to be confident in a business relationship.
- **Better decision-making.** Similar to gaining the trust of external business partners, better data security and oversight will promote trust with internal users. As a result, the data will be used more for making decisions in the organization.
- **Reduce costs.** Good governance processes will aid in collecting only the data that will be used and in disposing of data at the end of its life. The company can reduce related IT and personnel costs by not collecting extra data and storing it past its usefulness.

Data governance best practices encourage establishing and involving several individuals/committees within the organization. These individuals are:

- **Steering committee.** The committee should be senior management from the organization. This committee is responsible for setting data governance policies aligned with the overall organization's goals and strategy. The committee should have a broad view of the enterprise and a good understanding of data governance principles.
- **Data owner.** This individual is responsible for the governance of a specific data portion and is likely to be specific to a business function or line of business. The owner should be familiar with the processes that generate the data and the needed controls. The owner is responsible for overseeing a particular portion of the data.

- **Data steward.** This individual manages a portion of the data daily. They are responsible for understanding changes in the data environment, escalating them as needed, and resolving any data issues within their domain. The individual requires technical skills and detailed knowledge of the data within their area.

Data Governance Planning

When building a comprehensive data governance plan, managers should take a holistic view of data and align it with the organization's mission and strategy. Even though each organization's plan will be different, this guide will enable you to develop a data governance plan.

First, identify the overall goals for the data. For example, the goal is to increase the security of data and data integrity. The steering committee will set the goals and invite stakeholders throughout the organization to provide input.

Next, inventory the existing datasets throughout the organization. This is an essential step. To govern, protect, and control the data, you have to know what data is captured, how it is captured, when the data is created, where the data is stored, who the data owner is, and who the data stewards are.

Document the following key items about each dataset in your data inventory:

- The source of the data and, more specifically, how it is created.
- Who is the data owner?
- Who are the data stewards?
- Where is the data stored? Document details of the file storage, such as the location and type of data (flat file, relational database, graph database).
- What metadata should be added to the data, such as type, dates, and sources, to make it easier to locate at a later time?
- How often is data updated?
- Who has access to the data?
- What are the existing controls for this data?
- Will this data be consolidated into a data warehouse or lake?

It is essential that you do not rush through this step. If done properly, this task will reveal data sources previously not known to managers. Creating this inventory is the starting point for the rest of the plan.

Determine the priority of the datasets and focus resources accordingly. Higher-priority datasets should have more stringent levels of oversight. For example, changes to this type of data should receive a stricter review before making any changes to the data. Use automated processes to ensure that appropriate metadata is attached to the files for easy cataloging. Limit access to high-priority data to increase security.

Create an access matrix for significant data sources to determine who can use the data for analysis. Sensitive data may be limited to management or aggregated for broader use.

Determine the overall lifecycle for each dataset. How long does the data need to be stored and maintained? Even though data storage is historically relatively inexpensive, it is still costly to maintain, secure, and back up data that is no longer used. Depending on the type of data and the potential uses, the timeframe to store each dataset may differ. Also, the data can be stored initially on a high-speed server and later moved to secondary storage. Documenting this now makes the decision to purge the data easier later.

Work with an IT security team to provide proper security to the dataset. Data that is more sensitive, such as personal information, should be given a higher level of priority. The level of security required will be determined by the priority given to the dataset. If the data is of the highest value to the organization or is more sensitive, reduce access to the data and establish more security controls. However, be careful not to overlook securing less important datasets. Unauthorized access to these datasets can create indirect threats to the high-priority data in an organization.

Create an approval plan to document any changes to the criteria established in the previous step. Changes to the business are certain, and more data will likely be required to support the analysis. Designate a committee of cross-functional and data analytics experts to review the change requests. Be certain that changes to the plan are documented.

Ethics

To quote a *Harvard Business Review* article, "With Big Data Comes Big Responsibility."[7] Data collected today contains not only financial data but also behavioral aspects of customers, vendors, or employees. Therefore, when organizations use data, they must ensure that data is used ethically and socially responsibly. Decisions based solely on data can have negative impacts on people and society and reflect back on the company. We discuss several ethical considerations about data in the following sections.

Data Privacy

One of the biggest concerns about data is privacy of data, particularly about individuals, such as customers or employees. Companies can build goodwill with customers by demonstrating that it implements data privacy procedures. However, with the recent changes in data privacy laws, data privacy has become a legal issue as much as an ethical one. Controls around individuals' private data require more actions to protect the data than many other types of data.

Legal Environment

In recent years, several legal changes have required companies to take greater responsibility in protecting private data and ensuring that the individual has a more significant say in what is done with the data. The following briefly summarizes some of the most prevalent laws that affect organizations.

The **General Data Protection Regulation (GDPR)** is one of the most stringent privacy protection regulations worldwide. Although the law protects citizens of the European Union, any company that has collected data on EU citizens has to comply with the requirements of the regulation. Put into effect in 2018, the GDPR is the most comprehensive law for protecting individual data privacy. The regulation includes significant fines for noncompliance of up to 4% of global revenue or 20 million euros, whichever is higher.[7] The law requires that organizations provide users the ability to opt in to the collection of data rather than opt out. According to the requirements, data can only be used and stored according to the guidelines in the law.

The GDPR requires any company with EU citizen data to "by design and by default" consider how to protect data, establish "appropriate technical and organizational measures" to handle the data, and communicate with affected individuals of a data breach within 72 hours of the breach. Therefore, the law increases the need for good data security processes to meet these requirements. The law also permits individuals to have more control over their data by requiring companies to inform them of their rights and allowing individuals to request that their data be removed and have access to their data.[8]

The **California Consumer Privacy Act (CCPA)** is a law modeled after the GDPR, protecting California citizens. The law was put into effect on January 1, 2020, and amended with additional consumer protections on January 1, 2023. Unlike the GDPR, which applies to all organizations, the CCPA is for companies with annual gross revenue of more than $25 million or makes the majority of their revenue from selling personal information. The CCPA is the first major law in the United States to comprehensively address consumer privacy.[9]

Currently, the United States does not have an extensive privacy law that is broad in scope. The Federal Trade Commission, through the Federal Trade Commission Act, has some authority to enforce privacy laws when there is deceptive trade practice. This ability is, however, somewhat limited in scope.

Other federal laws have a specific scope and are limited to a particular record type, such as financial information or health data. A brief list of the most significant privacy laws include:

- The Health Insurance Portability and Accounting Act (HIPAA) – governs health information.
- The Gramm Leach Bliley Act – regulates the collection of financial information in banks and other financial institutions.
- The Fair Credit Reporting Act – controls the use of personal credit information.
- The Family Educational Rights and Privacy Act (FERPA) – restricts access to student education records.

Ethical Considerations for Data

Besides protecting a company from legal threats, protecting the privacy of individuals can be beneficial for many other reasons. Primarily, showing that the organization cares about privacy and takes extra steps to secure the data can help build its reputation. As privacy becomes more of a concern for most individuals, it can be a factor when choosing which company to buy from or work for. In a 2019 survey, 90% of respondents believed there is a connection between how their data is treated and how they are treated as customers.[10] So, protecting data can be good for your business.

Companies like Apple use their data practices as part of their marketing strategy. Apple's campaign emphasizes that personal data is not shared or sold to their parties. If customers see you doing the right thing, it matters.

There are several key things that a company can do beyond security measures to help promote ethical data practices in the organization.

1. **Build privacy into the design.** When designing a new process, system, or data collection stream, consider privacy from the start of the project. Before implementing a new system, create a plan for how to protect the data. Move privacy considerations from an afterthought to one of the primary actions taken during a project.
2. **Design with the individual in mind.** Assume the individual is the owner of the data. Design the data collection process to inform the individual of their rights, what data is collected, what it is used for, and how the data can be deleted.
3. **Be transparent.** Inform the individual how the data will be collected, stored, and used. Include how long the data will be kept and when it will be stored.

4. **Anonymize the data.** When possible, remove any identifying individual characteristics from the data as early as the process. Use the data to determine generalizations more than traits of a specific individual. When you are unable to use anonymized data, clearly inform the individual.

5. **Consider any unintentional consequences.** Review the intent of the data analysis. Are there any potential unintentional consequences that can be harmful to the individual? This can be a greater issue when using data to create a personalized experience.

Ethical Considerations for Data Analytics

Over the years, data analytics, if not critically evaluated, have led to discriminatory outcomes. Decisions based on various analytics can have harmful consequences for those included in a particular dataset. Individuals not in the original dataset as well as the general public may be indirectly harmed due to the infiltration of data mining practices into our everyday activities, such as marketing done through social media platforms.[11] Some factors that cause discriminatory outcomes are:

- Algorithmic mechanisms/bias that result in involuntary and accidental discrimination, causing harm to real people.
- Grouping data or creating profiles can cause direct discrimination against individuals of a certain race, ethnic group, or age.
- Including biased data in a data model. For example, using only white males in a dataset excludes females and other races. Bias data can come from historically biased data sets, bias in manually assigning class labels, or bias in data collection leading to under- or overrepresentation.
- Using proxies to represent certain characteristics, such as using the zip code for economic status or race of an individual.
- Creating unintended feedback loops. For example, notifications of crime increase police patrol, and when police patrol increases criminal activity reporting increases, creating a vicious feedback loop.
- Prior selection of certain attributes in data analytics causes a reductive representation of a more complex real-world scenario.
- Misspecification, which is not properly identifying features that represent the real world. The unintentional omission of data from the analysis can also cause bias.
- Masking, which is the intentional use of data analytics to exploit certain individual groups.

- Digital divide causing unintended discrimination. People who do not have access to the internet or a computer may not be included in datasets because their data may not be collected regularly. This may eliminate people from programs that may benefit them.
- Automatically obtaining and linking data about individuals may disclose personal information that may lead to discrimination.

Managers should be aware of and do their due diligence with the following to avoid ethical issues when using data analytics for decision-making:

- Be aware of systematic bias in data collection.
- Create the best practices for data collection and storage, being mindful of privacy issues.
- Be aware of systematic bias in data analysis during data extraction, transformation, and loading.
- Be aware that just because you have the data does not necessarily mean that it is ethical to use it.
- Provide ethical training for data scientists periodically.
- Create accountability within teams.
- Lead by example by creating an ethical culture and asking questions to uncover any intentional or unintentional discrimination.
- Be aware of misleading correlations. Analysts might be able to find various correlations when large datasets are used. However, these correlations may not make sense in the real world.
- Be aware of the sample size and the variables used to look for associations. When the number of variables increases, to ensure statistical significance, the number of data points needs to increase as well. Therefore, managers should consider whether the dataset used is large enough to derive accurate, reliable inferences.
- Be mindful of the type of visualizations selected to present the data and how they are created. If proper graphing techniques are not followed, visualizations can mislead managers and cause them to make the wrong inference from the analysis.

Notes

1. Ransbotham, S. (2015). Coca-Cola's Unique Challenge: Turning 250 Datasets Into One: Remco Brouwer and Mathew Chacko (Coca-Cola), Interviewed by Sam Ransbotham. *MIT Sloan Management Review* 56 (4).
2. White, A. (2019). Our Top Data and Analytics Predicts for 2019. Gartner. https://blogs.gartner.com/andrew_white/2019/01/0/our-top-data-and-analytics-predicts-for-2019.
3. EY. (n.d.). Academic Resource Center – Analytics Mindset. https://www.ey.com/en_us/about-us/ey-foundation-and-university-relations/academic-resource-center#.
4. Parra-Moyano, J., Schmedders, K., and Pentland, A. (2020). What Managers Need to Know About Data Exchanges. *MIT Sloan Management Review* 61 (4): 39–44.
5. FASB. (2021). Statement of Financial Accounting Concepts Statement No. 8—Conceptual Framework For Financial Reporting—Chapter 3, Qualitative Characteristics of Useful Financial Information (as Amended). https://fasb.org/document/blob?fileName=Concepts%20Statement%208—Chapter%201%20(As%20Amended).pdf.
6. The Data Governance Institute. (n.d.). Definitions of Data Governance. https://datagovernance.com/the-data-governance-basics/definitions-of-data-governance/.
7. HBR Editors. (2014). With Big Data Comes Big Responsibility. *Harvard Business Review* (November). https://hbr.org/2014/11/with-big-data-comes-big-responsibility.
8. GDPR.EU. (n.d.). What Is GDPR, the EU's New Data Protection Law? https://gdpr.eu/what-is-gdpr/.
9. California Department of Justice. (2023). California Consumer Privacy Act. https://oag.ca.gov/privacy/ccpa.
10. Redman, T., and Waitman, R. (2020). Do You Care About Privacy as Much as Your Customers Do? *Harvard Business Review* (January 28). https://hbr.org/2020/01/do-you-care-about-privacy-as-much-as-your-customers-do.
11. Favaretto, M., De Clercq, E., and Elger, B. S. (2019). Big Data and Discrimination: Perils, Promises and Solutions. A Systematic Review. *Journal of Big Data* 6 (1): 1–27. https://doi.org/10.1186/s40537-019-0177-4.

CHAPTER 5

Introduction to Artificial Intelligence

The True Meaning of AI

Excerpts from an interview with Ginni Rometty, former IBM CEO, during an interview at the 2017 World Economic Conference in Davos, Switzerland

"AI said replacement of people, it carries some baggage with it," Rometty said. "And that is not what we're talking about."

In line with what Rometty mentions, artificial intelligence has garnered a negative reputation over the decades as a force that will eventually destroy humanity. And part of that has to do with the nomenclature, which tacitly defines AI as something on par with the human mind.

That's why we call it narrow AI, or, better yet, "These are technologies to augment human intelligence," as Rometty said during her interview. "By and large, we see a world where this is a partnership between man and machine, and this is, in fact, going to make us better and allow us to do what the human condition is best able to do."

"You have so much information . . . so much that if you don't do something, your brain, us as humans, can deal cognitively with all of that," Rometty said. As an example, 8,000 medical papers are being published every day, an insane amount of information for any single doctor to read or review. And medical data is doubling every 60 days.

"You need a system that can understand all this data, could reason over it, and could learn, which means they do become more powerful with time," Rometty said. This is the basic description of how machine learning and deep learning algorithms work. Instead of embedding static

(Continued)

(*Continued*)

logic (if-else statements) into them, you provide them with samples and data from a specific nondeterministic domain and you teach them to come up with their own rules for running applications. These can be anything ranging from simple pictures to social media posts, news articles, and other unstructured data. The data goes through "neural networks," a software structure that roughly mimics the human brain and transforms into an intricate set of rules that maps inputs to outputs.

"I think these systems have the opportunity to do for some of what have been the world's most unsolvable problems, to find solutions to them," Rometty said.[1]

Artificial Intelligence

Some of the first concepts of artificial intelligence originated in the 1950s with Alan Turing's question on whether machines can think.[2] Since then, AI has moved from a theoretical concept to one many use daily. These AI applications are not similar to the images of robots like those depicted in science fiction movies. However, they exist behind the scenes and are now a part of the products and services we use daily, such as making recommendations for internet shopping, matching your interests in a search engine, or answering questions on a virtual assistant (such as Alexa). AI is also used to power self-driving cars and answer questions in chatbots.

Artificial intelligence is the study of how to make computers behave intelligently. Intelligent behavior uses perceptions, reasoning, learning, communicating, and acting in complex environments.[3] Therefore, the goal of AI is to develop machines that behave intelligently[4] and understand the behavior of other machines or humans.

In 2011, IBM's supercomputer Watson defeated two humans, former champion contestants in the TV game show *Jeopardy*, who had long winning streaks on the show. This demonstration showed the power of AI to understand the rules of the game show and language, search for an appropriate answer, and communicate the results in the proper format.[5] Although AI is used for *Jeopardy* and other games, such as chess, Go, and mahjong, AI is also useful in many business applications. In a recent PWC study, 52% of organizations accelerated their AI implementations due to the COVID-19 pandemic to increase productivity during worker and supply-chain shortages.[6]

Artificial intelligence is helping many businesses develop a competitive advantage by understanding their customers, predicting financial results, reducing potential fraud, and creating new products. Several new products, such as self-driving vehicles and voice assistants like Siri, have integrated AI into their functionality. However, developing an artificial intelligence process is not without its challenges. Before moving on, let's define several terms related to AI.

- **AI algorithm.** Algorithms are sets of instructions written using computer code that tells the computer how to perform specific calculations or operations. Therefore, an AI algorithm is a program, set of instructions, or code that tells the computer how to learn, calculate, and operate given specific criteria.
- **AI model.** A model is the output of an AI algorithm developed from analyzing data.
- **AI applications.** These are various software applications that use AI algorithms. We use the term AI applications to refer to software applications that have embedded AI algorithms.
- **Augmented intelligence.** These applications combine human knowledge with the output of the AI model.

How to Build an AI Model

In general, all forms of AI require existing data to build a model. This data can be in various forms, including structured data, such as databases and spreadsheets, or less structured formats, such as text, audio, and visual data. The data used to build the model is divided into training, validation, and test data. First, the AI algorithm imports the training data and then produces the model using various statistical and other model-building techniques discussed later in this chapter. Different algorithms may work better for different problems. Therefore, finding the proper method and other parameters requires trial and error.

Second, once the model is built with the training data, it is tested with the validation data. The analyst will evaluate the model for accuracy and prediction ability. Typically, an analyst will go through several iterations of building a model and testing with the validation data before finding and finalizing the optimal model. Once the model is finalized, the final step is to test the model with the test data. Figure 5.1 shows the three-step high-level process for building AI models.

This process describes the basic methodology used to build an AI model. Depending on the type of AI used, the process may vary slightly. However, the primary training, validating, and testing steps will remain the same. The models can be updated when new data is collected. Unlike most computer

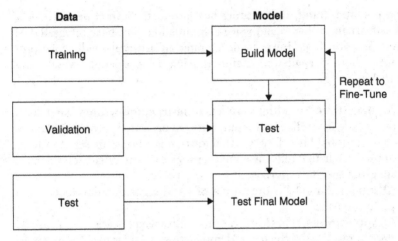

Figure 5.1 Three-Step High-Level Process of Building an AI Model

code that is static, many AI algorithms have a learning process, therefore, change with the data.

Types of Artificial Intelligence

Artificial intelligence mimics human intelligence and, in some cases, improves upon it. AI can be very broad, with the most simplistic form of AI that mimics human actions falling into robotic processing automation (RPA) and more advanced forms of AI using natural language processing (NLP) and deep learning neural networks. Even though several different types of AI algorithms exist, only the primary types are discussed in the next section.

Machine Learning

Machine learning (ML) is the most common subset of AI. ML uses technologies to help identify patterns and then uses the findings from the algorithm for either decision-making or improving user experiences. These algorithms rely highly on statistical methods to analyze patterns and similarities in the data and can adapt as it receives additional data. The output of AI provides insights and correlations that were likely unidentifiable by humans. The learning occurs when the algorithm adjusts based on new data it receives.

One of the critical advantages of ML over human intelligence is the lack of preconceived ideas of where possible correlations exist. Humans tend to focus on the linkages that they believe exist. Therefore, traditional statistical methods rely primarily on a hypothesis-first methodology to build a model. These methods are somewhat limited by what hypotheses the human analyst generates. Thus, the traditional approach relies on the judgment and experience of the analyst to provide the questions. Machine learning focuses first on the data and less on any a priori hypothesis. AI applications will analyze all possible correlations and statistically build models accordingly. Machine learning can identify patterns in the data by examining data otherwise overlooked due to human bias.

Behind each of these algorithms is a statistical function that helps to determine the connections and similarities between data points through various mathematical methods. The specific statistical method selected will influence the reliability of the model. The type of machine learning can also vary depending on the data available to build the model. Over time, the models improve as more data is analyzed; thus, the machine learning algorithms continuously learn and adapt to new data. In the end, machine learning applications can make decisions without human intervention. Figure 5.2 shows the different kinds of machine learning. Machine learning is categorized into supervised, unsupervised, and reinforcement learning.

Supervised Learning

Supervised learning applications use data that contains labeled or known values to build a model that can be used to evaluate future data. For example, the application receives data with the features of animals such as dogs, cats, or horses. After learning what each animal looks like with training data, the AI application builds a model to predict the type of each shape based on what it has learned. The model is then tested with additional labeled data to measure the accuracy of the model. Figure 5.3 shows an example of supervised learning.

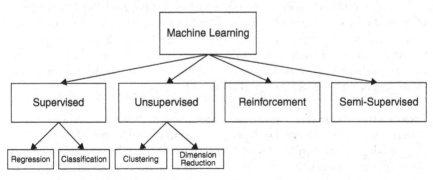

Figure 5.2 Types of Machine Learning

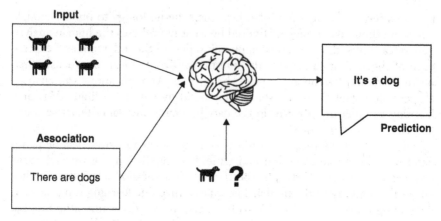

Figure 5.3 Supervised Learning

Another example of supervised learning is using a dataset containing millions of credit card charges. Each charge is labeled as either fraudulent or nonfraudulent. Using supervised learning, AI can build a model indicating the characteristics of a fraudulent charge versus a nonfraudulent charge. The algorithm can then use additional test data to evaluate the credit card charges. The model's efficacy is determined by calculating the correct number of responses, false positives, and negatives.

There are two main types of supervised learning: classification and regression.

Classification   Classification models are used to identify to which group an item belongs. The training and testing data are labeled with categories and used to build a model. The model identifies the most critical characteristics to place the item in the appropriate group.

Every day, the spam filter on your email uses this algorithm to determine whether the incoming email is spam. The filter uses an AI model to identify patterns in the language and format of emails previously labeled as spam or not. After testing, the model determines which incoming new emails are spam and places them in your spam folder. The model continues to learn as additional emails are received and marked as spam.

Regression   Regression uses techniques from statistics to determine associations between several independent variables and a dependent variable. This method uses similar calculations to what you learned in statistics courses. However, AI can analyze more variables and accurately determine correlations with large volumes of data. This type of AI is best used for forecasting models, for example, predicting a company's given net income based on several internal and external historical data. In real estate, this method is used to predict rental prices based on input factors such as square footage, location, and distance from the city.

Unsupervised Learning

Unsupervised learning does not use data with predefined categories like supervised learning does. The goal is to generalize a description of the data and group similar items together based on patterns discerned in the data. An unsupervised algorithm will not identify or name the groups but group them. An example of this type of unsupervised learning occurs in most social media platforms. Individuals are grouped based on clusters of individuals who know each other. From there, the output makes suggestions of possible friends or acquaintances. Figure 5.4 shows how unsupervised learning is applied to pictures of animals.

Building these models requires significant data and more computing power than supervised models. Thus, they can take longer to generate and add additional costs. However, unsupervised learning may be the best option depending on the end goal and available data.

Clustering These algorithms try to find commonalities between records based on the variables given. Clustering algorithms can be based on density, distribution, centroid, hierarchical, or K-means. For example, given transactional data from customers making purchases at your store, an unsupervised learning algorithm would group them into similar categories based on demographics, purchases, or other information. Marketing can use the model to generate targeted ads.

Dimension Reduction This form of unsupervised learning is a method to reduce the complexity of a dataset to build a simpler model. This method will take large datasets with many variables, determine the most relevant

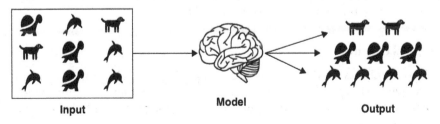

Figure 5.4 Unsupervised Learning

items, and eliminate the rest. Dimension reduction techniques are broadly categorized into linear or nonlinear methods. Several linear techniques are principal component analysis (PCA), factor analysis, linear discriminant analysis, and truncated singular value decomposition. Kernel PCA, multi-dimensional scaling, and isometric mapping are several nonlinear methods. Simpler models are less apt to be overfitted and thus can only be used in a particular scenario.

Reinforcement Learning

Reinforced learning is a machine learning technique that allows the agent to learn by trial and error in an interactive environment. Usually, this technique has a win/lose outcome or a desired type of outcome. The most common example of reinforced learning can be applied to learning to play chess or the game Go. The player can perform several different moves to reach the final goal of winning the game. In such situations, the AI algorithm learns from trial and error. The difference between supervised and reinforcement learning is that reinforcement learning rewards or punishes as a signal for positive and negative behavior. In supervised learning, we provide a correct set of actions for performing a task.

In business, reinforced learning applications are used for recommender systems, such as Amazon's "recommended other products" or Netflix's movie recommendations. The objective is to make the consumer buy or watch the recommended products. These algorithms continue to adjust until the consumer selects a suggestion.

Semi-Supervised Learning

Semi-supervised learning uses a combination of supervised and unsupervised techniques. For example, when the training data is missing or has incorrect labels on a portion of the data, the algorithm will build a base model with the labeled data and seek input from a human on completing the remaining data. Therefore, when using semi-supervised learning, the AI algorithm may require more supervision during the initial stages. The model will become more efficient as more data is completed or corrected. Some recommender systems use semi-supervised learning, at least in part.

Deep Learning

Deep learning is another form of artificial intelligence. The primary method for deep learning includes neural networks. Unlike machine learning, which requires human input regarding test data, neural networks find patterns and predict outcomes without any initial human input. Deep learning algorithms are more complex than other types of machine learning algorithms. As a result, they need more data to learn during the training process and more computing power for processing. Unlike many machine learning applications, a high-end computer is needed to perform complex calculations in the neural network. In addition, these systems are more complex and require a higher level of expertise to implement correctly.

Deep learning is superior to other AI types in analyzing unstructured data, such as video, text, and audio, and finding patterns. The primary deep learning method is neural networks built to mimic how the human brain works. These networks are frequently known as artificial neural networks (ANNs). Figure 5.5 shows the basic flow of data in an ANN.

ANNs consist of several layers: the input layer, several hidden layers, and an output layer. Each node, depicted as a circle in Figure 5.5, connects to every other node in the next layer. Each node is associated with a specific weight and threshold. When data passes to the next network layer, ANNs undergo many intensive training rounds to fine-tune the model. Each time, each node's weights and thresholds are tweaked until the model becomes efficient and accurate. The downside of ANN is that how the output is developed is largely unseen by humans. This black box effect hides the weights and thresholds used at each node and how the weights were determined. Therefore, ANN makes it difficult for anyone else to audit or validate the results.

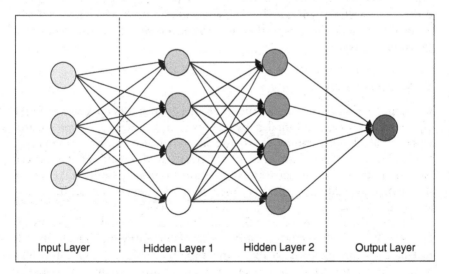

Figure 5.5 Artificial Neural Network

Natural Language Processing

Natural language processing (NLP) moves beyond basic speech recognition to converting spoken words to text and adding meaning based on the tone of the conversation. NLP can be combined with other types of AI and used in chatbots or intelligent voice assistants to respond verbally to questions. NLP applications can also evaluate text documents and provide a summary or extract key data for further processing.

Basic NLP software applications include text generation, which converts verbal communication to written text. The application must understand the basic nuances of language to convert verbal data to text data. For example, the application should be able to distinguish between "their" and "there." Another use of NLP is in content extraction. Software applications using content extraction must understand the language sufficiently to extract data from documents. An example of content extraction is examining contract documents to search for specific terms and conditions and copying them to a format that could be analyzed. NLP is also used for translation between languages. Translation requires knowledge of multiple languages and contexts to select the correct words depending on the context and apply various grammatical rules appropriate for that language.

The final example of NLP is the use of chatbots and voice assistants. These applications not only understand the language but can trigger additional AI applications as a response to a question. The chatbot's front end must understand the user's question but provide enough data to other applications to search the appropriate database and find the correct answer. Once an answer is found, NLP is further used to convert the answer into conversational text or voice.

Computer Vision

Computer vision is one of the more advanced AI and deep learning areas. These applications build models based on visual data. Using complex mathematical calculations, computer vision models analyze the differences in pixels to help identify images. Similar to other types of AI, thousands of images need to be imported into the software application to initially built an AI model. These model-building applications use a form of a neural network to understand how the pixels in the images relate to one another.

There are a variety of uses for computer vision models. This technology is used in facial recognition software to help identify individuals. In self-driving cars, computer vision allows them to differentiate a stop sign from a streetlight. Computer vision can also be used for quality control to compare newly manufactured items with images of finished quality items. Computer vision can be used in inventory management to identify empty bins or count inventory items in a bin.

AI Platforms and Software Applications

Many specific AI algorithms are unique and are developed for a particular purpose. However, there are a variety of software applications or artificial intelligence platforms that companies can use to implement AI solutions without starting from scratch. Table 5.1 lists some of the more common tools available for implementation. Before selecting an AI software application, management must carefully evaluate the purpose and goals for implementing an AI application and consider how AI models would help achieve the company's strategy. An advantage of many of these software applications is that they provide cloud infrastructure or storage.

Table 5.1   AI Platforms and Software Applications

Software or Platform	Description
Google Cloud AI	Offers a variety of AI products and algorithms
	Can use in the cloud or local network
	Focus on language products, including transcription, OCR, and NLP
	Scalable solutions
	Security solutions
Microsoft Azure AI	Offers a variety of scalable applications, including image processing
	Specializes in marketing and e-commerce applications
	Supports a variety of tools, languages, and framework
IBM Watson Studio	Offers prebuilt models to adopt, including code and no-code.
	Compatible with AWS, Azure, and Google
	Has deep learning integration
Salesforce Einstein	Focus on applications for customer relationship management
	Determines next actions for customers
Amazon Alexa	Virtual voice-based assistant
	Develop apps for customers to use via devices
TensorFlow	Consists of an open-source code library for building machine learning modules
	Portable to various platforms

Source: PAT Research. (2022). Top 18 Artificial Intelligence Platforms in 2022. *Predictive Analytics Today.* https://www.predictiveanalyticstoday.com/artificial-intelligence-platforms/.

Use Cases

AI models can be developed to help management decision-making in every area of an organization. We discuss a few use cases of AI in each functional area and the healthcare industry.

Accounting

Fraud discovery. One of the primary ways AI is used in accounting is fraud detection. For example, AI is heavily used to flag potentially fraudulent credit card charges. Credit card firms used data from historical transactions, including those known to be fraudulent, to build AI models. These models are used on real-time incoming transactions to flag potentially fraudulent charges. As additional data is generated, the models continue to evolve and adapt.

Auditors can use similar techniques to evaluate a company's transactions to determine which events are outliers and need further investigation. Using AI, auditors can evaluate entire populations of transactions rather than samples.

Forecast generation. By integrating data from various sources, AI can build models to predict future financial forecasts better. Once the initial models are created using a company's internal and external data, such as economic trends and weather patterns, social media data can better predict financial changes than traditional data sources can.

Inventory counting. Frequently, accountants require counting inventory items for audit or valuation purposes. Auditors can use computer vision to count items that are difficult to enumerate due to size, mobility, or volume. For example, AI can analyze animal pen photos for large farm operations. Rembrandt Farms developed a computer vision and AI system to count eggs as they passed on a conveyor belt. It could identify cracked eggs and estimate their size, even when the eggs overlapped on the conveyor belt.[7]

Marketing

Lead generation. Obtaining new customer leads is key to generating new sales growth. AI can analyze your current customer base and rank new potential customers based on their likelihood of becoming new customers. This ranking will allow salespeople to focus their energy on the potential customers most likely to convert. AI can also scour new sources to find names of other potential customers from various internet sources.

Personalized marketing. One of the newer trends in marketing is personalization. AI allows a marketer to adjust customer messages based on their current needs. The message can also remain consistent for individuals across a variety of platforms. Interaction data can be collected and analyzed to adjust the messaging to the individual customer.

Chatbots for customer support. Many organizations have web-based chatbots for customers and clients to ask questions. Although many have a human on the other end, more frequently, a chatbot that uses NLP does much of the initial screening and basic answering of questions. This allows the human representatives to spend more time resolving more complicated issues.

Production

Quality checks. Many differences in manufactured products are so small that they are difficult for experts to detect easily. Using imaging techniques and comparisons to specifications or perfectly completed products, AI can compare the images to see minor defects. AI can alert production managers about potential problems early in the manufacturing process and help correct deficiencies, thus eliminating waste and reducing future problems.

Preventive maintenance. Most machines in the manufacturing process need various preventive maintenance procedures performed to ensure long life and efficient operation. Many of these maintenance tasks are time-consuming and expensive. Delaying maintenance can damage machines but having downtime while performing maintenance before it is needed can increase costs. Using sensor data from the devices can detect changes in operations, operating conditions, and other factors that can affect the operation of the equipment. This application will help organizations perform maintenance when needed.

Human Resources

Resume scanning. Text-based artificial intelligence programs can extract keywords and phrases from resumes and match the skills with the required skills listed in the job posting. Additional forms of AI can then rank the potential applicants based on specified criteria. Some attempts have been made to compare incoming resumes with those currently working in the company; however, early attempts have led to misleading results.[8]

Recruiting. Artificial intelligence can help reach potential employees, even those not actively seeking new employment. AI searches various sources online for individuals with the needed skill. These intelligent bots can then reach out to the potential matches and prescreen the individuals with basic questions to determine whether the process should continue. From there, intelligent agents can aid in booking interviews, arranging travel, and completing any other logistical arrangements.

Healthcare

Image analysis. AI is used to analyze images, such as X-rays and ultrasounds, to help diagnose diseases. In a 2019 study, researchers found that diagnoses from AI were as good as those from human experts.[9] Using AI to evaluate images can allow doctors to focus more time on treatment and patient care rather than the diagnosis process.

Diagnosis. Often, diagnosing an illness in a patient can be a long process as medical professionals eliminate some potential causes while trying to find the correct one. AI can help provide medical professionals with additional information by evaluating patterns in health complications and comparing them with historical diagnoses. The additional information can provide more insight for the doctors to arrive at a more conclusive diagnosis sooner. This application exemplifies how artificial intelligence can work alongside human expertise to gain even better insights.

Notes

1. Dickson, B. (2018). What Ginni Rometty Teaches Us About the True Meaning of AI. *TechTalks* (8 May). https://bdtechtalks.com/2018/05/08/ibm-ceo-augmented-intelligence-ai/#.
2. Turing, A. M. (1950). Computing Machinery and Intelligence. *Mind* LIX (236, October): 433–460. https://doi.org/10.1093/mind/LIX.236.433.
3. Nilsson, N. (1998). *Artificial Intelligence: A New Synthesis.* San Francisco, CA: Morgan Kaufmann.
4. Ertel, W. (2018). *Introduction to Artificial Intelligence.* Weingarten, Germany: Springer.
5. Best, J. (2013). IBM Watson: The Inside Story of How the Jeopardy-Winning Supercomputer Was Born, and What It Wants to Do Next. *TechRepublic* (9 September). https://www.techrepublic.com/article/ibm-watson-the-inside-story-of-how-the-jeopardy-winning-supercomputer-was-born-and-what-it-wants-to-do-next/
6. McKendrick, J. (2021). AI Adoption Skyrocketed Over the Last 18 Months. *Harvard Business Review* (27 September). https://hbr.org/2021/09/ai-adoption-skyrocketed-over-the-last-18-months.
7. Smith, D., and Hoggard, G. (2022). Counting Eggs with AI. *Strategic Finance* (1 February). https://sfmagazine.com/articles/2022/february/counting-eggs-with-ai.
8. Amazon Ditched AI Recruiting Tool That Favored Men for Technical Jobs. (2018). *The Guardian* (10 October). https://www.theguardian.com/technology/2018/oct/10/amazon-hiring-ai-gender-bias-recruiting-engine.
9. Marr, B. (2020). *Tech Trends in Practice.* Hoboken, NJ: Wiley.

CHAPTER 6

Artificial Intelligence Implementation and Management

Instacart to Add Chatbot as Grocers Push Boundaries on Digital Content

This week in grocery, Instacart taps AI as supermarkets test shoppable content and new formats.

OpenAI, creator of artificial intelligence (AI) chatbot ChatGPT, announced Wednesday (March 1) that developers are now able to integrate the bot into their products, with one of the first companies to do so being Instacart.

The AI company noted that the grocery aggregator will add to its app the ability for consumers to ask questions related to recipes and inspiration, with the responses featuring shoppable suggestions. The feature will be added "later this year."

With this, the chatbot will have the opportunity to reach the 42% of men and 28% of women who purchase groceries online using a same-day delivery site such as Instacart, according to data from PYMNTS study "The ConnectedEconomy™ Monthly Report: The Gender Divide," which draws from a survey of more than 2,600 U.S. consumers.

Granted, ChatGPT has sparked concern among some.

Most recently, a report Thursday (March 2) by *The Wall Street Journal* (WSJ) said Apple has delayed the approval of an update to its BlueMail app that uses the technology due to concerns that it could generate content that's not fit for younger users. Additionally, a recent CNN report noted that JPMorgan Chase has restricted its global staff's use of the technology because of compliance concerns around the use of third-party software. Additionally, in January, a report noted mixed reviews from companies using the system.[1]

Implementation Framework

Many believe artificial intelligence (AI) has the potential to change the type of products and services provided by companies, how we work and make decisions, and how we spend our time at home. This great transformational power comes with a bit of caution. There are many risks associated with embracing AI. Unleashing an AI application without regard for the ethical implications can negatively impact internal and external stakeholders and society. Before beginning any AI implementation, management must understand and evaluate the implications of such adoption on various stakeholders.

Successful Artificial Intelligence Projects

Organizations have the potential to utilize artificial intelligence to find new products, increase efficiency, or provide better customer service. However, as with many technologies, management should follow several critical practices to increase the probability of a successful implementation.

Have a long-term vision. Investing in artificial intelligence can be expensive. These costs include hardware upgrades, software, and training costs. For this reason, you do not want to consider only the cost of your first AI project when making the initial investment. An organization needs to consider many potential uses of AI and develop a long-term strategy on how it can be incorporated to add business value. The strategy will help ensure that the investment in hardware and software is compatible with possible AI applications and allows seamless integration. Having a long-term vision will also help you determine and plan any hiring or training needs within the organization.

Based on the long-term plan, build processes for evaluating and approving future AI projects that are aligned with the organization's business strategy. A formal process will enable management to decide on significant projects and add flexibility to respond to changing business needs while providing an overall direction for innovation using AI.

Have clear requirements and goals. Especially when you start the first AI project, managers may become overenthusiastic and set unrealistic goals without fully considering the organization's requirements. Consider the requirements, such as whether this AI application will interact with employees using augmented intelligence or whether it can build models and evaluate solutions without human intervention. Similar to any other application implementation, having the overall goals defined at the beginning of the project will provide clear expectations for the project team, management, and other interested stakeholders. Clearly defined requirements will help management define the project scope, determine resource needs, and improve the success of the implementation.

Ensure proper skills. Before beginning, be sure you have sufficient personnel resources trained in AI. If the skills necessary are unavailable within the organization, consider initially hiring external consultants to provide the needed expertise. Consultants will help guide your internal staff in implementing a new area and supplement their training. Of course, technical knowledge is necessary, but don't forget that extensive domain knowledge is required to understand the processes before beginning a project. Employees beyond the technical project team should receive basic technology training if the long-term strategy is to implement several organizational projects. This strategy will help the organization to adapt and discover new activities if there is widespread knowledge of the capabilities of artificial intelligence. If augmented artificial intelligence is part of the strategy, employees will also need to be able to adjust to working with the technology to use it efficiently.

Create a data plan. Creating a robust artificial intelligent application requires significant data from internal and external sources. Before starting the project, make sure you can obtain the data in a format usable for building the AI model. Create a plan for maintaining data and adding new data to train the model further.

Evaluate the existing infrastructure. Before starting any AI implementation, determine the requirements for the infrastructure. Then decide whether your current infrastructure can handle an AI application or what new hardware needs to be acquired. A long-term view of the needs will ensure long-term scalability and compatibility for your applications. If the current architecture is not capable of the volume of processing needed, consider other cloud options to augment the current environment.

Buy-in from stakeholders. Like most projects that can directly affect employees, getting their buy-in from the start is helpful. AI is likely to change job requirements for many individuals within the firm. Consequently, employees can feel threatened or fear the loss of their jobs, so having clear expectations of what AI applications will and won't do can reduce stress and motivate employees to use AI outputs. Including key individuals from each business function in decision-making will help ease some reluctance to use AI models.

The overall acceptance of AI models will be greater if your organization already has a culture of data-driven decision-making and a data mindset. Table 6.1 offers a list of reasons why most common AI projects fail. Therefore,

Table 6.1 Why Do AI Projects Fail?

Technical factors contributing to AI failure

- Choosing a solution that requires intensive programming
- Not relying on AI third-party tools when available
- Choosing a solution that did not demonstrate scalability
- Using biased or the incorrect training data
- AI doesn't solve everything

Process factors contributing to AI failure

- Starting with a transformational change rather than a smaller goal
- Implementing AI without a clear goal in mind
- Not focusing on the business problem first
- Not taking time to properly clean and understand the data

Organizational factors contributing to AI failure

- Lack of leadership and stakeholder buy-in
- The company lacks a clear strategy
- Not measuring the ongoing accuracy of the model
- Not having a big picture view of the implementation process
- Poor change management process
- Ignoring the cultural shift required to use AI for decisions
- Fear of failure – AI sometimes needs experimentation

People factors contributing to AI failures

- Unrealistic expectations
- Lack of time commitment from business experts
- Trying to implement AI on your own without adequate expertise
- The project is driven by IT
- Lack of governance

managers should consider and address the following before beginning an AI project.

The benefits of AI on an organization can be categorized into the following.

- **Increased process efficiency.** AI can increase business process performance by automating tasks, performing tasks faster, and reducing the error rate.
- **Insight generation.** A major advantage of AI is that it can unlock patterns hidden in large sets of data. Organizations will be able to gain insight into patterns in behavior, buying, shipping, and manufacturing to help make better decisions about business operations.
- **Business process transformation.** AI can be used to help influence how resources are allocated, such as demand-driven scheduling.

- **Increase operational performance.** As in the opening story, organizations can use AI tools to create new services for customers, increase satisfaction in customer experience, and enhance the quality of products and services.
- **Increase financial performance.** The previous benefits affect the organization's underlying financial performance. Properly planned AI adoption can lead to better financial performance not only in the year of adoption but also the subsequent years.

AI Risk Management

Risks of AI can be broadly categorized into two areas: risks to the organization and to society.

- **Risk to the organization.** Most organizational risks can come from the factors listed in Table 6.1. Any bias in the data and algorithms can cost the organization its reputation and brand recognition and impact financial performance. Further, risks to the organization can stem from cyberattacks on data, lack of transparency on testing and AI models, and AI model self-adjustments, causing the models to be noncompliant with existing company policies.
- **Risk to society.** As responsible managers, it is important to consider how AI models used for business decision-making may have negative implications for society. AI can significantly increase automation, leading to job losses across the organization. Over time, an increase in job losses may lead to an increased disparity in the socioeconomic status of the general population. For example, the general population may be manipulated through AI algorithms to buy a particular product. As AI data needs increase, individuals may be burdened by continuous surveillance to provide location data. Therefore, if an organization is a socially responsible company, managers working for such organizations should consider hidden risks to society when implementing AI models for marketing and delivering services and products.

Singapore's Model AI Governance Framework, presented at the 2020 World Economic Forum in Davos, Switzerland, established several measures organizations could use to mitigate risks when deploying an AI model.[2]

- Understand that most datasets are, to some extent, biased. Keeping this in mind, organizations should implement procedures to mitigate bias and understand the potential risks. Evaluate the training output and consider whether there are any other unintended risks.

- Create a monitoring and reporting process to review any issues related to a deployed AI. The monitoring can include model accuracy, errors, explainability, and other specific insights as appropriate.
- Ensure that appropriate individuals receive training on how to use the results of the AI. In addition, implement processes to transfer knowledge on monitoring the AI model when key individuals change positions or leave the firm.
- Review the governance structure to ensure that it is still appropriate in the current business environment and staffing. In addition, conduct a review of the governance structure to ensure that it is still effective.

Implementation Lifecycle

Artificial intelligence projects present new challenges. Therefore, several unique key decisions should be considered at each phase to implement an AI project successfully. Even though the same implementation steps are followed as in traditional projects, some differences exist with AI projects. The significant difference is that there is more uncertainty in managing AI projects. First, the data is constantly changing and updating. As new data or additional sources are added, the models may change, and testing must begin again. Also, because the model can constantly be adjusted, there isn't a definite end to an AI project as traditional development. Models can always be adjusted and improved. Due to the continuous learning that occurs, the AI implementation lifecycle may take a more iterative, agile approach. The following discussion provides many significant items management needs to focus on during each stage of the implementation lifecycle.

Planning

The planning phase sets the direction for the rest of the project. During this phase, you should have a clear understanding of the end goal to be achieved by the new AI system and how feasible it is to use artificial intelligence. By the end of this step, you should be able to justify adopting an AI system by determining whether the AI project is economically and technologically feasible.

Most planning phase decisions are common to any implementation. The following are several important unique decisions to consider in the planning phase.

- **Identify the initial process for AI.** Similar to other implementations, finding an excellent introductory project is essential if this is the organization's first foray into using the technology. Several unique attributes that should be considered are whether the application will be fully automated and run independently or if it will interact significantly with human participants. Based on the scope, determine whether the project can be done with our current expertise and resources. Consider whether the scope and the requirements are scalable and easily modified to match any changes in the business environment.

- **Determine the economic feasibility.** Since the initial AI project can incur significant upfront expenditures, you want to make sure that those costs can be recovered. For example, given the relative novelty of AI development, training costs can be expensive but will be used over several projects. Will you be able to justify these types of upfront costs? Can the benefits expected from the new implementations exceed the expected expenditures? Can the project meet any anticipated return on investment?

  - **Quantify the expected benefits.** Some benefits may be increased sales, better customer satisfaction, fewer errors to correct, or staff reduction. Some benefits can be difficult to quantify financially, but they at least need to be included in determining potential value to the organization.

  - **Determine the costs of software and hardware.** When selecting an AI software package or platform, consider whether the platform can be used for multiple projects and whether the platform is scalable to larger projects. Using the same software for multiple models can reduce training and support requirements. Scalability is a particular concern given the large amounts of data and processing time required to build AI models.

  - **Maintenance.** Managers must do their due diligence to understand the maintenance and support agreements. Maintenance decisions should consider the infrastructure, hardware, software, and AI algorithms. Apart from support and maintenance costs common to any application, the cost of maintaining the application may include continuous training costs and testing or monitoring the AI algorithms.

  - **Training and upskilling.** Managers should not only plan technical training but also consider training users on how to use and interpret AI. Train business users to evaluate and understand the outputs provided by AI applications critically. Interacting and using the results from AI models will change the number of employees involved and how these employees work and interact. Therefore, managers should carefully consider training and upskilling nontechnical business employees.

- **Determine the technical feasibility.** During this part, you must determine whether adequate hardware or software applications fulfill the requirements. Some questions to ask:
  - Are the hardware and software available compatible with your current infrastructure? Does your hardware have enough processing power for the large amounts of data needed to build AI applications?
  - How much will customized development be needed? Many AI processes are unique and require customized development rather than off-the-shelf functionality.
  - Is the end-user interface, if applicable, user-friendly? Is the development environment user-friendly?
  - Are the data sources providing outputs compatible with the software used for AI?
- **Determine ethical issues.** It is essential to identify any ethical issues related to the use and development of any AI applications and consider the additional time and effort needed to address these issues. Therefore, managers should consider the following:
  - Who are the stakeholders that will be impacted by the development and use of AI?
  - What are the conflicting interests that may arise?
  - How do we plan to collect data to test the AI algorithms, or what data sources will we use?
  - Is there bias in the data?
  - Can we obtain any missing or underrepresented data and, if so, how?
  - What type of training is needed for developers to handle coding bias?
  - Do we need to hire an ethicist for the project team?

During this phase, it is essential to set realistic expectations of what AI can and cannot do. Although it can transform the business, it cannot overcome data quality issues, fix flawed business processes, or replace all human judgment. Setting realistic expectations at this stage will set the tone for the rest of the project.

One of the key components of this type of project is having the appropriate personnel available. Of course, individuals with technical knowledge in data management, data warehouses, and infrastructure must be a part of the team. In addition, there will be a need for data scientists or individuals who understand the complex analyses of artificial intelligence. Further, it is important to include experts in business functions to be part of the team. These individuals are essential in ensuring that the AI model's output makes sense from a business perspective. Even though an AI model can find patterns and correlations in the data to derive a model, some human judgment still needs to be applied. In addition, oversight of executive management and the board of directors is also important for AI projects. They should evaluate the potential risks to the organization, determine that proper AI ethical procedures are used, and review the outcome of AI from a firm performance and a social and ethical responsibility perspective. Other governance tasks are discussed later in this chapter.

Analysis and Design

The overall requirements and specific use cases are developed during the analysis phase. At this time, you should have a better understanding of the entire model, the input and training data, and the details of the algorithm. When analyzing and designing the process, consider the following.

- Is there an existing solution to adapt, or is development required?
- Who is the business owner of the process? Having an owner is particularly important if the application is used across many departments.
- What data will you need for the application?
- What data already exists within your company, and what do you need to obtain?
- How often does the model need to be updated or retrained?
- How much data cleansing needs to be done before use?
- What metrics will be used to determine whether the application is running properly? How will false positives and negatives be evaluated?
- Given the type of data that exists and the goal, what algorithm is best suited for this business purpose?
- Where is there potential for bias to exist in the data? How can that be reduced?
- What controls need to be put into place for appropriate implementation and use?
- What performance metrics should be developed and implemented to assess whether the model functions properly?
- Which users will be impacted by the use of this implementation? Start a plan for communication and training as needed for the end-users.
- Who will review the model to ensure that it is functioning correctly?

Implementation

During the implementation phase, you will start to create the model that will be deployed to production. During this phase, the data will be cleaned and the model built and tested, and it will be deployed for use in production. When developing a new AI model, a large dataset is needed. The actual size depends on the complexity of the end goal, the number of variables, and the desired accuracy.

Prepare Data

Depending on the solution you plan on implementing, you will need to collect a large amount of data to train and test your algorithm. This data may come from various sources and needs to be put into a format usable by the system. Take time at this step to ensure that you have the correct data and remove any irrelevant fields or records before beginning the modeling process.

The following are some considerations to complete this step.

- **Clearly define data.** Ensure that the team understands the data completely, as this may affect downstream steps. Consider the definitions of each of the fields. For example, the term *year* may seem clear to everyone, but is this the calendar or fiscal year? Many downstream errors can be avoided by having clear definitions.
- **Capture data.** Determine how future data will be captured. Will there be potential inadvertent bias in the capture? For example, capturing user preferences may bias the selection data if the products are displayed in the same order. Look for ways to eliminate these types of concerns at the source. In addition, is there a potential for errors due to missing data if the capture of new data is complete?
- **Coding data.** Carefully consider possible bias in coding the data. For example, say that you are coding a set of pictures with people as fashionable versus not fashionable. Fashion trends change over time; therefore, what you considered fashionable in the 1980s will not be fashionable in the 2020s. When you code the data, consider whether the coding scheme is specific to a time period, ethnic group, or social status.
- **Understanding historical data.** Depending on how old the data is, the individuals who made decisions about the capture, cleansing, and calculations may not be available to explain these choices. You may need to make assumptions about the options that were made in years past that may affect your decision-making. Understand that this may happen and try to reduce any related bias.

However you proceed with the data collection, this is the foundation of all artificial intelligence processes. Spending time to reduce errors here will ensure better accuracy in the modeling. Do not underestimate the time required to obtain and cleanse the data before building the model.

Training and Testing – Model Fit

Once the data is collected, you can start building the model. The previous chapter describes how the model is created by using training and test data. Several iterations are typically needed to find the right balance between accuracy and flexibility in the AI model.

The AI software applications can calculate the accuracy rates and create a confusion matrix using the testing data. The program parameters are altered by changing the calculation methods and other parameters to improve the model's accuracy. The model is then tested again until a desired level of accuracy is achieved. Table 6.2 shows a confusion matrix that displays the percentages of accurate and false predictions.

Determining the appropriate model tends to balance having false positives with false negatives, as no model can predict 100% accurately and consistently. The analyst will need to decide the proper level of error that is satisfactory for a given business problem based on other factors rather than statistical data.

For example, an AI model that identifies fraudulent credit card transactions may elect to have more false positives and reduce the number of false negatives. In this case, a decision was made to have more transactions identified as fraudulent, knowing that some would be proper transactions. The alternative would have more fraudulent transactions not flagged by the model and the customer not being notified. Even though a credit card company may decide to err on the side of false positives, having too many can be troublesome for the customer if they are asked to respond each time.

Finding the right balance will partly depend on the type of decision the model was developed for. There may be situations where the organization can have more false negatives without impacting decision-making.

Tweaking the model takes careful consideration to balance between accuracy and efficiency. Figure 6.1 shows underfitted, good, and overfitted models. If managers strive to achieve closer to 100% accuracy, they will likely end up

Table 6.2 Confusion Matrix

		Actual Values	
		TRUE	FALSE
Predicted Values	TRUE	True Positive (Correctly Predicted)	False Positive (Incorrectly Predicted)
	FALSE	False Negative (Incorrectly Predicted)	True Negative (Correctly Predicted)

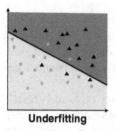 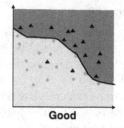 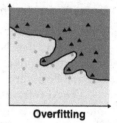

| Underfitting | Good | Overfitting |

Figure 6.1 Model Fit

with an overfitted model that matches the training data too closely. An over-fitted model based on a specific dataset will limit its use in the future, hence will not be efficient. Such a model will lack the flexibility to learn and adapt to the changes in the behavioral patterns reflected in the data. On the other hand, if too much emphasis is given to processing efficiency and simplicity, you may end up with an underfitted model at the expense of accuracy. The goal is not perfection but a good, acceptable model that provides a balance between accuracy and efficiency. A good model will increase its longevity by increasing flexibility to handle future differences in the data. Therefore, give careful consideration to the model fit decisions.

Maintenance

AI applications, by design, continue to learn independently and adapt to new data available to the model. However, this does not mean they can run continuously without any maintenance and monitoring of the output.

In the analysis phase, the team should have considered metrics for performance. These metrics will vary depending on the type of business process. For example, suppose the project's goal is to increase timely payments. In that case, the managers should consider whether they have data about how long it took to process payments before and after the implementation. Managers should continuously monitor the model's success rates and periodically review it to determine whether it needs to be retrained or tweaked.

AI Governance and Management

All AI applications require significant amounts of data to train. For this reason, management must take extra precautions to secure the data and ensure high data quality. Oversight of the data selection and processing will help ensure that the AI model provides the best results and is secure. AI has a higher risk than other technologies as it does not provide an audit trail of the model's construction or the logic behind the decision process. The lack of transparency in AI algorithms requires additional governance to ensure proper controls and oversight.

Governance Oversight

Because of AI implementation's complexity and ongoing risk, management should establish an oversight group to monitor and evaluate AI projects. This group could be part of a Center of Excellence for AI projects or a standalone committee. The committee should have AI technical specialists, business owners, an IT security expert, and a legal member. Due to the significant implications of an AI project, it is necessary to include a diverse range of expertise to oversee the use of AI within the organization.

The Artificial Intelligence/Machine Learning Risk & Security Working Group (AIRS) was formed to guide organizations on governance practices for those implementing AI processes. Even though the group focuses on the financial services industry, its recommendations are appropriate for all sectors. The group provides four key components for developing an AI governance plan for the company. The four main components are:

1. Definitions
2. Inventory
3. Policies
4. Framework

Using these to develop guidance within the organization will reduce the many risks with AI but can allow the flexibility required for each firm.

Definitions

AIRS recommends defining what constitutes AI and ML and what does not within the organization. This definition provides a clear roadmap for any governing groups on the boundaries of what will be covered in the governance plans. The definitions can provide transparency for the stakeholders throughout the organization. The definitions should include what techniques are used for training, how AI differs from other automation, and what processes are included. These definitions will be used in the next portion of the governance plan.

Inventory

Consider whether there are small AI models already being used in the organization. Use the definitions from the previous step to identify any AI models that have already been deployed or are being developed. For each of these AI models, note the following:

- The owner. Who owns the AI model will depend on who uses the results of the model for decision-making.
- Developers
- The software used
- The key data used, including sources
- Outputs

Taking an inventory of AI models will help managers keep track of all the models, plan for review and monitoring of the models, understand how business decisions are driven, and assess whether the same controls, principles, and policies are followed when developing and using the models. In order to govern and protect each process, management needs to be aware of how these models are used in business decision-making.

Policies

There are likely policies regarding data protection and system development that will also apply to artificial intelligence systems. Review the existing policies and determine which ones apply to AI and whether existing policies need to be updated. AI might also require managers to create new policies for transparency.

Framework

The framework provides the governance and monitoring of AI development and long-term maintenance. First, name the body of individuals that will be providing the oversight for AI development. Select a group of stakeholders from throughout the organization to guide the future of AI. The committee can be considered a steering committee or a center of excellence.

The group should review best practices for the organization, provide expertise on the controls for AI, and share knowledge between departments. The committee should consider all issues related to data ethics, privacy, compliance with regulations, and long-term monitoring of AI performance.

The central committee can be a clearinghouse for approvals for any new development using AI. It can also review controls to reduce risks for new developments or changes to AI processes. Other critical concerns of the central committee include the following:

- **Monitoring and oversight.** AI processes in production need to be monitored on an ongoing basis. Business experts should review changes to AI for compliance with laws, ethical concerns, and accuracy of the output. Procedures should be in place to override changes if necessary.

- **Address discrimination in AI models.** Consider whether a certain variable unduly influences the outcomes of an AI model and whether the data used is biased.
- **Enhance the interpretability of AI models.** Consider whether the explanations given for AI-derived outcomes are reasonable, reliable, and useful. The more transparent managers and analysts are about why a certain set of variables were selected, how the model derived the results, and what data was used to train the model, the more managers will be able to make responsible decisions.
- **Third-party risk management.** The steering committee should review contracts with outside parties and understand the testing/training methods and the system of controls at the third-party provider. When possible, allow your management team to review the supplier's controls or request a service organizations control (SOC) report.
- **Ethical review.** Consider implementing an ethics review board separate from the steering committee to ensure that all AI applications meet company policy and adhere to all other ethical principles.

Ethical Considerations

"Success in creating AI could be the biggest event in the history of our civilization," Stephen Hawking acknowledged, noting the unprecedented and rapid development of AI technology in recent years, from self-driving cars to a computer playing (and defeating) humans in a game of Go. "But it could also be the last," he warned.[3]

Experts recognize the many benefits provided by artificial intelligence. However, there are many ethical concerns that must be addressed about AI.

Amazon Scraps Its Resume Review System

To eliminate bias in reviewing resumes for technical positions within the organization, Amazon developed an AI application to screen resumes and rate each candidate on a one- to five-star system. The tech industry was long male-dominated, and Amazon was no exception. The AI-enabled system was meant to help reverse this trend.

To train the system, Amazon used the resumes of the primarily male applicants they received over the past 10 years. As a result, the system downgraded resumes with terms such as women's basketball team and two women's-only universities. Other language differences, including more masculine terms, affected the scores. Attempts were made to adjust the resulting algorithm, but the organization could not eliminate this and other biases and decided to scrap the system. Amazon assured applicants that the system was not used solely in hiring decisions.[4]

One of the components that an ethics review board can consider is the potential harm from an AI-generated/influenced decision. A simple way to approach this is to evaluate this risk as a form of probability and severity.[2] Figure 6.2 shows a simple matrix on how to assess the risk.

Based on this assessment, an organization can select the amount of human oversight required to reduce the risk of using this AI. The impact of a bad decision from AI can vary significantly depending on how it is being used. For example, an AI recommender system for a music platform may inadvertently recommend a song that is not in the expected genre. The harm from this is relatively low. The user may be annoyed or, worse, switch the music platform. On the other hand, an AI system that diagnoses patients based on medical data has more severe consequences if it is incorrect.

Applications with a higher probability of harm require constant human oversight. In the medical example, AI should not automatically take action without confirmation from an expert first. On the other hand, a recommender system can make a recommendation without any confirmation first. AI can use both machine and human expertise by engaging with a human for input when it reaches some unexpected or exceptional event. For example, an AI application that processes invoices may encounter a missing field. It can then stop and prompt a human expert for input.

An AI application does not have to make decisions regarding a person's physical well-being to be harmful. For example, models that monitor cash should be considered higher risk and possibly require human input, at least for large amounts. Managers should evaluate whether or not to integrate human oversight, depending on the industry and type of application.

Biases in AI Applications

Because AI applications must work with and are created by humans, you should reduce inserting any existing human biases into the application.[5] Ironically,

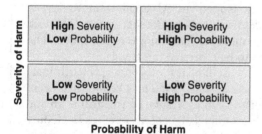

Figure 6.2 Matrix to Evaluate AI Risk

many AI systems are developed to remove human biases and inadvertently insert them into the model. Humans select the data for training, choose the processing models, and make many decisions on creating AI models. Because of our natural tendencies, a certain amount of bias will be inserted into the AI indirectly. Taking measures to reduce this bias leads to more responsible AI systems, providing better modeling and results. Several types of biases that can be inadvertently inserted into the applications are listed below.

- **Sampling bias.** The training and testing data do not accurately represent the population, future trends, and so on. At a minimum, this causes incorrect output and thus affects decision-making. Professionals should evaluate the selection of data used to train and test the models before making decisions. Ask whether there have been changes that would affect new data.
- **Confirmation bias.** We tend to believe outcomes that affirm our opinions or beliefs and ignore others. If an AI model produces results that are expected or match the user's beliefs, there is a tendency to accept the model at face value. On the other hand, if the output does not match our beliefs, there is a tendency to dismiss it. Users need to evaluate all output with skepticism.
- **Automation bias.** Individuals tend to trust information generated by a computer system without further evaluation. All output from AI models should be evaluated using judgment and expertise to ensure that it is reliable. This is especially critical when first using a new application, but it can continue through the life of the application. The more individuals understand some of the basics of how AI works will help reduce this bias.
- **Data bias.** Biases in the data used to create and train the model will incorporate the same tendencies in the output results of AI. Many AI solutions have been developed as a potential way of eliminating human biases. However, if the data selected to build an AI model is biased, the AI model will carry through with these biases. Data scientists must work to choose appropriate data that is representative of a larger sample.

Legal Implications

Integrating some of these biases may open up the company to legal implications. As shown in the Amazon resume case, introducing bias into AI modeling can inadvertently discriminate toward certain individuals.

In the United States, several federal statutes prohibit discrimination. For example, the Equal Credit Opportunity Act and the Fair Housing Act are a couple of laws that enforce fair and nondiscriminatory practices. Both housing and credit decisions use AI and analytics models to help justify the decisions and determine approvals. Although the intent of developing such a model is to reduce unfair treatment, using biased data or bad algorithms can create situations of either discrimination or disparate treatment of applicants. If managers fail to consider bias in the model, it may lead to legal implications for the organization.

Notes

1. Pymnts. (2023). Instacart to Add Chatbot as Grocers Push Boundaries on Digital Content. Pymnts (2 March). https://www.pymnts.com/news/retail/2023/instacart-to-add-chatbot-as-grocers-push-boundaries-on-digital-content/.
2. Personal Data Protection Commission Singapore. (2020). Model Artificial Intelligence Governance Framework. Second edition. https://www.pdpc.gov.sg/-/media/Files/PDPC/PDF-Files/Resource-for-Organisation/AI/SGModelAIGovFramework2.pdf.
3. Galeon, D. (2016). Hawking: Creating AI Could Be the Biggest Event in the History of Our Civilization. *Futurism* (20 October). https://futurism.com/hawking-creating-ai-could-be-the-biggest-event-in-the-history-of-our-civilization.
4. Dastin, J. (2018). Amazon Scraps Secret AI Recruiting Tool That Showed Bias Against Women. Reuters (10 October). https://www.reuters.com/article/us-amazon-com-jobs-automation-insight-idUSKCN1MK08G.
5. Zhou, N., Zhnag, Z., Nair, V. N., Singhal, H., and Chen, J. (2022). Bias, Fairness and Accountability with Artificial Intelligence and Machine Learning Algorithms. *International Statistical Review* 90 (3): 468–480.

CHAPTER 7

Cryptocurrency and Blockchain

According to Statista, there are more than 300 billion crypto users worldwide. Now, you can buy almost everything with cryptocurrency – from a cup in Starbucks to a private business jet. This excerpt includes several actual cases.

- *Clothes.* Cryptocurrency can be used to pay in Gucci boutiques and Off-White stores.
- *Education.* The University of Nicosia and the Lucerne University of Applied Sciences and Arts accept registration fees and tuition fees in bitcoin.
- *Tourism.* Alternative Airlines, a site for searching and booking airline tickets, accepts payment by more than 100 cryptocurrencies. The Travala.com platform helps travelers book hostels, hotels, villas, and apartments worldwide, as well as buy air tickets with virtual assets (more than 90). You can use 40 different cryptocurrencies to pay for accommodation in the Pavilions Hotels & Resorts hotel chain.
- *Cars, yachts, and planes.* Online dealer BitCars, car dealership Taabo Imports, and Californian manufacturer Karma Automotive accept payments in cryptocurrency. While trying to expand their audience with the help of the crypto community, business yacht reseller Aviatrade, yacht brokers Denison Yachting and the Yacht Break also added crypto payments.
- *Art.* Banksy's work "Laugh Now Panel A" has become the first lot of the Phillips auction house to be auctioned with cryptocurrency as payment. Sotheby's allows customers to pay in bitcoin and Ethereum and successfully sells gemstones with cryptocurrency.
- *Jewelry and precious metals.* Stephen Silver Fine Jewelry, REEDS Jewellers, Bitgild, and European Mint also accept crypto payments. In 2023, Tiffany & Co. will manufacture jewelry from the Crypto-Punks NFT collection that was sold online with ETH in 2022.[1]

Cryptocurrency and Blockchain

Cryptocurrency, a form of digital currency, became popular in 2009 with the introduction of Bitcoin. By the end of 2022, there were 21,844 different cryptocurrencies, with a total market capitalization of about $830 billion.[2] One distinct characteristic of cryptocurrency is the use of blockchain technology. Blockchain is a computer network that is not reliant on a central authority. Even though blockchain technology was initially developed to send and receive Bitcoin, the use of blockchain technology extends beyond cryptocurrency transactions.

A blockchain is a distributed network of computers that uses a consensus algorithm and encryption to process and store data in a distributed ledger. Even though the initial use of blockchain was to process and store cryptocurrency transaction data, it can store additional information, such as transaction data between business partners, ownership rights, and documents that require proof of creation. The characteristics that make blockchains optimal for cryptocurrency are the same features that will help blockchains transform many business processes.

History

In 2008, an individual using the pseudonym Satoshi Nakamoto published a white paper introducing Bitcoin and blockchain. The following year, the first blockchain was created and used as the public ledger for transactions using Bitcoin.[2] Since the introduction of blockchain, many have speculated about its benefits and impact on every industry. Many experts believe there are valid use cases in every industry, extending beyond cryptocurrencies. Table 7.1 presents some historical milestones in the development of blockchain.

During the first 10 years of blockchain, five major innovations have expanded the potential of blockchain technology. These innovations will help blockchain be a transformative technology for business.

1. **Introduction of Bitcoin.** The ability to send and receive money directly and securely without using a central authority and keeping track of these transactions using a distributed ledger solidified the use and potential for the technology.
2. **Separation of blockchain from Bitcoin.** The separation allows the expansion of the technology to other business transactions.
3. **Smart contracts.** Smart contracts allow the automation of business processes and the exchange of other assets, such as bonds, loans, products, or services.

Table 7.1 Brief Historical Milestones of Blockchain

1991	Stuart Haber and W. Scott Stornetta described a cryptographically secured chain of blocks.
1992	Merkle trees were incorporated into the design, allowing multiple documents to be collected into one block.
1998	Computer scientist Nick Szabo worked on "bit gold," a decentralized digital currency.
2000	Stefan Konst published his theory of cryptographically secured chains, plus ideas for implementation.
2004	Harold Thomas Finney II introduced a system called reusable proof of work.
2008	Satoshi Nakamoto released a white paper establishing the model for a blockchain.
2009	Nakamoto implemented the first blockchain as the public ledger for transactions using bitcoin.
2013	Vitalik Buterin founded Ethereum and designed Ethereum to be more than just a cryptocurrency.
2014	Blockchain technology is separated from the currency. Blockchain 2.0 was born, referring to applications beyond currency.

Source: The History of Blockchain Technology. CFTE (7 March 2023). https://blog.cfte.education/the-history-of-blockchain-technology/.

4. **Proof of stake mining.** Moving away from proof of work mining was an attempt to improve on cost and energy consumption issues during the mining process.
5. **Blockchain scaling solutions.** Since all the computers in the network must process transactions, transaction speed can be slow. Addressing scalability issues enables the widespread use of blockchain in general business transactions.

This evolution of blockchain technology has led us to a platform with many valuable applications, such as providing time and date verification for copyrighted works, securing the exchange of assets, and providing a central repository for transactions. In the following sections of this chapter, we discuss the fundamentals of cryptocurrency and blockchain technology and expand on the significant innovations mentioned above.

Cryptocurrency

Cryptocurrency is a digital or virtual currency that uses cryptography for security. Even though a digital currency was initially tied to actual currency held in a digital wallet, cryptocurrency does not necessarily reflect an actual

Figure 7.1 Popular Cryptocurrencies in Circulation by Market Capitalization (March 2023)

Source: Today's Crypto Price. Crypto.com. https://crypto.com/price (accessed 31 March 2023).

asset. For example, Bitcoin, the most popular cryptocurrency, is not tied to assets such as cash in a bank or gold. Figure 7.1 shows several popular cryptocurrencies in circulation as of March 2023.

The fundamental characteristics of cryptocurrency are:

- **Lack of central authority.** Cryptocurrency does not require a central authority to verify transactions. For example, the banking system acts as a central authority when we use cash and checks; cryptocurrencies do not require a third party to facilitate the currency transaction.
- **Anonymity.** The identities of users can be kept private. Transactions do not need to be tied to a person's identity.
- **Immutable or irreversible.** Once a transaction is committed, it cannot be changed or reversed.
- **Scarcity.** Most cryptocurrencies have a limited money supply.

These characteristics are discussed further in the subsequent sections of the chapter. Similar to a banking network, cryptocurrency requires the following several components to work together.

- **Payment network.** Cryptocurrencies need a payment network. In cryptocurrency transactions, a decentralized peer-to-peer network eliminates the need for a central authority, such as a bank.
- **Ledger.** The network needs a valid ledger to track accounts, balances, and transactions. For cryptocurrencies, this ledger is the blockchain. One significant difference from the traditional record-keeping system is that the ledger on the blockchain is distributed and public. The distributed nature means that every node on the network has access to the ledger, unlike the bank account at a bank. Since a blockchain is public, anyone can access the ledger and read the transactions.
- **Validation through consensus.** The current banking system creates accounts, records currency transactions, and maintains individual account balances. Further, the banking system provides a central authority to clear transactions between accounts by assuring that the payer has sufficient funds to pay. Cryptocurrency transactions and issuance of currency are validated based on a set of rules called consensus rules. Since there is no central authority to validate transactions, the decentralized network uses a set of mechanisms to arrive at a global consensus on the valid blockchain.

Both digital and cryptocurrencies use a digital wallet. A digital wallet is an application to store payment information. Even though both can use a digital wallet, there are several fundamental differences between digital currency and cryptocurrency.

- **Structure.** Digital currency is centralized, whereas cryptocurrency is decentralized. When a digital currency transaction is submitted, a central authority, such as a bank, validates the transaction. However, a cryptocurrency transaction is validated by the majority participating in the community.
- **Anonymity.** Similar to having a bank account, digital currencies require user identification. However, cryptocurrencies are not tied to a person's identity.
- **Transparency.** Similar to having a bank account, not everyone can look at your transactions when you use digital currency. However, anyone can see the transactions of any cryptocurrency user because all records are publicly maintained in a distributed ledger.

Before moving to the fundamentals of blockchain technology, let's look at the difference between cash, debit/credit cards, and cryptocurrency.

Cash, Debit/Credit Cards, and Cryptocurrency

Transactional and monetary properties distinguish cryptocurrency and traditional currencies. For example, cryptocurrency transactions are irreversible. Once a transaction is confirmed, it cannot be stopped or refunded. However, if a transaction is made to the wrong payee by a check, credit, or debit card, it can be stopped after initiating the transaction.

Most cryptocurrency transactions or wallets are pseudonymous, meaning they are not connected to actual identities. Traditional transactions with credit/debit cards or cash/checks require a central authority to clear and settle the system. Cryptocurrency transactions do not need a settlement system and are propagated through the network within approximately 10 minutes, providing a speedy transfer of funds. For international transactions, cryptocurrencies do not need to be converted to other currencies, making them more global.[3]

To create an account, the user needs to obtain authorization from a bank. However, cryptocurrency transactions do not need the permission of a central authority. For example, anyone can download a bitcoin wallet to receive and send bitcoins without obtaining authorization from a central authority to create an account.

Currencies, such as U.S. dollars, are fiat currencies that are issued by a government. Cryptocurrencies differ from fiat currency based on two monetary properties. First, some cryptocurrencies, such as Bitcoin, have a controlled supply. The currency supply created during mining will decrease over time and reach its final quantity during a specified year. Due to the controlled supply, the value of the cryptocurrencies will deflate rather than inflate. Second, most cryptocurrencies are not created by debt. Unlike balances shown in a bank account representing debt or liability for the bank, cryptocurrency is similar to having actual coins or gold.[3]

Cryptocurrency has several advantages over fiat currency. First, cryptocurrency does not require a central authority such as a bank. Without a central authority, a sender can send money directly to a receiver, reducing transaction fees and the time spent on a transaction. With a standard money transfer, once the sender specifies money to send to the receiver, the bank verifies whether the sender has enough money to send and communicates the transfer to the receiver's bank. The bank maintains a record of this transaction. Then the receiver goes to the bank to withdraw the money, whereas with cryptocurrency, the sender directly transfers money to the receiver using their digital wallet, and within minutes, the receiver will have the money in their digital wallet.[4]

Second, cryptocurrency solves the double-spend problem, where the sender spends the same cash twice. This situation can occur because of the delay between initiating, verifying, and finalizing a transaction. Cryptocurrency eliminates the double-spend problem by confirming that the sender has the funds before processing the transfer. Also, when you use a credit card at a grocery store, it is like handing over your wallet to the cashier and asking him to take the correct amount and return the rest to you. We trust that the grocery store or restaurant will only take what is owed to them. On the other hand, cryptocurrency eliminates the need for trust because the sender can specify precisely how much is transferred to the receiver.

Third, cryptocurrency provides privacy. When you send money through the banking system, the receiver has to share their bank account number with the sender. With cryptocurrency, the receiver can share their public key or address with the sender and conceal their private key. Even though this feature in cryptocurrencies increases data protection, it does not eliminate hackers from obtaining private keys using other means.

Fourth, cryptocurrency transactions have lower transaction fees. Even though transaction fees for cryptocurrencies are currently at a minimum, currencies with a cap on the amount of currency in circulation might produce higher transaction fees after the maximum amount is reached to compensate miners for the proof of work performed.

Fifth, the speed of transfer can also protect merchants from chargeback fraud. Unlike credit card transactions, where the funds are transferred several days after a transaction, a cryptocurrency payment can be confirmed within minutes. Therefore, the merchant can verify the fund transfer before the delivery of goods or services.

Sixth, the inflation rate will decrease, given the fixed supply of some cryptocurrencies in circulation. Even though the decreasing inflation rate is an advantage compared to fiat money, some inflation risk remains due to lost cryptocurrencies. For example, out of the 17 million bitcoins mined as of 2018, between 2.78 to 3.79 million bitcoins are lost due to various reasons, such as forgetting private keys, death, and losing or discarding hardware with bitcoins.[5]

Blockchain

Blockchain is not a single technology but a combination of different technologies working together. Blockchain is a data structure in which each block of transactions is linked to the previous block, creating a chain. In general, blockchain provides data validation, secure transactions, immutable data storage, and access to the data on the blockchain to any participant.

The characteristics that make blockchain useful for cryptocurrencies and other business uses are explained under the properties of the blockchain. First, the basic process for adding data and transactions to a blockchain is the same, no matter the type of blockchain. The following basic steps are common to recording transactions in any blockchain.

1. A transaction is initiated by entering data into an existing information system or manually using a specific application such as a digital wallet.
2. The data from the transaction is transmitted to all of the nodes (computers) associated with the blockchain network.
3. The network of computers validates the transaction and prepares to add it to the blockchain.
4. The network of computers comes to an agreement using a consensus algorithm specific to the blockchain.
5. The block is added to the blockchain, and the transaction is complete.

Properties of Blockchain

The working together of several technologies gives blockchain its unique properties and differentiates it from other types of data storage. The fundamental properties of blockchain are encryption, a decentralized network, distributed ledger, and the consensus algorithm. These properties make blockchain a unique method of storing information securely, sharing data among business partners, and automating the supply chain and business processes.

Encryption

Encryption, a subset of cryptography that dates as far back as the early 700s, is used to maintain the confidentiality of a message. Encryption is the primary way that blockchains secure data on the blockchain. In encryption, a message is encoded using a specific algorithm known only to the owner of the message. The readable text, known as plaintext, is converted to ciphertext, making the message unreadable to users. To convert plaintext to ciphertext, you need an algorithm and a key. Similarly, the algorithm and the key can be used to revert ciphertext back to plaintext.

There are different methods of encryption. To better understand the encryption used for blockchain, we provide a review of basic encryption methods. In *symmetric-key* encryption, the sender and the receiver of the message use the same key, as shown in Figure 7.2. A significant disadvantage of this type of encryption is the management of keys. Each distinct party needs a unique key to secure communication between the sender and the receiver.

In contrast, in *public-key* or *asymmetric encryption*, two different but mathematically related keys called private and public keys secure a message. With public-key encryption, the sender encrypts the message using the receiver's public key. The public key can be freely shared with all parties; therefore,

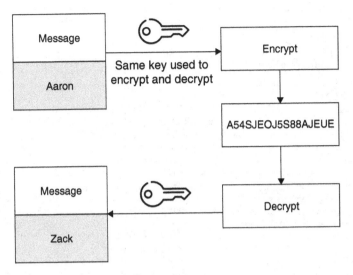

Figure 7.2   Symmetric Encryption

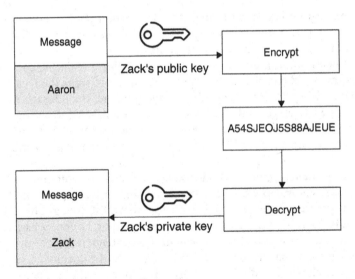

Figure 7.3   Asymmetric Encryption

a company can share the public key with all its vendors and customers. If a vendor or customer wants to send a message, they will use your public key to encrypt the message, and the receiver will use a private key to decrypt the message. Figure 7.3 shows the process for Aaron to send a message to Zack. Aaron uses Zack's public key to encrypt the message, and Zack decrypts the

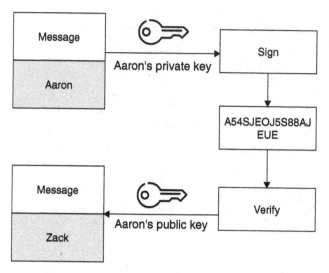

Figure 7.4   Using Public-Key Encryption to Sign a Message

message using his private key. Even though the private and public keys are mathematically related, and the public key is derived from the private key, others cannot derive the private key from the public key.

Public-key encryption is used to implement digital signatures, which are used to sign contracts in blockchain. The sender of a message signs the message using a private key. When the sender signs the message, the message is hashed or converted to a single code. The receiver verifies the message using the matching public key of the sender. As Figure 7.4 shows, Aaron signs the message using his private key, and Zack verifies the signature using Aaron's public key.

There are several encryption methods. Blockchain uses a cryptographic hash function to encrypt transactions. The cryptographic hash function takes a message of any length as input and converts it to a short, fixed-length hash or a string of random letters and numbers, which is the output. Different hash functions use different algorithms. Imagine you have a contract; it will be very difficult to detect if someone changes one word or space in the document. In blockchain, a simple change in a document will create a different hash. Therefore, the receiver can verify whether the document has been tampered with during communication by encrypting using a hash function.

Blockchain uses public-key encryption and a hash function to encrypt transactions. The hash of a block is created using *Merkle tree*. A Merkle tree is a hash-based data structure. Imagine a family tree where two people have a child, then children have children, and so forth. If you want to retrace your family tree, you might be able to get to one set of great-great-great-grandparents.

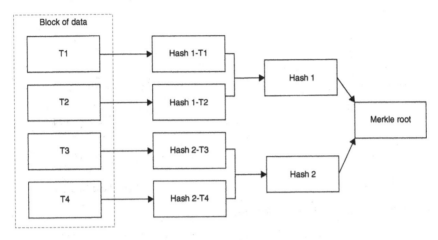

Figure 7.5 Merkle Tree

Similarly, a block in a blockchain contains many transactions. Each pair of transactions are hashed, then another pair is added and hashed together to create a Merkle root (great-great-great-grandparents). A typical Merkle tree has two branches; that is, each node has up to two children. In Figure 7.5, each transaction (T1, T2, . . .) is hashed. Then each pair of transaction hashes is hashed again until you reach the Merkle root.

Decentralized Network

A network is a group or system of interconnected things or people. When we refer to a network in technology, we refer to a group of computers connected to each other. Computers can be connected in many ways. A decentralized network is where each node (computer) in the network has the authority to independently make decisions on how it will interact with other computers in the network. Key elements of a decentralized network are:

- The nonexistence of a centralized authority monitoring how each node interacts with the other nodes.
- The lack of a single point of failure because the independent nodes can process data without depending on a single centralized server.
- Easy scalability.

One of the advantages of using a decentralized network for blockchain is system reliability. If one node fails or becomes vulnerable, the rest of the network will not be compromised because each node is independent. However, a decentralized system is very difficult to build and manage because it

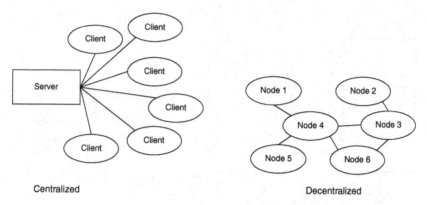

Figure 7.6 Centralized versus Decentralized Network

requires all nodes to keep up to date on patch management, updates, and security requirements.

A centralized network, on the other hand, is where the information technology architecture is built around a single server. The server handles all the processing; therefore, each node connected to the server depends on the server to host applications, process transactions, and store the data. An advantage of a centralized network is the ease of maintenance. However, the server's capacity will limit the ability to scale the network.

The blockchain was initially introduced on a decentralized network. The advantage of blockchain using a decentralized network is the lack of a central authority. The transactions are processed and stored based on a majority vote of the participating nodes. Therefore, a decentralized blockchain network should implement additional controls to ensure that the data being processed and stored are correct. The Bitcoin blockchain is a decentralized blockchain.

Distributed Ledger

Distributed ledger technology (DLT) is a database that is consensually replicated, shared, and synchronized across multiple geographies, sites, and institutions. It is important to distinguish the difference between a decentralized network and DLT. Decentralization refers to how the computers on the network process the data, whereas distributed ledger refers to how the database is stored. DLT is accessible by multiple people, and everyone will have a common view of the database.

The distributed ledger is not a distributed database. A distributed database is centrally managed even though parts of the database are stored in different locations or dispersed over a network of interconnected

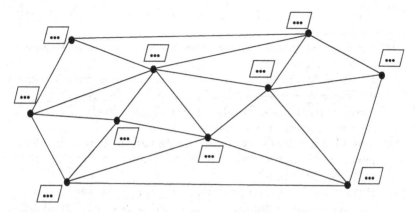

Figure 7.7 Distributed Ledger Technology

computers, whereas a distributed ledger is where all trustless nodes in the network maintain a copy of the entire database. When a transaction is received, depending on the DLT design, it is validated by a participating member(s) node(s) and appended to the distributed ledger. DLT designs differ in the way transactions are validated and stored. Blockchain uses some DLT concepts.

A major advantage of a DLT is that it does not have a single point of failure. Unlike a centralized database system, DLT is considered more secure and more resilient because DLT is based on a peer-to-peer network that maintains a copy of the database in every node on the network. Therefore, if a malicious actor attacks one node on the network and makes changes to the ledger, the other nodes will still have the time-stamped correct version of the database. Figure 7.7 shows how each node on the network maintains a copy of the distributed ledger (database).

DLT Properties   Each DLT design has certain properties that can be configured to fit the requirements of a given use case. All DLT designs consist of the following six properties.[6] Each property consists of various characteristics that have interdependencies and can either complement or conflict with each other, creating a cost-benefit trade-off when implementing a DLT.

1. **Security.** Preserves the following:
   - **Confidentiality.** Prevent unauthorized information access and release.
   - **Integrity.** Protect against unauthorized or accidental modifications.
   - **Availability.** The ability to access the system when needed.

- **Consistency.** All nodes store the same data in their ledger at the same time.
- **Level of encryption.** The level of security concerning authentication-related cryptography.
- **Level of decentralization.** The number of independent nodes participating in transaction validation and consensus finding.
- **Level of trust toward nodes.** The ability to identify the ownership of the nodes in the network.
- **The likelihood of forks and nonrepudiation.** Entities involved in communication cannot deny having participated in all or part of the communication.
- **Partition tolerance.** The system continues to operate correctly even if an arbitrary number of messages is dropped by the network.
- **Resilience.** The ability to return to a previous state.
- **Vulnerability resistance.** The system's degree of vulnerability to targeted attacks.

2. **Performance.** The performance of a given task in the system is measured against standards of accuracy, completeness, costs, and speed. System performance can be measured using the following:
   - **Block-creation interval.** The time between the creation of consecutive blocks.
   - **Block size.** The size of data that is stored in a block.
   - **Propagation delay.** The relative energy efficiency of a tool, the latency between the submission of a transaction, and the point in time where each node received the transaction.
   - **Throughput.** The bandwidth the DLT design's protocol requires for necessary data exchanges over the decentralized network, the capability of a DLT design to handle an increasing amount of workload or its growth potential, and the number of transactions validated and appended to the ledger in a given time interval.
   - **Transaction validation speed.** The duration required to verify transaction validity.

3. **Usability.** Users of DLT should be able to achieve specified goals. Usability is generally determined by the costs related to the implementation and usage, ease of node adoption, the ability to easily access and work with the DLT design, and the extent to which devices such as IoT devices can participate in a DLT.

4. **Development flexibility.** Development flexibility is determined by the possibilities, such as interoperability, modularity (modules can be exchanged), maintainability, and support for smart contracts offered by a DLT design for maintenance and further development.

5. **Level of anonymity.** The degree to which individuals are not identifiable within a set of subjects is a balance between transparency and unidentifiability.
6. **Institutionalization.** The embedding of DLT concepts and artifacts in social structures will be determined by how well the DLT is auditable, the resistance to censorship, compliance requirements, the level of development activity on the DLT design, the extent to which new nodes can join the distributed ledger without being verified, and the extent to which the organization that creates a DLT design's underlying code is responsible for its maintenance and functionality.

Consensus Algorithms

In a distributed network, all nodes process information and store it in the shared ledger. Since there is no central authority to oversee what is being added to the ledger, we need some way to make sure that all the nodes agree on how transactions are verified and stored in the distributed ledger. Mining is the process of adding blocks to the blockchain. A consensus algorithm is a mechanism to ensure that every participating node agrees on what and how a block is mined. The consensus algorithm is the most important control we have on a blockchain. Without it, we will have various versions of the truth. There are many ways nodes on a network come to an agreement. Several popular consensus algorithms are explained below.

Proof of Work   Proof of work (PoW) is the first consensus algorithm popularized with the Bitcoin blockchain. To achieve consensus, the participants in the network have to solve a complex computational problem. The node that wins the round of the competition has the authority to add transactions to the blockchain. Even though this method has been used since 2009 in the Bitcoin blockchain, it has several drawbacks. First, requiring the nodes to solve a mathematical computation takes up a lot of energy, having a negative effect on the environment. Given the time taken for computation, the processing of transactions can be slow and susceptible to economies of scale.

Proof of Stake   Proof of stake (PoS) is a consensus algorithm that selects the validator based on the proportion of their holding (stake). For example, if you have 10% of the cryptocurrency in a given blockchain, there is a 10% probability that you will be selected as the validator in the given blockchain network. The stake may be defined and implemented differently from blockchain to blockchain. Instead of simply the number of coins, for example, that number can be combined with how long someone holds these coins to calculate the stake a node has on the network. PoS is more energy efficient than PoW and can be more expensive for attackers to attack a blockchain. Also, PoS is not susceptible to economies of scale. However, since PoS nodes do not compete with each other to validate transactions, it makes it difficult for nodes to resolve forks because an equivalent amount of stake will be created in the forked chain. Therefore, a fork creator can start creating blocks in both chains.

Delayed Proof of Work The delayed proof of work (dPoW) hybrid consensus algorithm uses a secondary blockchain. A select group adds data from the first blockchain onto the second. The individual records are added to the first blockchain (i.e., the dPoW blockchain). The dPoW blockchain can use any consensus mechanism. The dPoW blockchain stakeholders then elect a set of nodes to add confirmed blocks from the dPoW blockchain to the corresponding PoW blockchain. This mechanism increases security because both blockchains have to be compromised to undermine the security of the transactions. However, this mechanism is energy-efficient and can only be used in blockchains using PoW or PoS.

Delegated Proof of Stake In a delegated proof of stake (DPoS) blockchain, the stakeholders in the system elect a block producer through a continuous voting system. The selected producers are scheduled in an order agreed upon by the majority. If a producer has not produced a block within 24 hours, this node is removed from consideration until it notifies the blockchain of its intention to start producing blocks again. Under normal conditions, a blockchain using DPoS would not experience forks because rather than competing, the nodes corporate to produce blocks. This mechanism is energy-efficient and fast compared to the other mechanisms. A disadvantage of DPoS is that it can be perceived as being more centralized and create circumstances where high stakeholders can vote themselves to become validators.

Proof of Elapsed Time Proof of elapsed time (PoET) is usually used in a permissioned blockchain where the participants must identify themselves. The PoET mechanism spreads the chance to add a block fairly across the largest possible number of network participants by requiring the nodes to wait for a randomly chosen time period. The first one to complete the designated time period wins the round to add a block to the blockchain. This mechanism has a low cost of participation and a low cost of verification of the leader selection process. A disadvantage of this mechanism is that it has to use specialized hardware, therefore, is not suited for a public blockchain.

Proof of Authority   In the proof of authority (PoA) network, approved accounts called validators validate the transactions and blocks. A validator must earn the right to add blocks by formally verifying the identity. Validators run software automating the process of adding transactions and blocks. Even though this process is fast and energy-efficient, it requires maintaining an uncompromised computer and can be centralized.

New consensus algorithms are developed every day. A few other algorithms that are currently in use are *proof of reputation, proof of weight, proof of space/capacity, proof of history, proof of velocity, proof of importance, proof of burn, proof of identity, proof of activity, proof of time,* and *proof of existence*. Further, many hybrid mechanisms are in use and under development today.[7]

Immutability

Immutability is the state of not changing or the inability to change. One of the drawbacks of current databases is that anyone with some technical knowledge can easily change the data in a database. Let's consider a straightforward example. Someone can easily make a small change in a single cell of an Excel worksheet without affecting the rest of the cells and without being detected. However, this single change can drastically change the analysis and mislead the decision-makers. This same situation can happen in relational databases as well. Even though system logs may be created about someone accessing the database and making a change, data can be easily manipulated after being entered into a system. Therefore, an unauthorized system state change can happen in a relational database without being detected easily.

Conversely, blockchain makes a state change very difficult by linking the previous state (block) to the most current state. The following features help create immutability in a blockchain.

- **Transaction hashing.** When transactions are ready to be included in a block, the node hashes the transaction. Creating a hash not only makes the transaction confidential but it also makes any subsequent changes to the transaction detectable. For example, an auditor can obtain transaction hashes from the distributed ledger and recreate a hash of the transaction, and see whether the hashes match.
- **Merkle root.** Transaction hashes within a block are hashed till one single hash is created. So even a small change, such as changing a single punctuation in the original data, can lead to a different Merkle root.
- **Block hash.** The consensus algorithm comes up with a block hash that meets specified criteria during the mining process. A small change in the block header details can lead to a different hash.

- **Parent hash.** Every block includes the block hash of the most recent block that is validated and added to the blockchain. This links the current block with the existing change.

The basic linking is done using block hashes. When the current block is prepared for mining, the parent hash (the block hash of the preceding block on the blockchain) is included in the block header. Therefore, the parent hash becomes part of the current block header and an input item that goes into creating the current block hash. This process ties the current block to the previous block, creating immutability. It will be difficult for a hacker to change data in a previous block because a small change will change the Merkle root, hence the block hash. This will affect the block hashes of subsequent blocks, breaking the blockchain and detecting that someone has tried to manipulate the data in the system.

How Does Blockchain Work? Cryptocurrency Example

Let's take a simple example to understand the basics of processing a transaction in a blockchain. Let's assume Tom wants to transfer 10 bitcoins to Andy. First, Tom should own some bitcoins. He can purchase some bitcoins in a cryptocurrency exchange, explained in the next chapter, or mine some bitcoins. When Tom is ready to transfer bitcoins to Andy, he logs into a cryptocurrency wallet and authorizes a transfer using his private key. Tom would indicate that this transfer should go to Andy using Andy's public key or address. Andy can then retrieve the funds using his private key by logging into his cryptocurrency wallet.

When Tom submits the transfer, the transaction is submitted to the decentralized network. When a node receives the transaction, the node performs several checks to validate the transaction. The node validates whether Tom has enough funds to transfer and whether cryptocurrencies are associated with the transaction, and performs various other checks to verify the completeness of the transaction. After validating, the node will add this transaction to a pool of transactions that are being prepared to be mined. When the node is ready to mine the transactions, it will hash the transactions in the pool and create a Merkle root, timestamp the batch of transactions, add the parent hash, the previous block hash, to the block header, and prepare the block for mining. Then the node will enter the competition in the Bitcoin blockchain to find a hash for the block that meets certain criteria. The node that wins by finding a hash that meets the criteria gets the privilege of adding the block to the blockchain. Once the block is added, the information is propagated in the network. When a node receives information about a block being added, it will verify the block and add it to its copy of the distributed ledger.

All transactions are recorded and validated using the basic process just described. However, depending on the consensus algorithm and type of blockchain, the way the blocks are validated, what checks are verified, and who gets the privilege to add a block to the blockchain will differ.

Notes

1. Barabash, Y. (2023). Cappuccino with Crypto. What Can You Buy with Cryptocurrency today? *FinExtra* (22 February). https://www.finextra.com/blogposting/23798/cappuccino-with-crypto-what-can-you-buy-with-cryptocurrency-today.
2. Howarth, J. (2023). How Many Cryptocurrencies Are There in 2023? *Exploding Topics* (14 March). https://explodingtopics.com/blog/number-of-cryptocurrencies.
3. Rosic, A. (2022). What Is Cryptocurrency? *Blockgeeks* (updated 18 October). https://blockgeeks.com/guides/what-is-cryptocurrency/.
4. Baggetta, M. (2022). A Concise History of Blockchain Technology. *Blockgeeks* (updated 19 October). https://blockgeeks.com/guides/history-of-blockchain/.
5. Delafont, R. (2018). Chainalysis: Up to 3.79 Million Bitcoins May Be Lost Forever. *NewsBTC*. https://www.newsbtc.com/news/bitcoin/chainalysis-up-to/.
6. Kannengießer, N., Lins, S., Dehling, T., and Sunyaev, A. (2019). Trade-Offs Between Distributed Ledger Technology Characteristics. *ACM Computing Surveys* 53 (2): 1–37. https://dl.acm.org/doi/pdf/10.1145/3379463.
7. Saini, V. (2018). ConsensusPedia: An Encyclopedia of 30+ Consensus Algorithms. *Hackernoon* (26 June). https://hackernoon.com/consensuspedia-an-encyclopedia-of-29-consensus-algorithms-e9c4b4b7d08f.

CHAPTER 8

Blockchain Developments and Governance

Cointelegraph *published an article about the use of blockchain in the gaming industry in July 2020. An excerpt of the article follows.*[1]

Blockchain technology has the potential to create a new era of gaming and drive true adoption in the industry.

The first true blockchain gaming application was Cryptokitties. While the platform itself is a technology demonstrator for collectible items, it quickly rose to prominence as the application representing the majority of transactions made on the Ethereum platform. Since its inception, the number of apps leveraging blockchain technology in gaming has exploded, with categories ranging from adventure games and card games to action games, role-playing games, and casinos.

Blockchain use cases in gaming are mainly constrained by the transaction capacity of blockchain platforms in the case of Ethereum. Current blockchain applications in gaming, therefore, are experimental tickets, with collectible platforms and mobile games leading the pack.

Card games are among the first games to use blockchain technology in gameplay. The unique feature presented by collectible cards is that the cards themselves, as non-fungible tokens (NFTs), become tradeable items. Most of the time, the NFTs are traded on OpenSea. One of the most popular collectible card games using blockchain technology is Gods Unchained.

Real-time strategy, or RTS, and massively multiplayer online, or MMO, games are ideal genres for testing blockchain technology in gaming, as the gameplay allows for the creation of multiple asset types and smart contracts governing the rules of the games themselves. While successful titles in gaming are increasingly massively

(Continued)

(Continued)

multiplayer, online, and feature group dynamics, the application of blockchain technology in gaming is probably going to gain significant traction in this segment.

Pixelmatic, a studio based in Shanghai and Vancouver that was founded by Samson Mow – current chief strategy officer of Blockstream and former director of production at Ubisoft – is working on a space-based MMO game with elements from the RTS genre and Eve Online and featuring a cryptocurrency for an in-game medium of exchange. While Eve Online features a marketplace for in-game goods, there's no news yet about the further development of crypto assets concerning in-game items. This is still pretty encouraging, and the game is the first step toward wider acceptance of cryptocurrencies among industry players in mainstream gaming.

Blockchain Layers

Blockchain consists of three layers, the protocol, network, and data layers. Each layer has a different role but works together to make the blockchain function.[2]

1. **The protocol layer.** This layer consists of software rules about how the system will operate. This layer is the foundation of the block-chain; therefore, it includes the initial codebase and architecture that specifies the rules of engagement within the system.
2. **The network layer.** This layer consists of all the interconnected actors of the blockchain. The network layer carries out the rules implemented at the protocol layer, such as how participants access the system, how the data is shared, and how the ledger is updated.
3. **The data layer.** This layer is comprised of the information processed and stored in the distributed ledger. The data layer consists of two components, the operations and journal components. Operations determine how creating new records, modifying existing records, and executing code are governed in the blockchain. The journal component determines what data is in the blocks on the blockchain.

According to this conceptual framework, the three layers are interdependent. The protocol layer defines the set of rules that are implemented in the network layer. The network layer is interconnected servers that carry out the rules defined in the protocol layer. The protocol and the network layers enable the maintenance of the data layer.

Types of Blockchains

Even though blockchain was first introduced as an underlying technology for cryptocurrency, many organizations are developing blockchain technology to facilitate many other transactions. One development we see is in the type of blockchains. There are public/permissionless, private/permissioned, and hybrid blockchains.

Permissionless versus Permissioned

A permissionless blockchain is a blockchain in which anyone can participate in the network to validate transactions, add blocks to the blockchain, and maintain a copy of the distributed ledger. A permissionless blockchain is also known as a public blockchain. For example, the Bitcoin blockchain is a permissionless blockchain.

In a permissioned blockchain, only authorized nodes can validate transactions, add blocks, and maintain a copy of the distributed ledger. Permissioned blockchains are also known as private blockchains. Table 8.1 summarizes the differences and similarities between permissionless and permissioned blockchains.

Table 8.1   Permissionless versus Permissioned Blockchains

Permissionless	Permissioned
A node does not require permission to join the network	A node requires permission to join the network
Is open to everyone	Is open only to selected organizations or individuals
The consensus algorithm brings trust to all	Nodes are known to each other, therefore do not need a trust mechanism
Offers high security because all nodes mine the transactions	Offers less security. It can be easily manipulated because only any one node will be responsible for adding transactions to the blockchain
Slow transaction speed because all nodes have to agree.	Fast transaction speed because only one node will be adding transactions to the blockchain
Harder to scale	Scalable network
Not energy-efficient	Energy-efficient
Truly decentralized	Not truly decentralized
Transparent network	Less transparent network
Immutable	Partially immutable
Governance structure imposed by the consensus algorithm	Governance structure imposed by the participants
Public transactions	Private transactions
Nodes are not authenticated	Has an established authentication process for the nodes

Hybrid Blockchains

Hybrid blockchains generally combine the features of permissionless and permissioned blockchains. A hybrid blockchain will allow controlled access while enabling freedom to decide which processes are kept private and which are kept public. Compared to a permissionless blockchain, a hybrid blockchain will offer more trust because you may have some control over who participates in the network. On the other hand, a hybrid blockchain will allow known nodes in the network; however, it requires a more stringent consensus algorithm, making it more secure than a permissioned blockchain. Hybrid blockchains are customizable, allowing blockchain members to decide who can participate and which transactions are made public.

Consortium Blockchain

Consortium blockchains or federated blockchains are a newer development. These blockchains fundamentally differ from hybrid blockchains. Consortium blockchains are networks in which a preselected set of nodes or stakeholders closely controls the consensus process. These blockchains are similar to private ones but are used by multiple organizations. Therefore, the network will be decentralized. Unlike a permissionless blockchain, a consortium will have preselected nodes that validate the transactions. Unlike a permissioned blockchain, even though it may be preselected, one node cannot add validated transactions and blocks to the blockchain without other validating nodes signing off on the block. Currently, we see three types of consortia blockchains: technology-focused, business-focused, or dual-focused (both technology and business). Technology-focused blockchain consortia provide help to develop the technology and gain global recognition. Business-focused consortia focus on solving a specific business issue such as banking, energy, or supply chain.

Smart Contracts

Simply stated, a smart contract is a computer program executed on a peer-to-peer network. When two parties to a contract agree, the terms of the agreement are written as a computer program. Once this program is executed, the subsequent steps can be automated, reducing any human contact. The peer-to-peer network will validate and verify the trigger events and subsequent transaction details, reducing the need for employees to match documents and verify events, such as the shipment of goods.

For example, let's say company A agreed to buy 100 widgets from company B. The two companies would negotiate and specify the terms of the sale and monitor each other based on the terms of the sales contract. A smart contract can be written based on the agreed-upon terms. Let's assume that according to the terms, company A must make an advance payment by the 15th of the month. On the 15th, the smart contract would inform company A that the payment was due, make the payment, and send it to an escrow account without the internal approval of company A.

Advantages of Smart Contracts

Smart contracts can simplify many types of transactions between business partners while adding an element of trust. There are several other advantages of smart contracts, as listed below.

- **Automation.** The contract terms are written as code/computer protocol and committed to the blockchain. The contract terms are executed automatically based on trigger events such as a date or receipt of goods.
- **No need to integrate.** If trading partners are to automate the entire supply chain processes, companies have to integrate their systems with the systems of all their trading partners. Integration is not feasible because of incompatibilities, cost, confidentiality, and time. Blockchain offers a common platform for smart contracts. Therefore, trading partners can maintain their systems and integrate data with blockchain.
- **Public availability.** The terms and events related to the contract are available to all parties.
- **Autonomy.** Since the contract terms are executed automatically and are publicly available, there is less room for manipulation by the other party.
- **Trust.** Since all terms and documents are encrypted on the shared ledger, documents cannot get lost or delayed. Therefore, there is a minimal need for trust. The automation of the terms eliminates the need for trust between two parties. For example, in a sales transaction, the two parties do not need to worry about receiving goods or cash, as the payment is triggered with the delivery of goods.
- **Backup.** The shared distributed ledger provides a layer of backup for the contracts.
- **Safety.** Encryption keeps the contract documents safe.
- **Speed.** Automated software code eliminates the need for human intervention to reconcile and verify whether particular events have occurred. All the verification is done using the peer-to-peer network.
- **Savings.** Savings can come from eliminating intermediaries such as banks and notary services.
- **Accuracy.** Well-written code can avoid errors that stem from manual data entry.

Smart contracts are not without any problems. The smart contract is only as good as the computer code written. If the programmer makes an error in the computer code, this error will trigger actions that will cost the parties involved money, time, and reputation. When developing smart contracts, key considerations should be given to all blockchain layers (network, protocol, and data) layers.

Other Developments

Oracles

An oracle, based on Greek mythology, is someone who can communicate directly with God. Blockchain oracles are systems or devices that enable the blockchain to communicate with external systems. To execute a smart contract, it needs to receive inputs from external systems, such as the date products are shipped. The shipping date may trigger a smart contract to execute to send payment to another organization. Using the earlier widget example, assume payment will be made once the goods are shipped. An external system generates the shipping date, and the oracle sends the date to the blockchain. Blockchain oracles, therefore, are devices or software that will capture data from external systems and feed them into blockchain smart contracts and vice versa.

Oracles enable blockchain to access data from various legacy systems, advanced computations, and the real world creating a unique ecosystem where on-chain code is connected to off-chain infrastructure. Oracles are categorized by the type of communication they have with other systems:

- **Input oracles.** Capture data from the real world and deliver data to smart contracts.
- **Output oracles.** Capture data from smart contracts and send commands to off-chain systems.
- **Cross-chain oracles.** Enable communication between different types of blockchains.
- **Compute-enabled oracles.** Provide secure off-chain computation that is impractical to do on-chain due to technical, legal, or financial constraints for data gathered from oracles.

Since most oracles are specialized devices, they are managed by third-party vendors. One of the biggest challenges of using oracles is ensuring the trustworthiness and reliability of various oracles that communicate with the blockchain. This problem of ensuring the trustworthiness and reliability of data is called "the oracle problem."[3] Blockchain, based on a decentralized network, attempts to solve the problems of trustworthiness and reliability. However, when data is captured by a single device/system, we are unable to completely trust the source of that data. One way to solve the oracle problem is to create a decentralized network of oracles.

For example, let's say that we need to monitor the temperature and input the current temperature into a smart contract. If the thermometer is located near a window, the average temperature may not be accurate; therefore, we may not be able to trust the input from the oracle. However, if we monitor the temperature in different areas of a room and use the average, we can receive a more reliable view of the temperature. Compute-enabled oracles address the oracle problem by collecting data from various systems/devices and using complex algorithms to come to a consensus about the accuracy of the data.

Exchanges

A cryptocurrency exchange is an intermediary that enables the buying and selling of cryptocurrencies. Some exchanges offer a variety of products and services, while others mainly offer the trading of digital assets. Crypto exchanges can be categorized into brokers and crypto exchanges. Traditional brokers can act as an intermediary between cryptocurrency markets and investors. A crypto exchange facilitates the buying and selling of digital assets based on market prices. These exchanges may only deal with cryptocurrencies or facilitate converting government-backed currency to cryptocurrencies.

A crypto exchange can be centralized or decentralized. A centralized crypto exchange is overseen by a third party called an operator. The operator ensures that trading runs smoothly. An advantage of a centralized exchange is that these exchanges enable smooth linking of your bank account or debit card to buy cryptocurrencies. However, these exchanges charge a fee for easy access. A decentralized crypto exchange does not require third-party oversight, is open source, and requires more technical skills to trade with cryptocurrencies. In addition to trading services, crypto exchanges offer secure storage of digital assets on behalf of their clients, insurance coverage of digital assets stored with the exchange, and easy access through mobile apps, portfolios, and investment management tools.

There are several factors to consider before choosing an exchange. Based on your particular needs, price range, tolerance for risk, and security expectations, consider the required deposit or withdrawal limits, transaction fees imposed by the exchange, payment methods available, any regional restrictions or regulations, the reputation of the exchange, and the verification requirements. Also, note that some exchanges may only offer a mobile option, whereas some exchanges may require specialized computers.

# ▲	Exchange	Score	Trading volume(24h)	Avg. Liquidity	Weekly Visits	# Markets	# Coins	Fiat Supported	Volume Graph (7d)
1	Binance	9.9	$10,620,125,016 ▼ 6.48%	938	14,204,559	1868	381	EUR, GBP, BRL and +6 more	
2	Coinbase Exchange	7.9	$775,171,413 ▼ 14.37%	716	26,876	600	242	USD, EUR, GBP	
3	Kraken	7.6	$322,766,977 ▼ 7.44%	744	989,079	698	222	USD, EUR, GBP and +4 more	
4	KuCoin	8.7	$514,394,808 ▼ 4.69%	490	2,081,582	1423	800	USD, AED, ARS and +46 more	
5	Bitfinex	6.8	$58,922,311 ▼ 4.51%	595	836,495	413	190	USD, EUR, GBP and +1 more	
6	Bitstamp	6.6	$50,398,778 ▼ 25.06%	600	296,817	163	73	USD, EUR, GBP	
7	Bybit	6.5	$277,344,182 ▲ 3.95%	615	3,370,105	535	356	USD, EUR, GBP and +3 more	
8	OKX	6.2	$1,004,972,369 ▼ 7.34%	514	1,668,695	792	359	AED, ARS, AUD and +43 more	
9	Binance.US	6.1	$232,892,815 ▼ 12.23%	680	522,649	325	155	USD	
10	Gate.io	6.0	$597,817,739 ▲ 2.00%	497	1,555,386	2658	1623	KRW, EUR	

Figure 8.1   Top 10 Crypto Exchanges as of February 2023

Source: Top Cryptocurrency Spot Exchanges. CoinMarketCap. https://coinmarketcap.com/rankings/exchanges/ (accessed 31 March 2023).

CoinMarketCap is the leading and trusted source for crypto market capitalizations, pricing, and information monitors. They rank 307 crypto spot exchanges. These rankings are based on liquidity, traffic to the exchange, trading volumes, and confidence in trading volumes reported. Figure 8.1 shows the top 10 exchanges in February 2023. These exchanges differ in where the exchange is based, the transaction fees charged, the number of cryptocurrencies offered, and the payment methods offered.

Crypto Wallets

Crypto wallets are applications that allow users to store public/private keys, execute transactions, and access transaction history. Crypto wallets do not store your crypto. Cryptocurrency is stored on the blockchain. The private and public keys required to access the crypto are stored in a crypto wallet. Blockchain-based wallets can be categorized into cold and hot wallets based on their internet connectivity. A hot wallet is always connected to the internet, whereas a cold wallet is not always connected. Hot wallets manage day-to-day transactions. On the other hand, cold wallets can be considered more like a vault where users can securely store their cryptocurrencies. There are three types of crypto wallets.

- ■ **Online wallets.** These wallets are connected to the internet, therefore, are hot wallets. Web-based, mobile, and desktop wallet applications are online wallets. Your private and public keys are stored in a software application.

- **Hardware wallets.** These are external devices, such as a thumb drive, that store your public and private keys. These devices allow you to store your keys offline, making them less likely to be hacked. Hardware wallets, such as Ledger Nano X, enable users to connect to the internet to send and receive crypto directly.
- **Paper wallets.** When private and public keys are written on paper, you are using a paper wallet. Even though it is harder for hackers to get your keys because they are stored offline, if the paper is destroyed or lost, you will not be able to access your cryptocurrencies.

If you create an account at an exchange, your wallet is maintained by the exchange. These types of wallets are also referred to as custodian wallets. Even though they are very easy to create and use, users do not have full control of their cryptocurrency because the exchange might hold the private keys. Most web-based crypto wallets are custodial wallets. Because of the ease of use, these types of wallets may be best suited for newer users.

Staking

Staking is locking up your cryptocurrency or other tokens for a fixed period. Let's say that you want to save money at a bank and you are given two options for where to save it: in a traditional savings account or in a certificate of deposit (CD). A traditional savings account allows you to save money and earn interest on your money. A CD offers an above-average interest rate. However, since the CD is for a fixed length of time, if you decide to take money out early, you will be charged a penalty. From the bank's perspective, the bank also benefits differently from offering these two options to you. When you deposit money in a CD, the bank can reinvest this money for the stated period and earn an income. Staking is similar to this scenario and is available only for blockchains using a proof-of-stake consensus algorithm.

In the proof-of-stake algorithm, the node that adds the block to the blockchain is determined by the stake it holds on the network. Therefore, block validators have to hold cryptocurrency in their wallet to be able to determine and increase the stake in the network. The greater the stake they hold, the greater the opportunity to mine the block. Therefore, if you are a fully participating node on the blockchain network, you want to have a higher stake to mine and earn a reward.

One way to increase your stake in the network is to buy more cryptocurrencies. However, this requires a larger investment, and, given the volatility of cryptocurrency, it can be riskier. Another way to increase stake is to pool resources from various users. Therefore, many exchanges, such as Binance, offer staking rewards to users. As a user, you agree to stake and delegate how much of your portfolio you want to allocate for staking. You can look up different staking pools and find a validator and delegate your funds for a fixed period to this particular validator. The validators combine cryptocurrencies with other users to increase their chances of mining blocks and receiving rewards.

Therefore, staking is a service offered to users to earn a passive income from the currency they hold. As a cryptocurrency holder, you earn a passive income from staking, and you also get to support crypto projects that you like. Also, since many exchanges offer this as a service, novel crypto investors can easily get started with staking. Many networks implement slashing or destroying some stakes as a punishment for improper actions. This mechanism is in place to incentivize users only to allocate funds to trusted validators.

Blockchain Coalition

A blockchain coalition is where multiple organizations maintain the blockchain network. Blockchain coalition is when various companies trade with each other. For example, supply chain partners form a network and use blockchain technology to communicate, share, and store data in the blockchain platform. A blockchain coalition differs from a blockchain consortium, where several firms in the same industry come together to communicate, share, and store data to achieve a common purpose and focus, such as technology, business, or both. Blockchain consortiums specify how a consensus is achieved in the network, whereas a coalition is simply the supply chain partners coming together.

Blockchain coalitions are implemented as permissioned private blockchains, permissionless public blockchains, a hybrid, or as a consortium. Figure 8.2 shows the difference between blockchain coalition and consortium. In Figure 8.2, the sample consortium is business-focused in the financial services industry.

Coalition with Suppliers (S), Distributors (D), Banks (B)

Consortium in the Financial Services Industry with Banks (B)

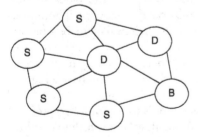
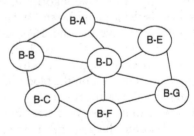

Figure 8.2 Blockchain Coalition versus Blockchain Consortium

Figure 8.3 Companies Invested in Blockchain

Source: What Companies Are Using Blockchain Technology? 7wData (29 January 2020). https://7wdata
.be/digital-transformation/what-companies-are-using-blockchain-technology/.

Use Cases

Almost every industry has invested or is looking to invest in blockchain technology. Figure 8.3 shows several industries and companies exploring ways blockchain can be applied to address various business problems. For example, the banking industry is investigating how blockchain can be used to manage payment systems, bond issuance, investments, and consumer lending. The healthcare industry is exploring how to share healthcare records among various stakeholders. Governments are looking into using blockchain to manage and digitize records of property rights. Energy companies are examining ways to manage the grid using blockchain.

Table 8.2 shows a list of top blockchain platform providers. Next, we discuss several use cases based on the functional departments of an organization.

Accounting

Blockchain-based accounting can be used for supply chain partnerships by enabling minimal human interventions, automation through smart contracts, and automated reconciliations through the audit trail between partners. The security offered through blockchain makes it useful for accounting and auditing because it significantly decreases the possibility of human error and ensures the integrity of the records. The immutability of records preserves the audit trail and provides an additional layer of control over financial reporting.

Table 8.2   Top Blockchain Platforms

	▪ Most established and oldest ▪ Platform and a programming language
	▪ Open source ▪ Modular architecture ▪ Permissioned and permissionless networks
	▪ Optimized for various decentralized finance applications ▪ Built-in security mechanisms ▪ Uses Stellar consensus protocol
	▪ For private blockchain networks ▪ Open-source project founded by JP Morgan

Source: Takyar, A. (2023). Top Blockchain Platforms of 2023. LeewayHertz. https://www.leewayhertz
.com/blockchain-platforms-for-top-blockchain-companies/ (accessed 31 March 2023).

Encryption is integral to the blockchain, making it exceedingly helpful in combating money laundering.

Financial

Blockchain simplifies and enables the secure and efficient transfer of funds internationally. Creating a tamper-proof log of sensitive activities is seen as a major advantage. Also, blockchain can be useful in creating a more efficient capital market system by enabling faster clearing and settlement of funds. Blockchain can streamline cross-border trade finance deals and simplify the process across borders. It enables enterprises to easily transact with each other beyond regional or geographic boundaries.

Marketing

Blockchain can also help marketing managers analyze a marketing campaign's effectiveness. Blockchain can strengthen digital marketing by forming a direct exchange between potential consumers, current consumers, and the brand. The ability to track user activity may result in greater trust and consumer data usability. Further, blockchain can be used to consolidate gift card merchants on one platform. Marketing can tokenize loyalty rewards to manage better, analyze, and take advantage of consumers' buying habits. Blockchain and digital tokens can enhance brand loyalty and prevent product fraud through brand verification.

Manufacturing

Manufacturing use cases for blockchain can be categorized into three areas – supply chain tracking and tracing, warranty management, and smart contracts – to minimize paper and turnaround times. Manufacturers can use blockchain to verify the reliability of parts, prevent fraud, increase the transparency of product origin, increase the transparency of the manufacturing process, and manage contracts using smart contracts.

Governance and Management of Blockchain

Even though the initial hype around blockchain has died down, development continues because of the benefits of blockchain. As a manager, you should know the various challenges of adopting blockchain technology. Before investing, the board of directors and executive management should consider the following key issues when joining a blockchain consortium or a coalition.

- **Understand the objective.** A consortium or a coalition will have a fundamental goal or objective for its existence. For example, a fintech consortium may focus on a specific category of transactions, such as bond issuance. Therefore, the board of directors and executive management should understand the objective of the consortium or the coalition before joining.
- **Consider the strategic alignment.** Do your due diligence about how joining the coalition or consortium is aligned with the organization's strategy. Consider the strategic benefits of the investment and how it will impact firm performance. Decide to what extent the company's board of directors should provide oversight of blockchain to create alignment with the company's strategy.
- **Understand the participants.** Organizations joining the consortium or coalition may have varying motivations. Some organizations may have more influence over the direction of the consortium or coalition, whereas others may join to keep up with supply chain partners. Therefore, it is important to understand who the participants are and their motives, how they will influence the direction of the consortium or coalition, how the decisions of significant parties will impact your

organization, and how the legal environment will impact your organization. Tension over the direction of the consortium or coalition can slow progress. See whether all members understand and agree on the direction before joining and investing heavily in a blockchain project. Consider whether there is a good operating structure. If not, decide on how to establish an operating structure with others.

- **Decide on intellectual property.** Especially for consortia, decide who owns the development and how they will exploit the technology. For example, if it is a technology consortium, determine who will own the technology, processes, and applications developed on the blockchain. The board of directors and executive management should do their due diligence and negotiate the terms and conditions under which member organizations can use each other's intellectual property for running the consortium and use the rights for any technology that is developed.[4]

- **Evaluate risk.** There is uncertainty with any new development. Therefore, the board of directors and the executive management should consider the risk of failure. Who will bear the loss in case of failure, and how will it be distributed among the participating firms? The board of directors and executive management should include terms and conditions addressing the above issues in their contract. The terms will enable better oversight of the consortium or coalition and incentivize participating firms to act responsibly and ethically. Consider whether the risk appetite is set as a collective. If so, what is management's role in defining risk? What risk exposure is imposed on participants? What is the benefit of alternative strategies to better prepare and plan for uncertainty with blockchain developments?

- **Understand the regulatory environment.** The board of directors and executive management should understand the regulatory environment and discuss whether sharing information among participating firms will result in claims of anti-competitive practices. Consider whether the consortium/coalition has documented guidelines to avoid such claims.[4]

Blockchain Governance and Management

Managers should address various concerns related to governance, performance, and monitoring of blockchain development and use.[5] Before discussing these concerns based on the three layers of blockchain, we should understand the nature of the overall development and ask specific questions related to the following.

- Are the company's objectives aligned with its business strategy and the blockchain consortium/coalition's strategy? Have the board of directors and executive management negotiated terms and conditions that align the company's strategy with the consortium/coalition's strategy?
- Do we have a set of performance measures designed to monitor the progress of the development and use of blockchain? What are those performance measures? Does the company have access to the data from the blockchain to monitor performance?
- What should be reported related to blockchain risks, and how should they be evaluated? What is the risk response for blockchain development failure? What is the risk response for any attacks on the blockchain once in operation?
- Are the development and use of blockchain sustainable? What are the real costs of operating on the blockchain? What should be disclosed or reported about blockchain development and use under sustainability requirements? How are these requirements measured?
- Do we have the relevant competencies within the IT department to evaluate, develop, manage, and operate blockchain and related technologies? What is the skills gap and training plan to upskill employees?
- How will blockchain impact the audit of financial reporting? Will auditors have access to the data? Can the auditors perform tests of controls and analytical procedures on the distributed ledger?

Protocol Layer

Since the protocol layer is the foundation of the blockchain, managers should consider the following aspects during the development and use of blockchain.

- How is the current blockchain linked to related technologies such as smart contracts, oracles, other IoT devices, or company enterprise resource planning (ERP) systems?
- Who is responsible for creating and maintaining the protocol layer? What skills are needed to develop and maintain the protocol layer? How is the maintenance of the protocol layer distributed among the participating organizations?
- What is the best consensus algorithm for the consortium or coalition, and why? What are the benefits and risks associated with the selected algorithm? Have we designed and implemented any controls to address threats related to the consensus algorithm? What is the protocol on how to handle future changes? How will any potential forks be managed?

- What transaction validation rules should be implemented? Are they adequate? If there are changes, how will these changes be managed in the future? Will all types of transactions require the same set of validations? If not, how will the protocol layer handle different requirements? How will the validation process address transactions that do not meet the validation requirements?
- How do we establish security and confidentiality of the data stored in the distributed ledger?
- Who should be responsible for determining the adequacy of built-in controls? How do we access the controls? How do we implement performance measured by the design of the protocol? How do we collect and disseminate the data to the appropriate companies for performance evaluation?

Network Layer

The network layer describes how participants communicate with each other. Therefore, managers should consider the following when developing and managing the network layer.

- How do we authenticate participating nodes? What is the process of authentication? The vetting processes will differ significantly based on the type of blockchain.
- Who is responsible for developing and managing the network layer?
- How will we evaluate the performance of the network layer? What metrics should be implemented? How will the data about the performance of the network layer be distributed?
- What communication channels should be established and how?
- What control mechanisms will we need to prevent, detect, and correct any attacks on the network layer?
- Who has access to the distributed ledger maintained on the network? How is access managed? Who is responsible for monitoring unauthorized access?

Data Layer

The data layer describes how data will be recorded, updated, and used as inputs to smart contracts. Several considerations related to the data layer are mentioned under smart contracts as well. Here managers should consider the following:

- How do we determine the integrity and quality of the input data? (We discuss data obtained from smart contracts and oracles under the subsequent headings.)

- How do we determine the integrity and quality of the data stored in the distributed ledger? Are there control measures in place to prevent and detect unauthorized browsing or copying of data?
- How do we determine the responsible use of data by the participating firms? Who is responsible for monitoring and enforcing actions against the irresponsible use of data?

Smart Contract Governance and Management

When developing and using smart contracts, managers should consider the following.

- Who should be responsible for the development of smart contracts?
- How do we establish the desired culture of a smart contract environment with multiple parties involved?
- What are the staffing needs for blockchain and smart contract development?
- If a company is not the initiator of a smart contract, how does it identify and analyze the risks and their impact on business strategy?
- If the company is not the initiator of smart contracts, what additional risks arise from participating in smart contracts?
- How will smart contracts and blockchain impact existing policies and procedures?
- Can we obtain performance data to assess the risks and performance of smart contracts?
- Will we know of any changes to smart contracts that may affect other business processes related to smart contracts?
- What criteria should determine the best controls applicable to a given smart contract?
- How will smart contracts and blockchain impact the existing general controls over technology?
- Since smart contracts may depend on inputs from external sources, how do we determine the integrity and quality of such data?
- How do we monitor whether smart controls built into a smart contract are present and functioning?
- Who should be responsible for monitoring if the company is not the initiator of smart contracts? Companies will have to consider whether the evaluation of internal controls should be done at the coalition level using, for example, a service organization controls report.
- Can the smart contracts be audited? How will we give auditors access to the terms and conditions programmed into smart contracts?

Oracle Governance and Management

Oracles provide and receive data from the blockchain. Therefore, managers should consider the following when developing and using oracles in the blockchain.

- What oracles input data into smart contracts? Where are they physically located? Where in the process are they implemented? How do we authenticate the oracle? Who is responsible for periodically evaluating the existence of physical devices?
- How do we validate the data provided by oracles? Should we have a single oracle or many oracles collecting data? How many oracles are implemented? How do we aggregate the results needed for the smart contracts?
- Who is the service provider for these oracles? What controls are implemented in the device to ensure the existence and accuracy of the oracle providing data into smart contracts?
- How do we audit the data provided by oracles? Do our auditors have access to the oracles' data?

Cryptocurrency and Wallet Governance and Management

Managers should have adequate control over the cryptocurrency held and the wallets used to access these cryptocurrencies. Therefore, consider the following:

- What type of wallet is most suited for the organization based on how many cryptocurrency transactions are done? What type of transactions are done, and on which blockchain?
- Who has access to these wallets? What access controls should we implement for private and public key storage? Do we have a way to secure access to the wallets when there is management turnover?

Future Trends

- Blockchain-as-a-service companies such as Amazon, IBM, and Microsoft may offer tools and platforms enabling organizations to leverage the technology without having to incur an initial investment for infrastructure and expertise.
- Metaverse (see the next chapter).
- Tokenization (see the next chapter).

- Enterprise blockchains – private blockchains will become popular in the recent future. With the rise of cryptocurrencies, the financial services industry will lead the way in deploying private permissioned blockchains.
- Mainstreaming of cryptocurrency – cryptocurrency will be accepted as a mainstream payment option by organizations and governments.
- Artificial intelligence and machine learning performed on blockchain data.

Notes

1. Kabanov, A. (2020).Gaming Industry Use of Blockchain May Lead to Mass Adoption. *Cointelegraph* (26 July). https://cointelegraph.com/news/gaming-industry-use-of-blockchain-may-lead-to-mass-adoption.
2. Rauchs, M., Glidden, A., Gordon, B., et al. (2019). Distributed Ledger Technology Systems: A Conceptual Framework (18 December, 2018). http://dx.doi.org/10.2139/ssrn.3230013.
3. Sheldon, M. (2021). Auditing the Blockchain Oracle Problem. *Journal of Infomration Systems* 35 (1): 121–133. https://doi.org/10.2308/ISYS-19-049.
4. Yaros, O., Pennell, J., and Marvin, M. (2022). Key Considerations When Joining a Blockchain Consortium. *Intellectual Property & Technology Law Journal* 34 (8): 3–5.
5. Vincent, N., and Barhki, R. (2021). Evaluating Blockchain Using COSO. *Current Issues in Auditing* 15 (1): A57–A71. https://doi.org/10.2308/CIIA-2019-509.

CHAPTER 9

The Metaverse and Non-Fungible Tokens

In October 2021, at Connect 2021, CEO Mark Zuckerberg introduced Meta, which brings together the company's apps and technologies under one new company brand.

"Meta's focus will be to bring the Metaverse to life and help people connect, find communities, and grow businesses. The Metaverse will feel like a hybrid of today's online social experiences, sometimes expanded into three dimensions or projected into the physical world. It will let you share immersive experiences with other people even when you can't be together – and do things together you couldn't do in the physical world. It's the next evolution in a long line of social technologies, and it's ushering in a new chapter for our company." Mark shared more about this vision in a founder's letter.[1]

Metaverse

Neal Stephenson first used the term metaverse in his 1992 novel *Snow Crash*. Even though he does not provide a specific definition, the novel portrays the metaverse as a persistent virtual world where one can work, relax, and engage in cultural activities or commerce. The metaverse interacted with and affected every part of human existence. Currently, there is no consensus definition of the word metaverse. Different industry leaders define the metaverse in a manner that fits their own company. For example, Microsoft's CEO defines it as "a platform that turns the entire world into an app canvas."[2] On the other hand, Facebook's CEO defines it as "immersive experiences with other people even when you can't be together – and do things together you couldn't do in the physical world."[1]

The major gaming technologies that contributed to the development of the metaverse are:

- Multi-user Dungeons is a multi-player text-based game. It is similar to a chat room. However, the focus here is collaborative storytelling and role play, for example, *Dungeons and Dragons*.
- Multi-user shared hallucinations allow multiple users to connect to a text-based online social medium. Emphasis is on solving problems together rather than embarking on a quest.
- Multi-user experiences.
- A multi-participant online virtual environment is an environment that is simultaneously accessed by multiple users and continues to persist once the users have logged in, such as the game *Habitat*.
- Virtual worlds such as *Active World*.
- *Second Life* in 2003.
- The rise of virtual world platforms such as Minecraft, Roblox.
- Cellphone inside Minecraft to make and receive live video calls to the real world.
- Fortnite is transforming into a social media platform where concerts are held.

The metaverse can be defined as:

a massively scaled and interoperable network of real-time rendered 3D virtual worlds that can be experienced synchronously and persistently by an effectively unlimited number of users with an individual sense of presence and with continuity of data such as identity, history, entitlements, objects, communications, and payments.[2]

The development of the metaverse may consist of the following three successive phases.

- **Phase 1.** Consists of digital twins, where a physical-world replica is created in the metaverse. In digital twins, virtual activities are an imitation of physical-world activities.
- **Phase 2.** This phase is called digital natives. The digital native phase allows innovative content to be created within the metaverse by avatars.
- **Phase 3.** Consists of surreality, where the scope of the virtual world will be larger than that of the physical world. In phase 3, there will be seamless integration and mutual symbiosis of the physical and virtual worlds.

These three phases are shown in Figure 9.1.

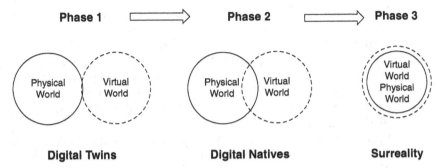

Figure 9.1   Three Phases of the Development of the Metaverse
Source: Wang, Y., Su, Z., Zhang, N., Xing, R., Liu, D., Luan, T. H., and Shen, X. (2023). A Survey on Metaverse: Fundamentals, Security, and Privacy. *IEEE Communications Surveys & Tutorials* 25 (1): 319–352. https://doi.org/10.1109/COMST.2022.3202047.

Major Elements of the Metaverse

For the metaverse to provide a fully immersive social experience, several major elements should work together. These major elements are briefly discussed below.

- **Scalability.** Scalability refers to the ability to contain many worlds within the metaverse. There may be metagalaxies, which are collections of virtual worlds connected by a visual layer that operate under the same authority.[3]
- **Interoperable network.** A novel concept of the metaverse, taken from virtual games, is the ability of the user to take personal virtual content across multiple virtual worlds. Consequently, a user's virtual activities should be tracked across multiple worlds, including the real world. To enable connectivity and tracking, the virtual worlds must be interoperable, meaning the computer systems or software can exchange and use the information sent from other systems.[3]
- **Real-time rendering.** In the metaverse, real-time rendering is another important specification. Rendering is the process of generating various objects using a computer program. The program uses different inputs, such as data, user instructions, and rules, to determine what and when things should be rendered. The computer program solves this problem using various computer resources such as graphics and central processing units.[2]
- **3D.** Even though virtual worlds can come in many dimensions, 3D is an important specification for the metaverse. According to experts, the digital platform needs to be more realistic to entice humans to place their real lives online. 3D enables a more realistic depiction of the real world.[2]

- **Virtual worlds.** Virtual worlds are computer-generated simulated environments. These environments can be fully immersive, layered onto the real world through augmented reality, or text-based and can have no users, a single user, or multiple users. Virtual worlds can reproduce the real world in a digital environment or be completely fictional. These worlds can be created by single or multiple users for profit or not-for-profit uses. Sometimes the virtual worlds may be limited to a specific platform or device.[2]
- **Synchronous.** The difference between the internet and the metaverse is that the metaverse is based on a shared experience. The internet was designed only to share static copies of messages and files from one party to another, not for a shared experience. The metaverse places a higher performance requirement on data transmission. One user's connectivity issues can affect not only that participant but all other participants, hence the shared experience. Therefore, the metaverse should function without users experiencing conflicting versions.[2]
- **Persistence.** Another element that will set the metaverse apart from virtual games is its persistence. Many virtual games reset after a certain period or after a certain goal is achieved. Similar to the real world, the metaverse should be able to continue and consider the consequences of many users' actions. Persistence requires massive amounts of data to be read, written, synchronized, and rendered to create and sustain the experience of many users. This introduces many challenges. For example, the system needs to decide whether to share a decision and consequence with other users, how many users will be affected, and whether it should continue to hold the decision in the memory of all the users.[2]
- **An unlimited number of users.** Currently, most virtual games have a cap on how many users can be in a specific virtual world. The metaverse should support many users experiencing the same event at the same time, in the same place, without substantially decreasing their functionality, interactivity, persistence, and rendering quality.[2]
- **An individual sense of presence.** Each individual can construct an online identity using a visible digital agent or a persona called an avatar. An avatar's characteristics can be personalized to reflect the user's self-expression freedom. The user's identification of their avatar can have a profound psychological impact on behavior. It can have a direct influence on human behavior in the virtual world and the physical world.[2]

Building Blocks of the Metaverse

Even though we don't have a proper framework for the metaverse, the building blocks can be categorized based on the platform needed, that is, infrastructure, how users visualize, how users interact with the metaverse, and how users interact with each other in the metaverse. S.-M. Park and

Y.-G. Kim built a taxonomy based on research about the metaverse. They categorized components broadly into physical devices and sensors, recognition and rendering, scenario generation, user interaction, technical methods, and metaverse applications.[4] The following is a basic list of building blocks of the metaverse.

- **Hardware.** The metaverse will require high-performing, powerful hardware to process user interactions and store massive amounts of data. Hardware needs will not be limited to data processing and storing but will also include mobile devices, wearables, augmented reality, or virtual reality headsets (explained in Chapter 13). Also, to collect and disseminate data from the real world, the metaverse must be connected to various data collection devices, such as surveillance cameras and thermometers, requiring IoT technology (explained in Chapter 12).
- **Network.** Another critical component necessary for the proper functioning of the metaverse is high bandwidth, such as 5G, for real-time connectivity.
- **Software.** The variety of software needed for the metaverse can be categorized based on activities performed on the metaverse. The software will be used to process/recognize languages, create avatars, create various assets, visualize images using 3D engines, relate various data back to the user through various senses, recognize voice and gestures, integrate biometric data, detect motion, and create other necessary content. The metaverse will depend significantly on artificial intelligence, cloud, blockchain, edge, and quantum computing, to allow users a seamless experience when interacting with the content of the metaverse.
- **User content.** The richness of the metaverse will be dependent on the content of the metaverse. User content will come in many forms, such as avatars, digital assets, and cryptocurrencies.
- **Services.** To facilitate interaction between users, the content, hardware, and the network, the metaverse will also include various services such as currency exchanges for buying and selling and a platform for employment.
- **Frameworks, tools, and standards.** ISO/IEC 23005 (MPEG-V) is the current standardized framework for networked virtual environments. The latest edition, released in 2020, aims to standardize the interfaces between the real world and the virtual world and among virtual worlds, to realize seamless integration, exchange of information, interoperability, and simultaneous reactions. However, this framework's focus is on sensory data. IEEE's 2888 project was launched in 2019 to standardize the synchronization of interfaces between the cyber and physical worlds and between virtual worlds.

In the future, the interoperability, operations, management, governance, and advancements of the metaverse will depend on how all the activities are supported coherently in the metaverse.

A complete architecture of the metaverse is presented in Figure 9.2.

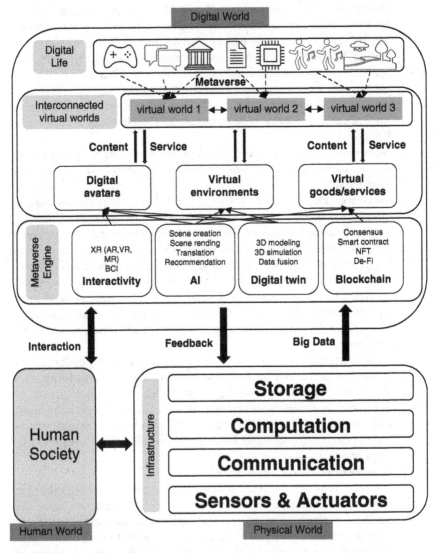

Figure 9.2 The Architecture of the Metaverse

Source: Wang, Y., Su, Z., Zhang, N., Xing, R., Liu, D., Luan, T. H., and Shen, X. (2023). A Survey on Metaverse: Fundamentals, Security, and Privacy. *IEEE Communications Surveys & Tutorials* 25 (1): 319–352. https://doi.org/10.1109/COMST.2022.3202047.

Figure 9.2 elaborates on the relationships between the three worlds (human, physical, and digital), the components in the metaverse (metaverse engine), and the information flow (interactions among humans and between humans and physical and digital worlds). Individuals with unique psychologies interact among themselves in human society. These interactions are extended to the digital world when individuals use various devices and avatars to store, compute, and communicate with others in the virtual world. The meta engine uses multiple inputs from the real and virtual worlds to create, update, and maintain virtual worlds. The meta engine uses various other programs such as artificial intelligence, blockchain, and cloud computing. The metaverse also should enable the information flow from humans to various devices in the physical world, between the physical and digital worlds, and between various digital worlds.

Challenges of the Metaverse

Many challenges and concerns need to be addressed in the development, diffusion, use, and operations of the metaverse. Most technological advances increase exponentially. Consequently, many businesses, governments, and users do not realize the full implications of using the technology until at least the first movers and most followers have embraced the technology. We can learn from past developments and consider the challenges and concerns we may face with the metaverse. We have broadly categorized these concerns into corporate governance, operations, and management, regulations, technical, and human.

- **Corporate governance.** Currently, a corporation centrally governs the developments of the metaverse. Can the metaverse be self-governed, or will the metaverse continue to be governed by a handful of metaverse corporations? Recent developments of the metaverse are either nonprofit or for-profit. Will there be different governance requirements for nonprofit versus for-profit? The metaverse does not need to be developed using a decentralized network, such as the blockchain. If the metaverse does not use blockchain, how do we establish trust among participants? Another aspect to consider is the interoperability of the metaverse. Who would build common standards around privacy, coding/program development, ownership records, payment processing, and digital communications? The metaverse will consist of many corporations; therefore, creating consensus among the participating organizations will be challenging.
- **Operations and management.** The metaverse will open new marketplaces for business. For example, many luxury clothing brands are creating digital clothes for avatars. The metaverse will pressure businesses to consider new revenue models, create digital storefronts

in the metaverse, and enable real-time monitoring for security and maintenance. Therefore, managers need to consider how they plan to move their business operations to the metaverse and consider how to manage business operations in the metaverse. Will human resource policies look the same in the metaverse? If customers buy items in the metaverse, are they purely digital products, or must they be connected to logistics for shipping and delivery?

- **Regulations.** There are significant regulatory concerns regarding the metaverse. If the metaverse is self-governing, who is responsible for regulation? Will governments regulate regulating the metaverse, or will a metaverse government be separate from national governments? Will all metaverses follow the same regulations? How can you uphold justice? These are just a few of the concerns that will need to be addressed as the metaverse progresses.
- **Technical.** The complete and optimal functioning of the metaverse requires many components, including hardware, software, network, standard, and protocols, to work together. Technical developments must consider whether the improvements are interoperable, sustainable, interpretable, secure, private, socially functional, and ethical.
- **Security and Privacy.** A major challenge for managers would be assuring the safety of the physical infrastructure, human bodies, and data. Data security and privacy should be addressed at the time data is collected. Policies on entering data or collecting behavioral data should include how data is accessed, aggregated, and stored, how data is created, and how data about interactions are processed and stored. Managers must consider a wide range of security vulnerabilities stemming from artificial intelligence algorithms, user-generated content, hardware, network, software, and various user devices, such as various wearables. Managers need to be aware of security threats to authentication, access controls, and data management and develop strategies to counter possible attacks on the metaverse.
- **Human.** Users can suffer from simulated motion sickness from imbalanced visual objects or errors in processing. Binocular-occlusion collisions and focusing displacement collisions can have negative side effects on humans. Cyber addiction and the inability to distinguish the real world from the virtual world are other challenges that need to be addressed.

Non-Fungible Tokens

"A non-fungible token (NFT) is a cryptographic asset on a blockchain with unique identification codes and metadata that distinguishes one asset from another."[5] Before discussing NFTs, it is important to understand the difference between fungible and non-fungible goods. For example, take a dollar bill. We do not differentiate between different dollar bills because all dollar bills have the same buying power and fulfill the same purpose or obligation. Therefore, a dollar bill is fungible, as it can replace or be replaced by another identical item. Fungible items are mutually interchangeable.

On the other hand, other goods, such as a bouquet, bread, or fruit, are not fungible because each bouquet, for example, may look different even if the same type of flowers is used. Some flowers may be slightly withered, or, for bread, some loaves might be crustier than others. These types of goods are non-fungible because they are not mutually interchangeable. Therefore, for some items, identifying each item uniquely, based on even slight differences, may be worthwhile from a business standpoint.

Types of NFTs

NFTs are used for various reasons, such as to display digital images using a digital frame, invest, trade, use as a profile picture, or decorate digital spaces. There are different types of NFTs, such as:

- **Digital art.** Art that is created using digital tools; therefore, the art exists in digital form only.
- **Digital collectibles.** Similar to digital art, they are created in digital form with the intent to remain in digital format. However, these are different from digital art because they do not necessarily have to be a picture.
- **Event tickets.** NFTs used for event tickets can verify people's identity and the ticket's authenticity.
- **Music and various media.** Music or other media converted to NFTs to verify provenance and ownership claims given to an individual.
- **Virtual fashion.** Clothes and accessories that are unique and can be worn by avatars.
- **Memes.** Sale of memes as NFTs.
- **Real-world assets.** NFTs that represent real-world assets such as diamonds and luxury items.

Advantages of NFTs

The advantages of NFTs can be considered using two perspectives, namely the content creator's perspective and the market participant's perspective. From the content creator's perspective, the most significant advantage is the ability to *showcase* and *earn* money for the digital content created. Since the resale or sale of content is easily traceable to the origin, NFT creators can retain their copyrights while generating revenue through royalties using smart contracts. NFTs are unique; therefore, content creators can differentiate each

NFT from the others. Some NFTs have multiple items, such as tickets to an event. Therefore, NFTs allow content creators *flexibility* on how they want to create the NFT. The scarcity of particular NFTs can *increase interest* and the price of the NFT. NFTs cannot be divisible; therefore, buyers may not be able to access an NFT until it is paid in full. The complete payment *reduces uncollectable accounts* to the content creators. NFTs cannot be stolen, broken, or destroyed, allowing NFT creators *visibility* in the marketplace.

From the market participant's perspective, the most prominent advantage of NFTs is their ability to *prove ownership*. The buyer can be assured that what they buy is an original rather than a fake product. Most NFTs are single products, such as a painting; however, some NFTs can be created with multiple replicas, such as tickets to an event. In either case, another important advantage of NFTs is the ability of the network to *authenticate*. Since NFTs are maintained on the blockchain and the blockchain is *immutable*, any modifications to the original can be detected. NFTs are also *transferable*. Once a buyer obtains an NFT, they can sell and transfer the ownership to someone else.

NFT Marketplaces

An NFT marketplace is a digital platform created to buy and sell NFTs. Apart from creating a meeting place for buyers and sellers, marketplaces offer other features such as displaying, storing, and minting or creating NFTs. Marketplaces also facilitate the buying and selling of NFTs by enabling participants to use a variety of cryptocurrencies and allowing currency conversions. The largest NFT marketplaces today are:[6]

- **OpenSea.** This is the oldest marketplace and was launched in 2017. OpenSea's core cryptocurrency is Ethereum, Solana, and USDC. In addition to a 2.5% transaction fee, OpenSea charges a gas fee for completing NFT transactions with Ethereum.
- **Rarible.** Rarible allows NFTs transactions in fiat currencies using credit cards. Common cryptocurrencies used at Rarible are Ethereum, Flow, and Tezos. Rarible also charges a gas and 2.5% fee on every transaction.
- **NBA Top Shot.** This is a marketplace for basketball fans to buy great moments in basketball history. You can buy video clips and play highlights. In February 2021, a LeBron James slam dunk video sold for $208,000. Purchases can be via credit or debit cards or cryptocurrencies, such as Bitcoin, Ethereum, Bitcoin Cash, DAI, or USDC.
- **Binance.** This is the largest cryptocurrency exchange. In 2021 Binance added the NFTs marketplace. The advantages of Binance are that it

has lower transaction fees (only 1%), offers typical digital assets, and is a large player in the cryptocurrency market.

- **Nifty Gateway.** This marketplace is known for exclusive and expensive NFTs. Nifty Gateway allows credit card payments. The largest transaction on this marketplace was $91.8 million to purchase digital artist Pak's "The Merge."
- **SuperRare.** This is a highly selective marketplace of art. Since SuperRare reviews the art before making it available, it charges 15% the first time an NFT is sold on the primary market and a 3% charge to the buyers of the transaction.

There are more NFT marketplaces, such as Axie Infinity Marketplace, Larva Labs/CryptoPunks, Foundation, Mintable, Theta Drop, Myth Market, BakerySwap, and KnownOrigin.

Creating/Selling and Buying NFT

An NFT can be created and listed for sale by following the steps below.

1. Decide what you want to create. The goal is to create a unique piece of digital media to sell.
2. Select the blockchain that you intend to use for your NFT. The process of minting or creating an NFT starts with this decision. The most popular blockchain technology used for NFTs is Ethereum. Other popular blockchains that can be used are Solana, Flow, Tezos, Polkadot, Cosmos, and Binance Smart Chain.
3. Create an NFT wallet that supports your chosen blockchain by downloading the crypto wallet app and providing a username and password. Make sure to store your private keys and recovery phrase offline. Popular wallets include MetaMask, Coinbase Wallet, and Ledger Nano X (a hardware wallet).
4. Select an NFT marketplace and connect your wallet with the marketplace. This step can be as simple as clicking and connecting the wallet on the marketplace site.
5. Create the NFT. If you want to create a series of NFTs, you can create a collection. Create the NFT by uploading your file and giving it a name, title, description, and other information.
6. List the NFT for sale. Choose how you want to sell and set a price for the NFT. Most platforms allow you to list the item for sale for free or with listing fees. This step is as simple as selecting the "sell" option and filling out the sale details in the selected platform.

Follow the steps below to buy NFTs.

1. Open an account in an exchange and buy Ethereum or any other cryptocurrency.
2. Create a crypto wallet and transfer the cryptocurrencies to your wallet.
3. Connect the wallet to an NFT marketplace.
4. Browse NFTs and make a purchase.

The Metaverse and NFT Economy

Similar to embracing e-commerce by developing a corporate website and offering products and services online, every industry and company will have to plan for the metaverse in the coming years. Unlike selling the same services and products online, the metaverse may challenge companies to develop new products, create new revenue models, and rethink the company's operations. The metaverse and NFT economy may include current organizations and create new types of businesses. Existing organizations may offer digital products and services such as digital clothing and accessories, digital art, digital furniture, digital landscaping, metaverse journalism, tourism, and social media. On the other hand, the metaverse will create opportunities for new businesses that will build, maintain, and support the metaverse ecosystem. Several current metaverse use cases are listed below.

- **Metaverse education.** The metaverse could change the higher education experience, where students from all over the world sit together in a classroom. The difference between current virtual learning and the metaverse university would be that the metaverse would give students a more realistic classroom experience. Further, higher educational institutions may have to reconsider how courses are structured, degree requirements are established, and the type of degree programs they offer.
- **Metaverse travel and tourism.** The metaverse may enable users to travel and experience real-life locations in the metaverse. Virtual tourism in the metaverse may not be limited to real-life digital locations such as Paris, New York, or London but also include digital worlds created in the metaverse.
- **Metaverse gaming.** Gaming is currently the primary investor in the metaverse. The social environment where every user stays connected distinguishes metaverse games from other VR games.
- **Remote working.** The metaverse will enable employees to work remotely while having the same experience as being at work and interacting with colleagues in real time.

- **Entertainment.** The metaverse enables users to attend concerts of their favorite artists from all over the world. Metaverse entertainment is projected to grow by $28.92 billion by 2026.[7] In November 2021 Justin Bieber performed his first live show as an avatar in his own virtual universe.[8] Ariana Grande and Travis Scott performed in Fortnite, reaching millions of plays.[9]
- **Retail.** Walmart's Roblox store is an example of a retail use case in the metaverse. In Walmart Land, users can explore various toys, appliances, home decor, and apparel before purchasing them.[10]

Ethical Issues

Before an organization moves to the metaverse, managers should consider the ethical issues. Although it is attractive and creates new markets, organizations should consider the broader issue of social responsibility and ethics of the implications of such decisions. We discuss several ethical issues below.

- **Code and rules.** The software code of the metaverse can constrain and influence users' social behavior. Therefore, developers and organizations should consider how to create a positive environment for the users and evaluate whether the code provides a positive experience for the users. Managers should critically evaluate whether there are gaps in the code where the organization allows certain behaviors that are unacceptable at the community level and vice versa. Managers should be aware of and avoid creating a "magic circle" where the game rules are different from the acceptable behavior in the real world.
- **Laws.** The laws of a land can be vastly different from country to country. What is law in certain countries can be frowned upon in other countries. A significant challenge in the metaverse will be deciding who will be responsible for governance. If using a metaverse platform, evaluate whether the current local laws apply to the metaverse. Also, consider how users from other geographical locations are treated. Is the metaverse based on a global set of rules and regulations? Is the metaverse centrally governed, or is it self-governed by the users? The governance structure may influence the organization's operations and impact real-world performance and corporate reputation. Managers should remember that the company's reputation may be damaged by engaging in questionable practices in the metaverse. Consequently, managers should evaluate whether the governance structure in the metaverse aligns with the social responsibility, vision, and mission of the organization.
- **Social good.** Managers should consider whether the organization's product and service offerings are socially good and instill positive

behavior. For example, is marketing to youth and manipulating behavior at a young age good for humanity, can acceptable behavior in the metaverse devalue fundamental human rights in the real world, and how will the trained behavior impact society in the long run?

- **Fairness.** Consider whether everyone will have access to the resources needed to participate in the metaverse or create NFTs. Moving business operations, products, and services to the metaverse may create a large disparity in a society in which one group of people has access to products and services, and another group is neglected. Managers should consider whether their decision-making is socially responsible.

- **Environment.** Managers should also consider the impact of engaging in the metaverse on the environment. Over time, what effect will the metaverse have on the real world? Will the focus be on beautifying the metaverse at the expense of the real world?

- **Enforcement of behavior.** It is important to consider the ethical implications of how rules will be enforced in the metaverse. Managers should consider whether certain enforcements have real-world consequences and how severe these consequences are.

- **Privacy.** Given the significant interaction with an avatar, is it admissible to collect data about individuals at a very granular level for user profiling? Is it permissible to collect and store data about user behavior, such as head movements and environments?

- **User licenses/consent.** Most often, users accept the terms of the agreement without reading them. Managers must consider whether terms of use are transparent and decide whether there is a better way to obtain user consent for terms of agreement rather than burying them in lengthy descriptions.

- **Racial and gender.** Managers will have to observe and address whether there are racial and gender inequalities in the creation and trading processes of NFTs.[11]

Notes

1. Meta. (2021). Introducing Meta: A Social Technology Company (28 October). https://about.fb.com/news/2021/10/facebook-company-is-now-meta/.
2. Ball, M. (2022). *The Metaverse: And How It Will Revolutionize Everything*. New York: Liveright.
3. Wang, Y., Su, Z., Zhang, N., Xing, R., Liu, D., Luan, T., and Shen, X. (2023). A Survey on Metaverse: Fundamentals, Security, and Privacy. *IEEE Communications Surveys and Tutorials* 25 (1): 319–352. https://doi.org/10.1109/COMST.2022.3202047.
4. Park, S.-M., and Kim, Y.-G. (2022). A Metaverse: Taxonomy, Components, Applications, and Open Challenges. *IEEE Access: Practical Innovations, Open Solutions* 10: 4209–4251. https://doi.org/10.1109/ACCESS.2021.3140175.
5. Miller, P. (2021). What Is an NFT? Value the Markets (27 September). https://www.valuethemarkets.com/education/what-is-an-nft.
6. Rodeck, D. (2023). Top NFT Marketplaces of March 2023. *Forbes Advisor* (updated 3 March). https://www.forbes.com/advisor/investing/cryptocurrency/best-nft-marketplaces/.
7. PR Newswire. (2022). Metaverse in Entertainment Market 2026, Rising Consumer Spending Across Virtual Concerts, Events, and Others to Boost Growth (27 September). https://finance.yahoo.com/news/metaverse-entertainment-market-2026-rising-011500073.html.
8. Gomez, S. (n.d.). Justin Bieber – Ghost (Live from the Metaverse Virtual Concert. YouTube. https://www.youtube.com/watch?v=d3vnxPq0meE.
9. Chen, H. (2022). Virtual Concert in the Metaverse: The Future of the Musical Industry. EventX (20 June). https://www.eventx.io/blog/virtual-concert-in-the-metaverse-the-future-of-the-musical-industry.
10. Case, B. Walmart is Making Its First Move into the Metaverse with Virtual worlds on Roblox. *Bloomberg* (26 September). https://www.bloomberg.com/news/articles/2022-09-26/walmart-is-making-its-first-move-into-the-metaverse-with-virtual-worlds-on-roblox.
11. Zhang, Y., Chen, Z., Zhang, L., and Tong, X. (2022). Visualizing Non-Fungible Token Ethics: A Case Study on CryptoPunks. arXiv preprint arXiv:2206.12922.

CHAPTER 10

Introduction to Robotic Process Automation

On February 18, 2020, the Wall Street Journal *published an interview with the deputy CFO of the U.S. Food and Drug Administration (FDA) on RPA implementation. An excerpt from the article follows.*[1]

Soon after Sahra Torres-Rivera joined the U.S. Food and Drug Administration (FDA) in 2016 as deputy CFO, her boss, CFO Jay Tyler, asked her to take on the task of improving the agency's inefficient and highly manual vendor invoice and payments processes. In this Q&A, Torres-Rivera discusses the planning and execution of the FDA's robotic process automation (RPA) implementation and lessons learned. She also explains how an initial pilot evolved into a scaled robotics capability in a managed service – the largest RPA deployment in the federal government.

How has applying RPA to vendor invoice processing improved performance?

Torres-Rivera: Our invoice and payments process is high volume, both in terms of the number of invoices and the amount of transactional, manual, and repetitive work required to process them. For example, we have to ensure the line totals match the total amount on each invoice, a highly manual and error-prone task because the invoices can be 50 pages long, with 500 or more lines of data, and come in multiple formats. With RPA, we now have bots performing the data entry and doing those calculations. People come into the process to validate the bots' work and to perform analytical steps to ensure timely processing of payments.

RPA is also cost-effective. The bots can operate 24/7, 365 days a year, without interruption as long as the information and the environment they rely on are available and working properly. Since implementing RPA, we have been able to process more than 500,000 lines of

(Continued)

(Continued)

unpaid invoice data, and have saved about 6,000 hours of manual labor, freeing up employees to perform higher-value work.

Our vendor payments process uses several disparate IT platforms that don't communicate with each other. We developed bots that bring together those different data points and systems to automate the creation of reports that communicate to the FDA program and acquisitions offices what they need to do to process the invoices. We also deployed bots to automate data collection for employee performance metrics associated with the vendor invoice and payments process; the bots use these metrics to create a performance measurement dashboard. The enhanced reporting capability aligns with goals established in the Department of Health and Human Services strategic plan aimed at improving performance and meeting government-wide objectives such as modernization, improved transparency, and accountability to Congress and taxpayers.

Robotic process automation (RPA) is rapidly changing how businesses carry out mundane, repetitive tasks. In organizations, back-office employees spend a significant portion of their time gathering data from different sources, copying and manipulating data, filling out forms, and generating standard reports, most of which are repetitive tasks. RPA enables the automation of such repetitive tasks. RPA has the potential to transform many back-office functions by reducing the mundane to allow employees time to focus on tasks requiring human knowledge.

RPA uses specialized software that requires little or no coding expertise to automate a process and moves task automation previously done by information technology (IT) staff into the hands of the end-user. This shift, of course, comes with many opportunities and risks. The software is not limited to a single software platform but can cross multiple platforms, such as enterprise resource planning (ERP) systems, email, or legacy systems. RPA works similarly to an Excel macro but with the ability to download emails, extract data from attachments, open the ERP system, and enter data into an invoice, as it works across multiple systems. These automated processes, called "bots," can work nearly 24/7, reduce errors, and improve accuracy. According to one study, firms found RPA processing to be seven times faster than manual processes, making RPA a viable option for automation.[2]

McKinsey refers to RPA as a process that "takes the computer out of the human."[3] Unlike many forms of artificial intelligence (AI), traditional RPA cannot learn as it processes data, and there is very little intelligence; instead, RPA follows the steps the user provides. RPA will significantly impact businesses by automating many processes and allowing employees to do other, more significant tasks.

In a 2020 Deloitte survey of executives, 53% of firms have started RPA projects, with expectations of increasing to 72% in the next two years.[4] Many organizations using RPA have reported a payback of fewer than 12 months. The time office workers spend on manual and recurring tasks is driving much of the movement to more efficient automation. According to a 2020 study by RPA provider Automation Anywhere, workers spend 40% of their workday on manual digital processes.[5] The time workers spend on these processes means less time spent using the skills you hired them to perform. Businesses that want to start process automation will likely turn to RPA. It is a straightforward technology to learn quickly and can frequently have a quick return on investment compared to other automation methods.

How RPA Works

Many back-office functions in an organization consist of repetitive and mundane tasks. Some tasks done by knowledge workers (experts) can involve repetitive steps. RPA excels at automating back-office, end-user-oriented tasks. Every day, rules-based and repetitive tasks are ideal processes that can be automated to save time and money for the organization. Process automation is not new to organizations. Many manufacturing processes, even some document management processes, are currently automated. Before RPA software, process automation required expert knowledge from IT professionals such as software engineers and programmers. The business user, who knew the process, would describe it to an IT professional who would write the code necessary to develop the program. With RPA software, an end-user does not need programming knowledge to automate a process.

Using RPA is similar to creating a simple macro in Excel. For example, if you want to copy and paste data from one sheet to another and format every row, you could write a macro in Excel to repeat the first instance. You can create the macro simply by pointing and clicking. The macro records all the steps you follow and repeats these steps when you run the macro. However, most macros are limited to a single application, such as Excel. RPA is separate from the applications it controls, making it easier to apply it across applications. So, a bot can retrieve data from an Excel workbook, enter data into your ERP system, and send a confirmation email using Outlook.

RPA uses software that allows users to define a process across multiple software programs using a graphical user interface (GUI). Then the RPA software converts the graphical diagram of the process into code in the background, makes changes in the GUI interface, then updates the code as needed.

Therefore, for simple RPA, the user does not require any technical knowledge of programming.

There are three primary components for most RPA automation:

1. **Studio or bot designer.** This interface is used to design the process. The user can point and click and emulate human interactions with other applications. These steps then get converted to computer instructions.
2. **Bot orchestrator.** This application is the control hub to deploy, schedule, and monitor the execution of the bots. The bot orchestrator will start the bot based on the specified trigger, such as receiving an email, initiating the bot through user interaction, or creating a new file.
3. **Bots.** The bot is the executable code that performs specified tasks.

There are two different ways a user can create an RPA script. The first way is to record the steps of the process, similar to how a user records an Excel macro. The user will initiate a new process in the RPA software and perform the necessary steps. The RPA software will capture the actions performed by the user and record the steps in the sequence of the tasks performed. Recorded bots do precisely as the user does, no more and no less. Scripts generated by recording are linear in nature, without any decision points or logic. Bots created using this method are the most basic kind and may be limited in what they can do. These types of bots are usually best for small, individual tasks. Users must be careful in performing the tasks because any mistakes made during the process will be recorded and played back during subsequent deployments. Users can jumpstart their script development by recording some steps and then making modifications or additions to the RPA designer software.

The second way is to manually program the steps using an RPA software application. The steps can be added using either a user-friendly graphical interface or a developer platform. Most RPA software packages offer both a graphical and a developer platform. The graphical interface is more end-user-friendly, with graphical controls and drag-and-drop functionality. The developer platform is more suited for someone with technical knowledge and possibly some coding experience.

Figure 10.1 shows an example of the end-user-friendly interface for generating bots. This interface comes with several different tools, from Excel, File Management, and email, which can be used to automate a process. The commands are easy to add with the graphical depictions. Within each of these subsets of tools, there are several actions the user can select to create a bot. A user can start by walking through the actions to record the steps and then add additional logic, such as loops and decision points, using the RPA interface to handle more advanced rules applied in a process.

Figure 10.1 Screenshot of UiPath StudioX

Figure 10.2 Screenshot of UiPath Studio

Most RPA tools offer more robust and complex designer software as well. This software allows users with more coding and development experience to add additional functionality to their bots. There are more options to give more control over the bot's functionality. Figure 10.2 shows the same bot as Figure 10.1. This interface has additional technical features to add to the bot.

However, the interface is less graphical. End-users can create a basic bot using the graphical interface and then work with their IT department to add additional functionality not available in the basic designer interface.

RPA bots are categorized into two groups based on how they are executed:

1. **Attended bots.** These bots work with humans in a process that cannot be fully automated. In general, they work as virtual assistants. These bots can retrieve information on-demand and give it to the user for the next step. Even though attended bots require interactions with employees, there is still potential for significant return on investment. Workers using these bots can experience less fatigue and accomplish more than those working without a bot. For example, a bot could assist an agent at a call center. When the customer's phone number appears, the bot could automatically retrieve the customer information across various systems to present to the agent. The agent can enter information triggering the next step for the bot.

2. **Unattended bots.** These bots execute without any interaction from the user. These bots have a scheduled time to run or may be triggered by an event on the process flow; therefore, they can start running independently without human interaction. These bots can monitor a folder or an email account and start execution when there are new items.

German RPA consultancy Roboyo raised €21 million in funding from growth capital specialist firm MML Capital in this excerpt from a news media outlet, September 18, 2020.[6]

Since launching in 2015, Roboyo has fast accumulated a market share in the global RPA landscape. The three co-founders – former management consultants Nicolas Hess, Christian Voigt, and Sven Manutiu – came together to establish the firm after noting that RPA sales across the world were doubling each year.

In an interview, Nicolas Hess pointed out that most organizations nowadays have a use case for RPA. "Many companies are fully automated in the factories, but many processes in the back office are still running as they were 30 years ago." Supporting modernization, Roboyo currently operates with a team of 120 professionals across six geographies, including its headquarters in Nuremberg and other offices in Europe and the United States.

According to director at Alantra Simon Roberts, RPA's wide applications make it a market to watch out for. "RPA is one of the fastest-growing software sub-sectors and is expected to receive significant attention over the coming years as businesses look to increase their RPA adoption and develop their digital transformation strategies."

RPA Software Applications

Automation Anywhere

Background

The company was founded as Tethys Solutions in 2003 but renamed itself to the current Automation Anywhere in 2010. Automation Anywhere offers a variety of solutions in the RPA realm to provide automation services to beginner and more advanced users. They offer a free Community Edition of the RPA platform to small businesses. The software is available to companies with less than 250 employees and $5 million in annual revenue. The free edition allows many start-ups to initiate automation from the very beginning and expand later as needed.

Automation Anywhere was one of the first RPA software companies to move into the cloud-native architecture space.[7] Besides their traditional RPA software, they are expanding their suite of products from strictly RPA to various automation tools.

Products

Automation Anywhere's primary RPA product is Automation 360, a cloud-based platform that integrates solutions from basic RPA to AI-integrated automation solutions.[8] They offer a full suite of products to help companies with their entire automation processes. The suite of products includes the following.

- **RPA Workspace.** This is the central component that lets the user automate and transform digital processes.
- **Process discovery.** This component records and documents existing workflows to guide the user on which processes are opportunities for automation.
- **Bot insight.** This provides operational data on the existing bots to optimize them further.
- **AARI.** This connects humans and bots through an interface. This works for tasks that require human input.
- **Bot store.** Predeveloped bots are available to plug and play in your organization.

The software solutions promote ease of use by individuals with any skill level. The Automation Anywhere software is accessible through various online training and tutorials.

Training and Certifications

Automation Anywhere University (university.automationanywhere.com) includes several learning paths of online instructions.[9] Many beginner and developer learning paths, called trails, are free. The more advanced-level self-study courses are available by subscription. Badges are available for those who complete the courses. There are over 20 learning trails available online. In addition, Automation Anywhere has some certifications available for business analysts and bot developers. See the additional resources at the end of the chapter to obtain the most recent information on training and certification options.

UiPath

Background

UiPath, the world's leading RPA software provider, started in 2005 with a team of 10 in Bucharest, Romania. UiPath's desktop automation product was launched in 2013 and incorporated in the United States in 2015.[10] Since then, the company has grown its global presence and product offerings. The CEO, Daniel Dines, has set a goal of creating a robot for every person, just as Bill Gates dreamed of having a computer in every home. In 2023, UiPath was the largest RPA software vendor.[7]

The UiPath platform and the automation cloud are the two product lines offered. The UiPath platform is an open, extensible, end-to-end automation suite. This platform provides core capabilities and tools to build, manage, and run robots and evaluate the business impact using analytics. The automation cloud offers the infrastructure necessary to build robots. UiPath offers solutions for various processes, industries, and technologies.

UiPath has grown from strictly an RPA software company to an overall automation platform. They have added functions like process mining, low-code app development, and intelligent document processing. UiPath is also known for its strong governance features, supporting various organization models.[7]

Training and Certifications

UiPath offers a free trial, learning programs, video tutorials, and certification to demonstrate RPA expertise.[11] The training can be used to prepare for one of the certifications offered by UiPath. UiPath offers two tracks of certifications – the Associate and the Advanced Developer. The general track requires strong foundational technical knowledge and is designed for anyone who works with the platform. The developer track evaluates the complex design and development of RPA solutions.

SS&C Blue Prism

Another large RPA software vendor is SS&C Blue Prism. They offer several products addressing the entire lifecycle of automation. The newly merged company of Blue Prism and SS&C now focuses on broader automation platform functions rather than solely RPA software. Their current software offerings can be grouped into the following categories.[12]

- **Create journeys.** The tools in this function help demonstrate value and assess which processes are candidates for building an RPA script. Tools include a process assessment tool and tools to document the current processes.
- **Accelerate work.** These are the typical RPA tools. These tools automate tasks and process documents.
- **Transform experiences.** These tools build user interfaces to enable interaction with the bots. Many of the tools here provide support for customer service types of tasks.
- **Unify operations.** These tools monitor bots throughout the organization, providing the orchestrator functionality found in most RPA software.

Like other software providers, Blue Prism also offers free training to users. There are several Blue Prism certification paths available for individuals. The certifications are for all skill levels, from individuals starting with RPA to advanced developers.

Microsoft Power Automate

In 2016, Microsoft released an automation product called Microsoft Flow as a cloud application. Then in 2019, Flow transitioned into Power Automate, one of Microsoft's Powertools. The Automate software added no-code or low-code RPA functionality in the application.

Windows 11 includes Power Automate as a standard feature for the automation of tasks for individuals. In addition, a mobile app is available to monitor and manage bots. This mobile app cannot be used to build or design RPA scripts. For enterprise bots, Power Automate is available via the web and Microsoft Teams.[13]

Power Automate has connectors to use many common business systems beyond Microsoft products. Using their standard connectors allows for the easier creation of bots without additional programming. Microsoft also provides several standard templates that users can modify for easy automation. Most of the bots are for personal productivity applications rather than business tasks.

Similar to the other RPA applications, Microsoft offers several training modules and learning paths online. The learning paths range from beginner users to advanced developers. Microsoft offers the following two certifications to demonstrate proficiency with the software.

1. **Power Platform Fundamentals.** To obtain this certification, professionals must demonstrate knowledge of building solutions in the platform. It is also necessary to be able to build a basic bot.
2. **Power Automate RPA Developer.** To obtain this certification, professionals must demonstrate the ability to create more complex solutions from design, development, and deployment.

Future Trends

RPA, in its current state, is simply the use of robots (small programs) for rule-based activities that are labor-intensive and repetitive. However, organizations will increasingly adopt RPA technology in industries and sectors such as oil and gas, retail, manufacturing, analytics, and legal services. In the future, RPA will manage most computer-managed processes with frameworks and protocols. RPA will enable organizations to increase efficiency and reduce costs by eliminating repetitive, manual processes. Further, RPA will integrate with other technologies to enhance the automation of manual, simple, and highly complex tasks over time. Experts anticipate that smart process automation will integrate with artificial intelligence and external processes.

Smart Process Automation

Smart process automation (SPA) is an extension of RPA. Currently, RPA is used to automate repetitive, labor-intensive, manual tasks. SPA extends the use of RPA to automate more complex tasks that require cognitive ability. SPA will utilize artificial intelligence and machine learning to develop cognitive bots that can handle unstructured data. Algorithms based on machine learning and natural language processing (NLP) can be used to understand unstructured data contextually and extract relevant data points for further analysis. Once the relevant data is extracted, it can be processed like any other machine-readable data. SPA is an evolving technology. Companies like Blue Prism, UiPath, WorkFusion, and Automation Anywhere are currently developing capabilities for SPA. The organization may be able to use different products and combine them to maximize the benefit of SPA.

Focus on External Processes and Customers

RPA use cases and developments are currently implemented for back-office repetitive processes. However, organizations will be able to develop automated external and customer-oriented processes in the future. The automations using machine learning and artificial intelligence can span external processes to integrate with third-party systems.

Process Improvement

Business processes change over time to adapt to new situations, regulations, or business models. Consequently, RPA is expected to adapt to external changes focusing on business process improvement. Once a process is automated, it is essential to periodically evaluate its efficiency, accuracy, and effectiveness and modify it to meet current needs. The future of RPA will focus on process improvements that can be derived from the application of other emerging technologies, such as cognitive automation, machine learning, and artificial intelligence.

Use Cases

Every functional area of a business can benefit from RPA. This section discusses how RPA can help automate various repetitive tasks in different functional areas in a company.

Accounting

Reconciliations

Account balances need to be frequently reconciled between control and ledger accounts or between different systems. Reconciling account balances requires comparing two or more outputs to see whether transactions are recorded in both systems/accounts and updated accurately. Accountants can use RPA to automate this time-consuming, tedious task.

Document Processing

Businesses receive many types of documents, as either paper or image files. Paper documents can have multiple formats or be written in various languages, and scanned documents may have varying image qualities. Preparing these documents into usable data for data entry is typically done manually. Companies can use optical character recognition (OCR) devices embedded in RPA tools to mitigate image format and quality challenges. OCR devices can help digitize the invoice into a consistent text format. RPA tools can then translate documents into different languages and map the fields to ERP applications for data entry. The RPA bot can be designed to handle missing data and exceptions for error processing.

Reporting

RPA can be used to automate report generation for both external and internal reporting. Accounting departments often receive data from multiple internal and external systems. RPA can extract data from various systems, clean it, and organize it into presentable formats. RPA can significantly reduce the number of manual, repetitive, and time-consuming tasks accountants perform to focus on more valuable activities, such as data interpretation.

Audit

Auditors serve vital roles in identifying suspicious transactions and ensuring that organizations comply with internal policies and financial regulations. Using RPA, auditors can gather evidence from various systems, format the data, perform simple comparisons, and so forth. Auditors can also use RPA to perform tests of controls and create detailed reports.

Finance

Investment Applications

Investment applications and new customer onboarding are tedious and drawn-out processes. Strict regulations like Know Your Customer (KYC) and anti-money laundering (AML) laws make collecting and processing investment applications more time-consuming. These processes make it difficult for banks to expedite the application process. RPA can eliminate manual review and data entry tasks by capturing data from KYC documentation. Banks can use RPA to notify customers of application decisions, making the communications' process more cost-effective.[14]

Capital Expenditure Process

In most organizations, the approval processes for capital expenditure are highly inefficient, requiring requests to pass through multiple departments. The request typically identifies the asset, the cost, and the anticipated return on investment (ROI). Management determines whether the acquisition falls within the organization's budget. If approved, the procurement team sends the request to get estimates and arrange payment. RPA can automatically route approval requests to the appropriate party and send subsequent reminders, allowing the requestor to track the proposal's status in real time. With RPA, organizations can easily design and implement approval processes that meet their unique business needs.[8]

Marketing and Sales

Customer Service Operations

Before answering a customer inquiry, customer service representatives need to collect data about the customer to access the customer account. Customer service representatives may use one system/module to manage customer service inquiries while the customer information resides in a different system/ module. RPA can retrieve and verify the information and route the request to a specific representative for resolution, reducing time spent accessing information and decreasing tedious data entry and retrieval.

Customer Relationship Management: Lead Generation

Sales representatives spend most of their time searching and collecting the information they need for lead generation on potential prospects and businesses. RPA tools can automatically acquire data from any website and integrate it with internal sources such as CRM systems. This integration gives the sales team the necessary lead-generation tools. RPA tools can convert incoming leads from various channels, such as social media, TV, and print, into a standard format. Further, RPA tools can automate the data entry process into a CRM system.

Advertising and Marketing: Data Manipulation

Consumer product companies consistently change their advertising campaigns based on market reactions. The amount of data available for analysis can sometimes be daunting to the company. RPA tools can help employees sift through data, combine it with data from multiple sources, and provide an output for decision-making. RPA, in conjunction with data analytics, can pinpoint actionable tasks for improvement and optimization and expose deficiencies and hidden patterns.

Manufacturing

Streamline Bill of Materials

Bills of materials (BOMs) are the source document that specifies the list of raw materials, components, and subcomponents needed for new product creation. Changes to the bill of materials can affect many decisions made in purchasing and production. Therefore, changes should be monitored and reported. RPA can monitor BOM systems, send automatic change alerts and notifications, ensure regulatory compliance, and provide real-time reporting and analytics.

Automate Reporting and Administration

Manufacturing managers need to coordinate labor, material, and equipment to eliminate interruptions in the manufacturing process. Managers depend heavily on data from various systems to adjust, coordinate, and facilitate an uninterrupted manufacturing process. RPA can help integrate the data arriving from multiple systems. RPA bots can clean the data, organize, analyze, and create reports that help daily administration and decision-making. RPA can help get timely data and increase visibility across production and business systems.

Transportation Management

Managing the logistics in manufacturing requires companies to perform various manual tasks such as scheduling shipments, monitoring changes, updating customers on statuses, and handling exceptions. RPA can automatically acquire, integrate, and deliver data across the supply chain to efficiently exchange information with shippers, carriers, logistics partners, freight bill payment processors, and other trading partners. RPA can automate manual shipping tasks such as checking the initial pick-up request and reporting shipment status between internal systems. RPA can automatically perform rate look-ups from multimodal carriers, eliminate manually copying data from load boards and emails into internal systems, and copy it back into business-to-business portals to report shipment status.

Human Resource Management

Resume Screening and Candidate Shortlisting

Human resource (HR) employees spend significant time reviewing resumes and application forms for open positions. RPA tools can quickly gather applicant data and compare it to the list of job requirements. These requirements can be established as predefined rules in RPA that guide the selection procedure. RPA can be used to automate the receipt of applications and rejection notifications.

Offer Letter Administration

Generally, employment offer letters need to comply with different regulations (company, legal, etc.) and be tailored to the particular candidate. These regulations are stored in various systems and databases, making manual verification and cross-checking time-consuming. Therefore, RPA bots can quickly gather all the needed information, create the offer letter, send it to the candidate, and monitor whether the candidate returns the appropriate documents.

Onboarding New Hires

Onboarding new hires requires creating a new user account and email address and providing access rights for applications and IT equipment. RPA can help activate a particular template for the onboarding workflow, make rule-guided decisions about which credentials need to be assigned to the new employee, determine which onboarding documents should be sent, and schedule appropriate initial training programs.

Attendance Tracking and Payroll Management

Large companies with many employees struggle to keep track of employee time spent at work on various activities. An RPA bot can help cross-check self-reported time against time logged in the company systems and report inconsistencies to HR staff. Robots can be built to monitor workflow resources and recommend reallocation of the workforce when confronted with absenteeism. Payroll processing typically involves significant data entry, increasing the risk of error. An RPA process can use OCR devices to read manual time cards and update time tracking applications, reducing data entry errors and increasing the efficiency of the process.

Travel and Expense Management

Manually processing expense reimbursements encounters many challenges, such as late expense submissions, missing receipts, and unclear expense justifications, which negatively impact compliance and employee satisfaction. RPA tools can make the process more efficient by creating bots to check expenses against company policies and external systems, such as checking per diem rates.

Additional Resources

UiPath Academic Alliance
Learning RPA – automation courses: https://academy.uipath.com/

Automation Anywhere University
Free RPA training and courses: https://university.automationanywhere.com/

Blue Prism University
RPA training and certification: https://www.blueprism.com/resources/university/

Microsoft Learn
Power Automate training: https://learn.microsoft.com/en-us/training/browse/?products=power-automate&WT.mc_id=webupdates_GEP_PowerAutomate-web-wwl

Notes

1. Marks, A. (2020). RPA on a Grand Scale at the FDA. *Deloitte Insights for the Wall Street Journal* (18 February). https://deloitte.wsj.com/articles/rpa-on-a-grand-scale-at-the-fda-01582056126.
2. Sandy, D., Ritchi, H., Adrianto, Z., and Alfan, A. (2022). Robotic Process Automation in Action: A Use Case in Accounting Task. *Center for Digital Innovation Studies* 1 (1).
3. Lhuer, X. (2016). The Next Acronym You Need to Know About: RPA (Robotic Process Automation). *McKinsey Digital* (6 December). https://www.mckinsey.com/business-functions/mckinsey-digital/our-insights/the-next-acronym-you-need-to-know-about-rpa.
4. Deloitte. (2020). Deloitte Global RPA Survey. https://www2.deloitte.com/ro/en/pages/technology-media-and-telecommunications/articles/deloitte-global-rpa-survey.html.
5. Automation Anywhere. (2020). Global Research Reveals World's "Most Hated" Office Tasks (21 January). https://www.automationanywhere.com/company/press-room/global-research-reveals-worlds-most-hated-office-tasks.
6. Consultancy.eu. (2020). German RPA Consultancy Roboyo Lands €21 Million Investment (18 September). https://www.consultancy.eu/news/4886/german-rpa-consultancy-roboyo-lands-21-million-investment.
7. Schaffrik, B. (2023). The Forrester Wave™: Robotic Process Automation, Q1 2023: The 15 Providers That Matter Most and How They Stack Up. Forrester. https://reprints2.forrester.com/#/assets/2/666/RES178434/report.
8. Automation Anywhere. (n.d.). https://www.automationanywhere.com/products.
9. Automation Anywhere University. (n.d.). RPA Training and Certification. https://university.automationanywhere.com/.
10. UiPath. (n.d.). The UiPath Purpose: Accelerate Human Achievement. https://www.uipath.com/company/about-us.
11. UiPath. (n.d.). Business Automation Proficiency Starts with Our Free RPA Courses. https://www.uipath.com/rpa/academy.
12. SS&C Blue Prism. (n.d.). Product Portfolio. https://www.blueprism.com/products/.
13. Microsoft (n.d.). Take Care of What's Important. Automate the Rest. https://powerautomate.microsoft.com/en-us/.
14. Eisner, M. (2020). Most Commonly Automated Financial Processes. ProcessMaker (12 November). https://www.processmaker.com/blog/most-commonly-automated-financial-processes/.

CHAPTER 11

Robotic Process Automation Implementation and Management

The excerpt from an IT consulting blog highlights the importance of companies developing policies and oversight for end-user development of RPA processes. The interview is with Marcelo Blbajari, the RPA Service Practices director at IT Convergence.

Our main stakeholder, the IT director of the company, discovered that several business owners had executed automation projects without the IT department's involvement or approval, funding the activities with their own budgets and without even notifying IT about the initiatives.

This was done as a proactive activity from those business owners who could not afford to wait for the next yearly round of evaluation for candidate projects, which is the official process in the company to define and fund the projects that will be executed during the year.

Automated processes (usually referred to by the fancy name of "robots") imitate the actions carried over by a human user to complete an activity, like entering an invoice into an application, or downloading files from different sources to consolidate a period closure report.

In order to be able to do that, robots hold passwords and system access credentials and have access to sensitive personal and company information.

The IT department has strict rules about how all types of security threats are handled and has some very specific processes that apply to system security, like password requirements, periodic regeneration, the prohibition to share passwords, tools to securely store the passwords, etc. It also has many processes that define how systems must log all

(Continued)

(Continued)

types of user activities as well as login attempts, login failures, password changes, etc.

Without considering security policies or letting IT know, the business departments gave robot processes the same system credentials and passwords used by human users. They thought that if John Doe enters invoices, a robot that does the same job could use the same user and password as John Doe, as it was doing the same activity.

What if fake invoices are entered by an automated process that was tweaked to do that?

What if the real human user approves payment for an amount higher than he's allowed to, and then blames the robot that uses his same credentials?

What are your key recommendations for companies in a similar situation?

If you face the same situation, where your business departments are ahead of IT and start automating processes without IT participation, you can still get back on track by defining the governance plan for automation processes and then adjusting the already existing processes as needed.[1]

RPA Framework: Successful RPA Projects

Robotic process automation (RPA) can help increase the efficiency of business processes in an organization. However, to reap the benefits of cost savings and efficiency, you should consider the following vital factors before implementing RPA.

Select the right process for automation. If you are using RPA for the first time, start with a well-documented, simple, and repetitive process. Simple tasks that can be easily defined and translated into the software are good first candidates. Select a repetitive process that does not require additional thought or judgment. If the process and the related software are constantly changing, the process is not ready for RPA. Automating an unstable process will require significant ongoing maintenance and will likely create problems and inefficiencies. Therefore, carefully select the first candidate process. Once the process is identified, document the process's activities using a documentation technique such as flowcharts. Then sequence the activities, possible exceptions, and rules for each step. Choosing a more straightforward process as the first candidate will help the organization better understand the RPA development process and become familiar with the RPA software tool. If the first automation project succeeds, it will help obtain employee and management buy-in, thus gaining momentum for future projects and seeing a faster return on investment. Allow time for employees to learn the RPA software and gradually move into more complex processes. However, remember that complex processes well-suited for RPA should be repetitive and rule-based.

Determine the goal(s) of RPA. Like any other IT implementation, determine the overall goals for implementing RPA. Is the project goal to reduce human errors, improve back-office processing, increase the processes' efficiency, or reduce staffing costs? Once the goals are identified, determine a plan of action. For example, if error reduction is the primary goal, first establish the source of the error. Then decide whether you need to modify tasks or business rules. Determine whether the business rules are followed consistently. If not, do the rules or the process need to be changed? Any changes to the process or business rules must be changed before implementing RPA. If incomplete and inaccurate upstream data are the source of the issue, RPA will not fix the problem. Finally, create several performance measures based on the goals to identify whether RPA implementation achieves the set objective.

Think long-term. RPA can help bridge the gap between newer systems and legacy systems. Although RPA can increase the lifespan of legacy systems, dependence on legacy systems can become a point of pain in the long run. Organizations should not consider RPA to be a quick, short-term fix but part of their long-term IT and business strategy plan.

Remember employee concerns. Similar to other software implementations, management should also consider several organizational issues. A significant component of RPA success relies on employee buy-in. When employees hear about automation, they may have a natural fear of job loss or job changes in the future. Management support for RPA and clear communications about RPA implementation goals will help reduce anxiety among employees and potential sabotage of RPA bots. Getting employees involved in RPA projects through training and education can also create employee acceptance of RPA.

Have a long-term maintenance plan. Once the bots are developed and deployed, they will need ongoing maintenance and oversight. Businesses frequently change, and your bots may need to update accordingly. Be sure to allocate staff to ensure that your RPA scripts are running efficiently and meet the business's needs.

Table 11.1 Why Do RPA Projects Fail?

Technical factors contributing to RPA failure

- Choosing a solution that requires intensive programming
- Not relying on RPA marketplaces and other readily available tools
- Choosing a solution that did not demonstrate scalability
- Not testing your software bots thoroughly

Process factors contributing to RPA failure

- Not choosing the right processes to automate
- Choosing a process that changes frequently
- Choosing a process with insignificant business impact
- Choosing a process where errors are disproportionately costly
- Choosing a process that involves higher-level cognitive tasks
- Choosing a complex process. Although its subprocesses are simple, the process itself may be complex if it has too many subprocesses
- Choosing a process for which better custom solutions exist
- Striving for end-to-end automation when it is not cost-effective

Organizational factors contributing to RPA failure

- Lack of leadership buy-in
- Company is lacking a clear RPA strategy
- Lack of management of RPA bots once deployed to production
- Not setting clear objectives for the automation strategy
- Not having a big picture view over the implementation process
- Poor change management process
- Third-party problems if using a third party to develop the bots

People factors contributing to RPA failures

- Shadow development by end-users
- Unrealistic expectations
- Lack of time commitment from local team
- Trying to implement RPA on your own without expertise
- Relying solely on the IT department
- Lack of governance

RPA projects can fail due to various reasons. In Table 11.1, we organize factors contributing to failure into four areas: (1) technical, (2) process, (3) organizational, and (4) people.

RPA Lifecycle

RPA projects will also follow the development lifecycle process. A typical technology development lifecycle has planning, analysis, design, implementation and testing, and maintenance stages. In the following sections, we discuss specific concerns, issues, and important decisions related to RPA in each stage.

Plan

Planning is the first essential step in an RPA project. At the end of this step, you should be able to answer why you are using RPA and whether it is feasible to do so. Planning also requires a firm to evaluate the strategic impact of the RPA project and categorize projects into programs and portfolios. You want to justify to management that RPA is the best solution and to support its economic feasibility. During the planning stage, you would:

- **Identify candidate processes for RPA.** The first step is to identify the business processes that can be automated using RPA. As mentioned in the previous section, use the guidelines provided to evaluate whether a business process is suited for RPA. Next, determine whether each process will be a single project or whether you can group related processes to create portfolios. Determine the project or portfolio scope to understand the boundaries of what will be included or excluded in the automation.
- **Determine the technical feasibility of RPA.** Consider whether RPA is compatible with existing technology. When deciding on the RPA software tool, you should consider the following:
  - Is the software compatible with the existing applications?
  - What features are available for development?
  - Does the tool meet the demands of the process, such as whether it can handle the volume of transactions?
  - Is it user-friendly?
  - Do we need in-house expertise to use the tool? Do we have the necessary expertise internally, or can we hire staff?
  - Can we obtain a free trial version to test the application before committing?
  - Can the application handle complex business processes?
  - Are there developer forums? If so, how extensive are they?
  - Is there training available for employees?
- **Determine the economic feasibility.** You do not want to spend on an RPA software tool to automate one process. Therefore, consider the following to determine the economic feasibility:
  - How many processes are good candidates for RPA? Are these processes in one department, or can the RPA software be used in other departments?
  - How much does the RPA tool cost? What is our expected return on investment?
  - Do we have access to support and maintenance? If so, how much does it cost?

■ **Develop a project plan.** Planning includes developing a project plan indicating the various RPA development lifecycle stages. The project plan should include a task breakdown of the activities, resource requirements, cost and effort estimates, likelihood and impact of identified risks, and a risk response plan.

Analyze

The next stage in the RPA lifecycle is the analysis stage. Like other technology development projects, RPA projects require considerable time to analyze. This phase aims to identify the system's requirements and use cases.

Evaluate the Business Process

Ask the following questions to understand the business process better and develop the use case and the relevant requirements for the process.

■ What are the primary steps in the business process? For example, consider a business process to update the customer relationship management (CRM) system from emails received. We can define the primary steps: open the email, identify emails with potential customer information, open the CRM, and update the necessary fields.

■ What are the decision points in the business process? Are there exceptions to the typical business process? How are the exceptions handled? Should exceptions exist? What are the consequences of eliminating any exceptions?

■ Who owns the business process? You should establish a process owner if a business process spans many departments.

■ How many stakeholders are involved in the business process? Simple automations, such as updating CRM and generating mass emails, may have only one user. However, more complex automation spanning various departments may have several stakeholders. Stakeholders may be individuals who provide input into the process or use the information generated. Therefore, it is essential to identify all the stakeholders involved and recognize each individual's role in the business process.

■ What are the existing internal controls in the business process? Identifying controls built into the current process is crucial to see whether they can be maintained as is or need to be modified to fit the automated process. Sometimes, manual controls may be replaced or eliminated since automation eliminates human interactions.

■ Should additional internal controls be designed and implemented? Even though RPA automates a process and minimizes human interactions, it does not mean that the need for controls is eliminated.

Therefore, while understanding the steps in the process, you need to think about how to avoid inaccurate, incomplete, and irrelevant data from being processed.

Design

The goal of the design phase is to create a blueprint for the requirements identified during the analysis phase. To complete the design, gain an understanding of the process's interrelationships, dependencies, rules, triggers, and the current infrastructure.

Business Process Design

When automating a process, there is pressure to replicate tasks exactly as they are currently done. Therefore, when considering a process for automation, it is necessary to analyze each step's validity in the process critically.

Therefore, during the design stage, you should ask similar questions as the following:

- What are the steps in the process?
- Why is a certain step important?
- How is this step related to other steps?
- If this step is eliminated, how will it impact subsequent steps?
- Is there a better way to organize the steps in the process?
- Is there a process that can be used as a benchmark? If so, how different is the firm's business process from the benchmark?
- What are the advantages of the existing process? Does the process add value to the customer?
- Will automation hinder positive customer experience and reduce customer satisfaction?
- What aspects of the process should be maintained to maintain customer satisfaction?
- What aspects can be improved to enhance customer satisfaction?

Once you have addressed these issues, you should have a good understanding of the existing business process; hence, you will be able to develop a vision and a strategy for the automation of the business process.

Conceptual Design

Conceptual design is a blueprint of what we are going to develop. Flow charts are a good documentation tool that can be used to create a blueprint. For example, a system flow chart can display how data is processed in the bot, and a program flow chart can depict the rules the bot will apply to control the flow of data and events.

Figure 11.1 shows an example of a potential RPA process. Cindy is responsible for reconciling intercompany transactions every week. Intercompany transactions are recorded in a control account and debited or credited to

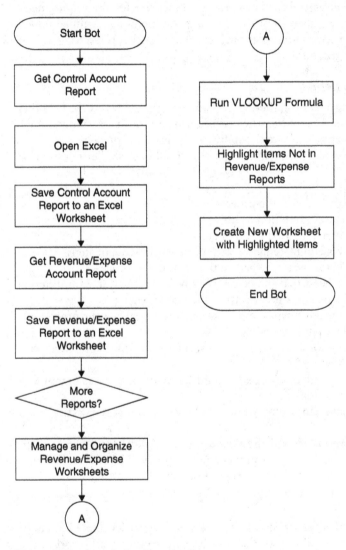

Figure 11.1 Sample Bot Flowchart

revenue and expense accounts. To ensure that all intercompany transactions are recorded each week, Cindy has to retrieve a control account report and a detailed transaction report for revenue and expense accounts from the corporate ERP system. Then she uploads these to an Excel workbook. She then merges the revenue and expense accounts into one file before starting the reconciliation. Cindy uses the VLOOKUP formula in Excel to compare the merged file with the control account report using a common reference. Even though the actual reconciliation using the VLOOKUP formula is fast, Cindy spends significant time downloading, merging, and organizing the data. She would like to automate this manual process to help her save time. Figure 11.1 shows a conceptual design of the bot to be developed to help Cindy retrieve, merge, and organize the data.

Implement and Test

Creating the Bot

In the implementation step, you will develop the bot using your chosen RPA tool. Depending on the tool selected, you might have to design and develop additional steps during the implementation stage. If the design steps are modified or added, remember to change the systems flow chart to reflect the necessary changes. Here are some guidelines for developing the bot:

- **Start simple.** Start by creating a simple bot. Consider the major steps and address those first. Add exceptions and controls in subsequent iterations.
- **Use a built-in script.** You can start from scratch or use sample scripts readily available in some RPA applications. If you are new to RPA, the sample scripts may help you develop the bot faster. However, there are some disadvantages to note:
  - You might not be able to modify the sample script.
  - You might mistakenly change the script and initiate an action that is not observed immediately.
  - You might spend more time trying to figure out how to modify the sample rather than starting from scratch.
- **Extend the bot.** Once the basic bot is developed, extend it by adding additional commands. Consider any internal controls to ensure accuracy, completeness, security, privacy, and availability.
- **Consult with IT.** If a business user does RPA development, do not hesitate to ask IT for guidance.

Testing

Testing is essential even if the RPA bot performs a simple process. Do not deploy your RPA bot into a live production system without thorough testing. There are five factors to consider for a successful RPA test plan:

1. **Understand the requirements.** The testing employee/team should understand how the process should work.
2. **Test data.** Invalid or incomplete test data will generate incorrect results, derailing the testing timeline and impacting the RPA implementation's efficacy. Hence, it is necessary to know clearly what data variations will be needed in terms of types and formats for the test cycle to be productive.
3. **Test scripts and test cases.** To generate complete test scripts, generate different test cases with specific outcomes. Document the test cases in a simple Excel spreadsheet that includes a list of test scenarios, the scenario-specific input data required to execute the testing, the output to be expected, and the output that displays. It should also include a status column denoting whether this test was a success or a failure. It is best to have the test script reviewed and approved by the design team and the subject matter expert. This extra step will ensure that there are no gaps in the test cycle.

   When developing test scripts, consider varying the following:
   - The file type uploaded.
   - The data type and format (text, numeric, date) to see whether the file will get processed. If you have two columns in which the data type is important, you should write test scripts holding each column and data type combination constant.
   - The business process with missing data in each field.
   - The business process with exceptions.
   - The number of users accessing the bot simultaneously.
4. **Execution.** Execution of the test script will be smooth if the test scenarios are documented clearly and concisely. Include each business rule defined in the business requirements in the test script.
5. **Defect management.** Defects are a general expectation with every testing cycle. The testing team should document each defect and notify the development team.

Ensure that you have considered all exceptions and errors and have built adequate controls to prevent, detect, and correct any exceptions or errors that may occur during the normal course of use. Testing should start during development. Each component or step of a bot should be tested and retested during the development stage to ensure that the bot functions as intended.

However, formal testing should be done once the bot is developed to ensure a smooth transition into production.

The best option would be to get a third party, rather than the user developing the bot, to test the process. Another essential factor to remember is to test the performance of loading files if needed. Focusing only on the process performance and not considering the loading of files as inputs or outputs can cause significant delays. Understanding the limitations before introducing the process to production is vital to avoid system overload.

Further, run the RPA bot parallel with the manual or existing operations as part of testing. As you go through the test scripts, document the test results. Like every technology, you will find defects/errors while you test. Errors should be noted, communicated to the development team, and addressed before deploying the RPA bot to production.

Some common mistakes in RPA bot development are:

- Implementing incorrect programming or process logic. Always check whether the program logic is accurate by running the bot several times with various data.
- Focusing only on the standard process and not paying attention to possible exceptions. Make sure you have considered many exceptions and possible errors and develop the program and process logic to handle these exceptions.
- Developing everything from scratch when there are reusable components readily available.
- Not using a standardized naming convention for workflow files, activities, arguments, variables, and so on.
- Not performing unit testing on each component developed and relying on the system integration test (SIT).
- Not demonstrating the RPA bot frequently. If you develop an RPA for other users, do frequent demonstrations to verify the outputs.
- Not keeping the development, test, and production environments separate.
- Not implementing version controls. If modifications are made after implementation, make the changes to the RPA bot in a new version.
- Ignoring the importance of logging for debugging and troubleshooting, especially after deploying the bot to production.
- Assuming that development will be complete once the bot is in production.

Maintain

Once the testing is complete, the next stage is implementing, using, and maintaining the RPA bot. Like any other process, RPA bots must be monitored to ensure that the bot performs without issues. You can observe a bot using the following methods:

- **Periodic parallel processing.** Periodically compare the output of the RPA bot with an output processed using an alternate method, such as the prior manual process.
- **Exception monitoring.** Identifying an event that is an exception to the normal business process and evaluating the bot's steps and the final output to ensure that the program logic remains intact.
- **Audit trail.** Evaluate the system log for the bot to identify any issues and red flags.
- **Subsequent audits/compliance testing.** Continue to review and test the bot, even once it is in production.

As with any other IT project, RPA projects can fail due to a lack of RPA maintenance and support needed for bots in production. Like any other application, RPA bots will also need to be modified after some time. These modifications can stem from changing business requirements, policies, regulations, user interfaces, missed requirements during development, or changes to the underlying information technology. Therefore, the RPA support and maintenance stage should include a process for change management.

Change management should follow the RPA lifecycle and consist of the following steps.

- **Step 1: Defining the change.** The first step is identifying and defining the change. Why is the change necessary, what needs to be changed, what steps in the bot should be modified, who is authorizing the change, and are there other processes affected by this change are some questions to consider when defining the change. Every new change should be approved by all stakeholders and documented before moving to the next step.
- **Step 2: Modify the RPA bot.** The necessary modifications will be developed and documented during this step. Remember to make a backup before making any changes and not make any modifications directly in production.
- **Step 3: Test the modification.** Even if it is a minor modification, the RPA bot should not be released to production without thorough testing. Rigorously test the modification following the steps discussed in the earlier section.
- **Step 4: Release to production.** When releasing the modified bot to production, remember to maintain proper versioning of all the tasks and comply with security protocols in the latest versions.

Governance and Management

As more users embrace business process automation, a firm may decide to deploy RPA projects in a centralized, decentralized, or hybrid manner. Regardless of the method chosen for RPA deployment, firms should ensure that these bots are properly managed and governed. Management of RPA involves implementing and monitoring projects throughout the RPA lifecycle. Governance of RPA consists of overseeing the strategic implications of RPA deployment; therefore, it involves asking questions such as:

- What is the impact of RPA projects on strategic objectives?
- How will RPA add value to the customer?
- Will RPA change customer satisfaction?
- How will RPA make non-value-added processes more efficient?
- What is the impact of RPA on financial and nonfinancial performance?
- What is the impact of RPA on the firm's reputation?
- Will RPA affect the employees' morale and the company's culture?
- How do we ensure ethical decision-making with RPA?
- How do we ensure that RPA bots are not discriminatory?
- Will RPA increase the company's risk exposure?
- Will RPA have an impact on financial reporting?
- What is the best sourcing model for RPA?
- Does the company have proper controls implemented for RPA?
- How significant is RPA within the company? Do we need a center for excellence? Who should be in charge of RPA?
- How does RPA impact any compliance requirements?
- What is the best method of RPA development (outsourcing vs. in-house)?

Even though RPA is more end-user-oriented, the management should communicate RPA-related decisions and challenges to the board of directors. Depending on the extent of the use of RPA, board involvement may be limited. However, these broad questions should be discussed among the board of directors and senior management. We explore various aspects related to these questions in detail next.

Strategic Objectives

Many firms may look to automate back-office non-value-added processes to minimize cost. Even though some processes may not be value-added to the customer, these back-office activities provide necessary services. Therefore, the executive management must understand the strategic impact of automating back-office processes.

Therefore, firms should carefully consider the strategic impact of automating value-added and non-value-added processes before deploying RPA bots and evaluate whether RPA will help the company achieve the set strategic objectives. Before starting an RPA project, carefully consider the strategic impact of the RPA. The board of directors and management can use COBIT 2019 as a guide and ask similar questions such as the following:[2]

- Will RPA help the firm tap into currently untapped markets?
- Will RPA reduce costs in the short term and the long term?
- Will RPA enable the development of new and innovative products?
- Will RPA enhance customer services, and how?
- Will RPA require the firm to change its internal organizational structure?
- Will RPA be able to enforce the existing internal principles, policies, and procedures?
- Will principles, policies, and procedures enforced in the RPA process have a negative impact on the business strategy?
- Will RPA affect the firm's culture?

RPA Development

Many RPA development issues need proper oversight and management. The board and executive management should select the right RPA vendor, enforce good change management and continuous improvement controls, establish long-term support, and emphasize the need for proper documentation of the RPA process.

Management must first consider which RPA vendor is most suitable for the company's needs. During the analysis stage of the RPA lifecycle, evaluate vendors based on the company's requirements. Management needs to consider the following to select the best vendor for their needs:

- Understand the processes selected for automation.
- Create a list of vendors and the functionality of the RPA platform offered by the vendors.
- Evaluate the vendors based on criteria such as price, licensing requirements, support and maintenance, whether the RPA process is stored in the cloud or on-site, the experience of the vendor in the firm's industry, the compatibility of the RPA software with the existing technology, the functionality of the RPA platform, user-friendliness of the user interface, scalability of RPA software, and the ability to monitor the automated processes.
- Conduct due diligence on each potential vendor before selecting a vendor.

Traditionally, when companies wanted to focus on value-added processes rather than reparative back-office functions, companies considered outsourcing non-value-added tasks to a third party. RPA can be regarded as a substitute for outsourcing. One of the benefits of RPA over outsourcing is that the company maintains the process and the ownership of the process in-house. Further, RPA is easily scaled to handle more transactions without substantially increasing costs. However, combining RPA with outsourcing can also maximize returns. Since RPA is ideal for repetitive logic-based tasks, these can be automated. In contrast, other tasks, such as exception handling that requires critical thinking or a personal touch, can be outsourced.

RPA Center of Excellence

If the company rapidly adopts RPA throughout the business, the management should consider establishing an RPA center of excellence (COE). A center of excellence provides the structural framework for directing, planning, implementing, managing, and monitoring the adoption of RPA within an enterprise. The center of excellence will help the company take a holistic view of RPA adoption and implementation throughout the company. The center of excellence can:

- Establish the policies, procedures, and standards for bot qualification, development, and deployment, and monitor compliance with audit, regulatory, and information security requirements.
- Select the right RPA tools and support the tools throughout the company. Further, the center can ensure the integration of RPA tools into the IT architecture of the company.
- Manage the RPA development lifecycle.
- Analyze the effects of RPA on people and culture and make the necessary changes to retrain employees.
- Define the organizational structure. Automating processes may eliminate the need for the company to have many levels in an organizational structure. Therefore, the center can help assess and recommend changes to the organizational structure to enhance business operations.

The COE can be organized in one of two ways. If the COE is considered a business support function, the COE can be viewed as the central RPA provider. Then the COE will be comprised of a combination of business and IT members who will manage all aspects of RPA for the company. Alternatively, the COE can be placed within IT, where IT will manage the COE.

RPA Performance

Once an RPA bot is in operation, an important next step is to measure the bot's performance. Similar to other activities performed in a business, it is necessary to quantitatively demonstrate its financial, business, and operational impact on the company. Quantifying the benefit of the bot will enable RPA champions to convince management and other stakeholders to buy into the idea and invest in RPA. Measuring performance will also verify whether the anticipated benefits have been achieved.

The following key factors should be considered when determining whether RPA implementations are effective.

Productivity. The company should also consider any additional benefits or productivity gains from implementing RPA. Did the RPA bot improve productivity? Unlike human workers, RPA bots can work around the clock. Further, the RPA bot may be able to complete the process faster. The time necessary to complete a process is called the process velocity. To evaluate productivity based on velocity, compare the number of times the manual process ran during a period with the number of times the automated process ran. Since productivity gains are most often achieved due to the reduction in manual labor hours, productivity can be calculated by observing the following:

1. The number of processes that were automated.
2. The number of hours saved from each process.
3. The number of times a process runs per period.
4. The costs per hour to run the process.

The number of errors. Errors can take place for various reasons. Most errors are due to human negligence or carelessness. Fatigue caused by repeating the same manual task and snap judgments about missing or incomplete information on a form can slow down the process and increase errors in the final output. Therefore, when measuring RPA performance, compare the number of errors detected in the manual process with those detected in the automated process to see whether there are cost savings due to reduced error handling. Cost savings are calculated as follows:

Cost savings due to the reduction in error handling = (Cost of handling an error × Number of errors detected per hour or period in the manual process) – (Cost of handling an error × Number of errors detected per hour or period in the automated process).

Consistency. Consistency is achieved by coding a set of instructions to the RPA bot. Since the bot will always follow these instructions, it streamlines the process and limits exceptions. Therefore, automation can increase consistency and compliance with management and regulatory requirements. To evaluate whether consistency has improved, compare the number of items processed as an exception in the manual process with items the bot rejected for not meeting the specified criteria.

Employee satisfaction. RPA can free up employee time and allow them to dedicate that time to more meaningful tasks. When evaluating the performance of RPA, it is essential to consider the qualitative effects of RPA on employee satisfaction. Collect qualitative information by talking to employees to solicit feedback.

Availability. Consider comparing the downtime of the manual process with the RPA process to see how much RPA has increased systems reliability and availability. Unlike humans who take vacations, sick days, and breaks between tasks, the RPA process can be available 24/7. Therefore, assess the increased availability by introducing RPA to evaluate the performance of RPA.

As with any other investment, RPA performance can and will be evaluated based on its return on investment (ROI). The ROI of RPA allows management to plan and measure the performance of RPA using a set benchmark. Managers will compare the ROI of RPA with the desired ROI to evaluate whether the investment in RPA will be worthwhile. RPA performance can be evaluated using the balanced scored approach as well. Table 11.2 shows several performance measures in each category of the balanced scorecard.

Table 11.2 Performance Measures Using the Balanced Scorecard Method

Financial perspective	■ Average annual cost savings ■ Five-year cost savings ■ Payback period ■ Five-year return on investment
Internal process perspective	■ Process efficiencies: processing time ■ Process efficiencies: daily throughput ■ Improvement in data analytics capability ■ Improvements to compliance/accuracy
Learning and growth	■ Employee satisfaction rate ■ The number of employees reallocated ■ The annual labor hours saved ■ Reduction in task/case workload per hour
Customer	■ The number of complaints received ■ Customer satisfaction ratings ■ The time taken to serve the customer

Risks and Controls

RPA reduces human interaction with a process. Humans increase risk exposure by doing things such as writing the password on Post-it Notes, taking shortcuts to manage their daily workload, or installing malware without realizing it. Therefore, there is a common understanding that RPA will be more secure, hence will reduce the risk exposure. Even though a lack of human interaction can reduce errors caused by negligence and fatigue, RPA can also introduce another set of risks to a firm. Decentralized RPA development by business users can increase the overall IT risk exposure of the firm. Lack of compatibility, lack of inbuilt controls, inadequate testing, lack of continuous improvement and change management controls, and unclear process ownership are a few reasons that RPA may increase IT risks for a company. Since RPA is popular as a business user tool that can be used with minimum assistance from the IT department, leaving the IT department in the dark can have some negative implications in the long run.

RPA projects have inherent risks. Inherent risks can be identified based on the RPA lifecycle, namely analysis, design, development, testing, and maintenance. Several inherent risks can arise during the analysis phase, including selecting the incorrect process for RPA, conducting a preliminary cost–benefit analysis, having inadequate oversight of the development process, and providing insufficient expertise with licensing or regulatory requirements. During bot development, risks can arise from insufficient evaluation of RPA technology and partner selection. Additional risks include a lack of evaluation of whether the technology architecture enables RPA and RPA tools to be compatible with existing technologies, inadequate or inaccurate translation of user requirements, and incorrect assessment of the likelihood and impact of risks throughout the project. Risks arising during the testing phase are associated with insufficient testing of the RPA bot. Insufficient testing can result from not fully understanding the underlying logic or algorithms. Inadequate RPA bot ownership, insufficient training, errors from improper integration, unauthorized changes to the deployed RPA bot, inadequate RPA bot monitoring and data validation, and overreliance on the RPA bot can increase risks associated with the operations and maintenance of the RPA.

Further, if third-party vendors are involved, monitoring third-party activity on the deployed RPA bot is important to reduce risk exposure to the company. Another critical aspect to consider when evaluating risks is identifying how an RPA bot may be retired. Therefore, a company should create a process of how to retire an RPA bot, deactivate access privileges, and migrate the data from the old bot to the new one. The lack of a formal process and risk response can increase RPA risk exposure for the company.

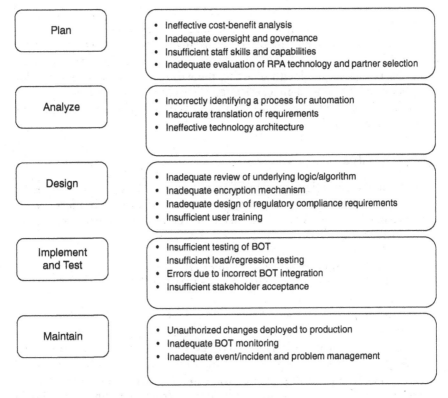

Figure 11.2 Risks Associated with the RPA Lifecycle

Organizations should evaluate the business risks in the strategic, technological, financial, operational, and regulatory environment associated with RPA. Figure 11.2 presents several risks identified in each of the RPA lifecycle stages.

RPA risks should be assessed holistically. When considering RPA risks, it is important to consider risks associated with RPA strategy, RPA sourcing, tool selection, stakeholder buy-in, and project, operational, and change management. Suppose companies fail to consider the strategic impact of RPA and view an RPA project as an isolated event. In that case, the company may not be able to reap the full potential of RPA and miss creating value for its stakeholders. This may increase the risk of exposure for the company and damage the company's reputation. When considering an RPA project, the company should also consider how they plan to develop the RPA bots and whether the development is outsourced or uses existing employees. Risks associated with the selected sourcing model can range from lacking internal skills, to choosing the wrong RPA vendor, to not having the required expertise, to not being able to comply with laws and regulations. Further, companies should consider risks associated with selecting the wrong tool or the wrong vendor, employee resistance to change, selecting the right use case, managing expectations, maintaining the bots once they are deployed, updating and improving the bots, and so forth.

Ethics and RPA

Automation cannot ignore ethical implications. What we create has a positive or a negative impact on employees and other stakeholders. When considering RPA, firms should understand the ethical implications in two important areas:

1. Ethical implications of engaging in RPA.
2. Ethical implications of developing RPA bots.

Given the increased awareness of corporate social responsibility, customers are increasingly inquisitive about where a company's products come from, how the company treats its employees, and how socially responsible the company is. Therefore, people are starting to pay close attention to the consequences of RPA processes on employees and the wider public. Even though every firm has a responsibility to shareholders to grow the business, this should not be at the expense of existing employees. Consequently, firms should consider some ethical implications of deciding to embrace RPA. Automation may spread fear among employees and increase concern that robots will replace humans. Therefore, companies should consider retraining staff who may be impacted by reduced workload due to increased automation. Managers should support employees by showing how RPA can create better job roles and provide training when and where necessary so that these employees will succeed in their new roles. Another aspect to consider is whether the bots are staying true to the organization's brand personality. Consider whether your firm takes pride in interacting with customers; if so, RPA may not align with your company's brand name.

When building bots, it is important to remember that the logic in the bot's code will be based on the existing rules. If the current rules are biased, an RPA process will perpetuate those biases. Therefore, before developing an RPA process, critically evaluate the rules applied to the bots. Therefore, consider the following when developing bots:[3]

- Do RPA bots have a positive impact?
- Are the rules applied in RPA bots free from bias?
- Are RPA bots trained and tested on verified data sources?
- Are RPA bots designed with governance and control in mind?

RPA bots should be developed with increased transparency. The bot should be able to show you why it did what it did. This should include the decisions the bot made, why the process followed a certain path, and how it arrived at the final outcome. In the artificial intelligence chapter (Chapter 6), we discuss additional ethical issues related to intelligent RPA bots.

Notes

1. Albajari, M. (n.d.). A Real Customer Case Study: The Importance of Governance in RPA. IT Convergence Blog. https://www.itconvergence.com/blog/a-real-customer-case-study-the-importance-of-governance-in-rpa/.
2. ISACA. (2019). COBIT 2019 Framework: Governance and Management Objectives. https://www.isaca.org/resources/cobit#.
3. NICE. (n.d.). NICE RPA Robo-Ethical Framework. https://www.nice.com/resources/nice-rpa-robo-ethical-framework.

CHAPTER 12

Quantum and Edge Computing

Excerpts from an interview with Professor Sándor Imre, the director of research and development at the Quantum Informatics National Lab of Hungary, in July 2022.[1]

What quantum networks are used at the moment? Quantum test networks are under deployment all around the world. They are used to collect experiences and reveal technological challenges to be solved. The primary application scenario of these networks is quantum key distribution, which will revolutionize the state-of-the-art security solutions. However, the midterm goal is to connect quantum computers to a global network and let them communicate directly in a quantum way.

What possibilities will open up when quantum computers and networks will spread? According to the history of info-communications, the success of every new technology depends on one or two "killer" applications. For example, GSM offered phone calls from and to everywhere. The cheap and quick email and its attachments result in the unbelievable fast spreading of the internet all over the world. One already-identified driver of quantum communication is the strong security it can provide. Task-oriented (i.e., not universal) quantum computers are already used in medicine research where combinations of various molecules are tested by simulations instead of mixing them in real laboratories. Of course, new killer applications will emerge as quantum devices and systems evolve. I am sure that the direct connection of quantum computers will somehow create a new paradigm in computation.

What do you think, how many years will we have to wait until quantum technology is ready for use on a big scale? Quantum computers accessible via the internet are already available with certain limitations but by 2030 everyday users will have the possibility to

(Continued)

(Continued)

use applications running on them. The advent of personal quantum computers is not so clear. Similar to the development of classical computers, this phase requires significant steps forward in technologization. Concerning quantum networks, big players such as governments, multinational companies, and banks will use them for secure communications by 2030.

Will quantum computers and networks be more efficient in completing everyday tasks? Will they be available for office and home use? It depends. Computationally complex problems such as weather forecasting, healthcare diagnostics, etc., will be more accurate; thus all of us will make a profit personally. Secure quantum communication will save our data and privacy against malicious hackers. I expect that home applications will mainly cover remote access and usage of central quantum computers in the forthcoming decade.

New developments such as driverless cars, space travel, blockchain, cryptocurrency, and artificial intelligence applications depend on complex and voluminous data processing that traditional computer processing cannot handle. To address the need for faster, more complex, and large data processing, computer scientists have developed newer computing techniques. In this chapter, we discuss two techniques: quantum and edge computing.

Quantum computing uses quantum mechanics to solve complex problems faster than conventional computers can. Quantum computing enables the processing of complex algorithms and simulations by combining concepts from computer science, physics, and mathematics. Edge computing brings computer processing to the edge of the network. In other words, some computing capabilities, such as data storage and computation, reside near Internet of Things (IoT) devices rather than at the center of the network. Edge computing is transforming where and how data is processed, allowing for more data collection and processing from all types of devices.

Conventional Computing

Before learning about quantum computing or edge computing, we must look at how traditional computers work to understand the differences and the unique power of quantum and edge computing. We are all familiar with conventional computers such as desktop or laptop computers. When storing or sending data in a conventional system, data is represented by strings of 0's and 1's, called bits.

Several bits are combined to represent letters, numbers, line feeds, or other characters. Conventional computers use transistors on the electrical circuit, which can have only one state at a time, either off or on. The 0 and 1 indicate whether the state is off or on. Therefore, if you want to increase power in a conventional computer, you must increase the number of transistors in the system.

Because of the nature of the circuits, computer instructions are processed one at a time in a sequential sequence. Suppose a conventional computer is trying to find an optimal solution to a mathematical problem. In that case, it must calculate all possibilities one at a time to find the best answer. For example, let's say that there are 256 routes a car can take between point A and point B. A conventional computer would need to calculate each route's distance or time to travel and then compare each solution with the others to find the optimal solution. However, a quantum computer can calculate the 256 routes simultaneously to find the fastest or the shortest solution.

Even recent developments, such as cloud computing, are based on conventional computing. For example, cloud computing sends data via the internet to central data centers. At the central data centers, the servers perform all necessary calculations and processing of the data using bits and transistors. Once the processing is complete, the results are distributed back to the original device as needed. Edge computing differs from conventional computing in central processing.

Quantum Computing

In 1994, Peter Shor discovered the foundation of quantum computing applications by developing an algorithm that reduced the time to find the prime factors of large numbers. Finding the factors would generally take billions of years on a conventional computer, but now with quantum computing, the time is reduced to only a few days. At the time, this was strictly theoretical, but seven years later, IBM demonstrated this algorithm on a quantum machine, proving that quantum computers were possible.

Although quantum computers are not readily available, several companies offer quantum computing as a service. A 2022 Quantum Readiness Survey by EY revealed that 81% of UK businesses expect quantum computing to disrupt business by 2030.[2] Like every technological advancement, quantum computing will also gain the attention of market influencers. Therefore, managers should be cautious and aware of the technology, its benefits, and risks to make an informed investment decision.

The ability to process large volumes of data will entice managers to consider quantum computing for their organizations. As these computers become more widespread and economically feasible, managers must be ready to evaluate the benefits and possibly implement quantum solutions. Therefore, managers should keep abreast of the advancements, evaluate the need for faster computing based on business and market requirements, and create a strategic plan to adopt and implement quantum computing to create a competitive advantage for the organization.

Quantum Computing Concepts

Quantum computing uses properties from quantum mechanics and is based on how matter behaves at a subatomic level. At the foundation of quantum computing is the qubit. Similar to bits in conventional computing, qubits help process data. Unlike a bit, which can only be a 1 or a 0, a qubit can hold multiple states simultaneously, that is, a qubit can be a 1 and a 0 simultaneously. Thus, a qubit holds more data than is possible with a traditional computer. For example, in a conventional computer, 8 bits form a byte and represent a number between 0 and 255, but only one at a time. On the other hand, an 8-qubit quantum computer can represent every number from 0 to 255 at the same time. This function allows the computer to analyze several scenarios one at a time.

Therefore, adding more qubits will exponentially increase the amount of computing power. Then, using the properties of subatomic particles, a qubit takes on all possible combinations of the qubit at the time. This phenomenon is known as superposition. Groups of qubits in a superposition state are "multidimensional computational spaces."[3] These principles are also used in MRI scans, lasers, and atomic clocks. By trying to control the unique functions of the subatomic particles, quantum computers can perform these calculations and analyses faster and more energy-efficiently than classical computers can.

Quantum computers also use a feature called entanglement. Entanglement is the inability to explain the state of one particle independently of the quantum state of other particles when pairs of qubits are forced to exist in a single state. When linked, changes to one qubit affect the other. Therefore, when the number of qubits increases, the computing powers also increase.

One of the most significant downsides of quantum computers is the feature of decoherence. This state is when the normal quantum behavior deteriorates. Qubits require a steady state, which is only obtainable at near absolute zero (–460°) temperatures. Thus quantum computers must be in large cooling rooms with no vibrations. Needing to be kept in this state makes these computers more expensive to operate and maintain.

Limitations of Quantum Computing

Even though quantum computing holds several advantages over conventional computing, there are some limitations of quantum computing.

- **Decoherence.** Decoherence causes a qubit to decay due to a disruption or temperature change. This decay is a concern, as it disrupts processing and loses data. Any fluctuation in temperature or vibration will cause decoherence. Therefore, it can be challenging for organizations to keep the computer environment stable and at an extremely cold temperature. The computer must also be free of any vibration or other changes in the environment. These computers are frequently located in supercooled insulated vacuum chambers to maintain a steady state. Failure to maintain a controlled environment may result in loss of computations and errors.
- **Security.** Security features for quantum computers have not been fully developed. The lack of security makes these computers impractical for some business solutions.
- **Limit in qubits.** Currently, qubits are restricted to 128, limiting their use to less complex problems.[4] The real strength of quantum computing will occur when the number of qubits can grow to thousands, if not a million.
- **Cost.** The cost of purchasing and maintaining quantum computers is a limiting factor for many organizations. Although a starter quantum computer is available for only $5,000, it is limited to 2 qubits. A commercially available D-Wave computer with 50 qubits is currently available for $10 million.[5] This cost does not include maintenance and operation costs, such as the energy cost to cool and maintain the equipment. In the United States, cooling costs alone per unit will cost an additional $25,000 annually.

Due to these limitations, quantum computers will likely only be used for the most complex problems in the near future.

Quantum Computer Architecture

The five main components of a quantum computer architecture broadly fall into two layers, namely the classical and quantum computing layers.[6] The classical computing layers consist of the following:

1. **Software applications.** These are software applications written to address business problems. In the future, new applications will be developed or upgraded to connect to the quantum computing programming environment.
2. **Quantum programming environment.** The quantum programming environment provides users with tools to access the quantum layer. The tools include quantum assembly languages to write instructions for the quantum processing unit, quantum programming

languages to develop high-level programs, quantum algorithms to solve various computing problems, and quantum circuits.

The quantum layer consists of three main components.

3. **Quantum-classical interface.** This component, consisting of hardware and software, enables quantum and classical layers to interface.
4. **Quantum logic gates.** Similar to classical computing, quantum computing also uses logic gates, which are the building blocks of processing information. However, unlike logic gates on classical computers, quantum logic gates can superposition 0 and 1.
5. **Quantum hardware.** This layer includes the physical building blocks of a quantum computer, such as qubits, qubit connectors, circuits, and memory.

Quantum Computing Services

Although most organizations cannot afford a quantum computer's initial cost or maintenance costs, they can still use some of its computing power through third-party services. There are several quantum computing service providers in the market today.

Qiskit

Qiskit is an open-source software development kit for developers. Since quantum computers work differently from conventional computers, the logic and programming used in these computers are also different. Qiskit is a library of tools that translate programming languages such as Python into quantum machine language. It also provides tools to create, manipulate, and test quantum programs. Qiskit is used to access IBM quantum computers or to simulate how a quantum computer works in a local computer. Using Qiskit is an excellent opportunity to learn how quantum computing works without the expense. If you use a local computer, you may not be able to solve complex problems, but the simulations will help you understand how quantum computers work.

Amazon Braket

Amazon released a complete quantum computing service in 2020 for researchers and system developers. The system contains a complete development environment to create, test, and execute quantum algorithms. Braket provides access to various types of quantum computers, including IonQ, Oxford Quantum Circuits, and Rigetti processors. In addition, Amazon Bracket also provides several developer tools, development kits, and tutorials. Some functions are free with Amazon Web Services (AWS), while other functions are available on a pay-as-you-go basis.

IBM Quantum

IBM's online platform, IBM Quantum Experience, allows free and pay-for-access to quantum computer services. Of the 20 devices available, six are free to the public. Users can develop, test, and execute quantum solutions on several quantum computers available. Developer tools, such as Qiskit Runtime, tutorials, and learning options, are available to the users.

Quantum Computing Use Cases

In general, the advantage of quantum computing is its speed in processing complex algorithms such as those used in machine learning and more extensive Monte Carlo simulations. Several areas that can benefit from faster and more complex processing are artificial intelligence, cybersecurity, encryption, drug development, blockchain consensus algorithms, the Internet of Things, 5G networks, and financial modeling. The following subsections discuss several industries and functional areas that can benefit from quantum computing.

Healthcare

Quantum computing can be used to test new pharmaceuticals and medical procedures by making clinical trials faster and safer. Quantum computers can simulate portions of the human body to test how a particular drug will interact. For example, the human immune system can be replicated while testing a specific drug. This simulation can eliminate some initial and more dangerous testing on humans. This type of simulation is only possible with the speed of quantum computing. Similar processes can aid medical diagnosis, gene sequencing, and disease prediction.[2]

Logistics and Manufacturing

One of the key features of quantum computing is the ability to compare many scenarios at once. This feature makes quantum computing ideal for analyzing optimization problems, such as determining the logistical route to move goods. Lisbon, Portugal, uses quantum computing to determine optimal bus routes.[7] Similar applications could determine the most efficient route for shipping goods or complex commercial airline routes.

Similar to determining routes for transportation and moving goods, a similar process can help to streamline manufacturing operations by selecting the best order of operations and factory design.

Financial Services

Finance is one of the areas primed to benefit from quantum computing. Many of the financial applications are what-if scenarios with hundreds of variables. Quantum computing can help with risk management and portfolio analysis to find the optimal combination of holdings to create the best investment portfolio based on the desired risk level.

In addition, banks could use a similar simulation to balance loan portfolios to maximize interest earnings.[8] Additionally, quantum computing modeling can help determine the optimal pricing for financial instruments. Due to the nature of various states, quantum computing techniques could model entire financial markets to analyze what-if models further.

Cybersecurity

Quantum computing can both help and hinder progress in cybersecurity. Quantum computers will likely be able to break many encryption schemes that are unbreakable by conventional computers. With today's processing power, a traditional computer would take 300 trillion years to decrypt the same algorithm. However, some estimate that by 2030 a quantum computer will be able to decrypt the standard encryption algorithm in seconds. The increased speed will be harmful if today's standards are continued.[9] On the other hand, quantum computing enables the development of quantum encryption algorithms. Therefore, organizations depending on classical computing for all their cybersecurity needs will increase their risk exposure if they do not embrace encryption and cybersecurity based on qubits.

Governance and Management of Quantum Computing

Even though quantum computing is still developing, managers should not disregard quantum computing but should prepare for the future by taking the following actions.

- **Be aware.** Managers should be aware of technological developments. Do not disregard technology advancements because you don't understand what something does the first time you hear about it. Even though you may not need to understand all the technical details, educate yourself about how experts anticipate the technology will be used in the future. Given the rapid change, quantum computing may be more accessible faster than expected.
- **Include it in the strategic plan.** Managers should consider including quantum computing in the organization's strategic plan. Start by considering which areas will benefit from quantum computing and how and assess which areas will have the highest priority based on

the potential business impact. This foresight will allow the organization to be a first mover, gain market share, and create a competitive advantage.

- **Train.** Encourage your IT staff to update their skills. Building a quantum-aware workforce, including IT staff and key business professionals, will help you quickly take advantage of quantum advances. Given that many quantum computing services are already available, encourage your IT staff to experiment with the simulations and shared cloud resources to understand the technology better and identify possible use cases for your organization.

Most governance and management practices for quantum computing is like other current or emerging technology. The World Economic Forum developed and published a set of quantum computing governance principles in 2022.[10] The following underlying nine themes are based on the core values, goals, opportunities, and risks of quantum computing and inform stakeholders of corresponding actions to take to manage and govern quantum computing:

1. **Transformative capabilities.** Managers should recognize the transformative capabilities of quantum computing and adopt the technology responsibly. Therefore, managers should do their due diligence to identify and minimize potential risks such as the risk of unknown transformation impact, lack of a clear chain of responsibilities, and absence of a comprehensive framework.
2. **Access to hardware infrastructure.** Managers should consider whether they have access to hardware and whether it will lead to uneven distribution of resources, skills, and knowledge among organizations.
3. **Open innovation.** To enable faster development, encourage collaboration among developers.
4. **Creating awareness.** The framework encourages stakeholders of quantum computing to be aware of the development and engage in responsible dialogue over its use and development.
5. **Workforce development and capability-building.** Managers should understand the different levels of knowledge required to work with quantum computing. Managers should consider strategic partnerships with higher education institutes and governments to prepare and plan for the need for a quantum-ready workforce.
6. **Cybersecurity.** Managers should direct and plan to secure their digital assets from cyberattacks that may derive from advanced quantum algorithms' availability.

7. **Privacy.** Even with quantum computing, managers should proactively mitigate potential data privacy violations during processing or because of theft.

8. **Standardization.** Standardization, like other technologies, accelerates development and enables easy adoption. Therefore, managers should encourage quantum developers and programmers to follow best practices and coordinate efforts in their specific industries, states, or countries.

9. **Sustainability.** Managers should consider whether developing a quantum computer is sustainable and whether the organization can contribute to creating a sustainable future using quantum computing.

Edge Computing

The following is an excerpt from the Wall Street Journal, *October 20, 2022.*

Taco Bell is making aggressive use of edge computing to support the many digital ways customers can place orders, the fast-food chain's head of technology said.

Part of Yum Brands Inc., Taco Bell is processing customer requests and account data using a mix of central cloud services and connected devices and software at its local restaurants. Though this edge-computing setup hasn't been easy to implement, the ability to offer consumers technology options is a business advantage, said Vadim Parizher, vice president of technology, speaking at a WSJ Pro Enterprise Technology virtual event on Thursday.

At Taco Bell, a computer server at each location ingests data from in-person and digital orders and customer loyalty accounts, as well as kitchen operations, and uses custom algorithms to make decisions about, say, when to tell employees at the fryer to sink the potatoes for an order of Nacho Fries so that they are warm when a delivery driver arrives for pickup, Mr. Parizher said.

The so-called edge isn't a place but a computing model, said Lynda Stadtmueller, senior vice president of the research, information and communication technology practice at Frost & Sullivan, a market research firm.

Key aspects are sensored devices, connectivity, analytics and responsiveness, Ms. Stadtmueller said, speaking at the same event.

The goal is to improve the performance of applications by processing data where it is generated, such as within a local Taco Bell, and applying it at lightning speed. Energy companies, retailers and industrial manufacturers are using edge computing to take advantage of fast internet speeds, including 5G networks, and a growing range of connected devices. General Electric Co. and Siemens AG, for example, are using edge computing to optimize factory machines in real time.

The team had to consider how to protect personal data about customers in Taco Bell's loyalty program. "For security purposes, we don't want that information to be at the store," Mr. Parizher said, so it is stored in the cloud. "You don't keep data at the edge for any longer than you have to."

With edge-computing foundations in place, he said, Taco Bell can experiment with connected robotic equipment that can fry food, warm up tortillas or pour drinks. "Now it gets a bit more exciting," he said.[11]

Edge computing is not necessarily a location but is processing data closer to the device collecting the data. Moving data processing closer to the devices enables these devices to respond to complex queries faster. This type of computing is referred to as edge computing because it shifts some computing capabilities away from a central server to the edge of the network where the devices are. Real-time, faster processing at the devices can respond to user queries and increase personalized experiences, productivity, data sharing, and efficiency that would not be otherwise possible.

Consider your smartphone; such applications perform some data analysis, processing, or storage on the device. Your phone is an example of edge computing. However, devices such as sensors on manufacturing equipment, in automobiles, point of sales systems, robots, and medical devices in patients are smaller than smartphones. Generally, such small devices are limited in the volume of data they can process and store on the device. With the growth of the Internet of Things (IoT) requiring small devices, the need for these devices to process, store, and share data among devices is becoming more prevalent. Therefore, edge computing is a paradigm that enables and shifts the processing from cloud servers and data centers closer to the devices. This paradigm is made possible with advances in mobile communications, such as 5G networks.

The ability to combine this technology with other emerging technologies makes edge computing even more powerful. When combined, these technologies enhance each other and provide complex solutions. One reason for the need for edge computing stems from the advances in IoT devices. Therefore, it is important to understand what IoT is before discussing edge computing in detail.

Internet of Things

The number of devices that collect data has grown exponentially in the past decade. Everything from appliances to smartphones and manufacturing equipment collects data that can be used for analysis.

IoT describes any physical object that can collect and store data and communicate with other devices via the internet. Although many devices connect via the public internet, that is not the only requirement for a device to be considered IoT. IoT devices can connect to any network. We have likely been in contact with one or more of these devices without realizing that they are IoT devices. Besides the increase in personal devices, IoT has also changed how data is collected in manufacturing, healthcare, and city planning.

The growth in IoT can be attributed to the advances in other technological areas, such as the following.[12]

- **Low-cost sensors.** The ability to manufacture sensors at low costs has made it affordable to integrate technology on a wide variety of devices.
- **Connectivity.** Advances in network communication make it faster and easier to connect devices to the internet and cloud services.
- **Cloud computing.** Developments in additional cloud platforms have enabled easier access to the infrastructure to store data.
- **Machine learning and analytics.** Developments in machine learning algorithms and analytic tools have increased the demand for source data. We need IoT devices to collect various data, such as current traffic conditions and the speed of a car in real time, that are used in machine learning algorithms.
- **Natural language processing.** The developments in natural language processing to understand written and spoken language have also made IoT devices more desirable.

Edge computing enables IoT devices to be more usable by providing easy access to processing and storing data faster. Therefore, the two technologies complement each other and cannot exist separately.

Edge versus Cloud Computing

Let us compare cloud computing to edge computing to understand this new paradigm better. As shown in Figure 12.1, the primary difference between cloud and edge computing is where the data is processed or calculations occur.

In cloud computing, data is transferred from remote devices back to a central server or data center. Data processing and computation are performed at a central server or a data center. With edge computing, the majority of the processing is done on a device, such as a smartphone or a server placed closer

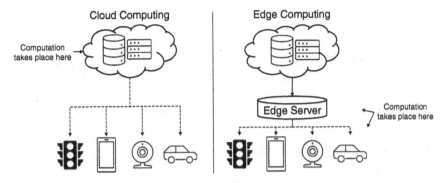

Figure 12.1   Cloud Computing Versus Edge Computing
Source: Jackson-Barnes, S. (2022). Edge Computing vs Cloud Computing: Differences, Benefits and Best Practices. *Orient Software* (9 June). https://www.orientsoftware.com/blog/edge-computing-vs-cloud-computing/.

to the device. Edge computing uses specialized hardware designed for limited spaces or harsh unprotected locations. In the Taco Bell example, local servers at different locations enabled devices at a specific location to communicate with each other efficiently and effectively.

Some benefits of edge computing over cloud computing are:[13]

- **Latency.** Latency is the time delay between placing a request and receiving an answer. With IoT devices, transmitting data across the network to a central server and receiving a response takes longer than sending and receiving data from a local server. With edge computing, some data processing is done at the source, meaning a local server, known as an edge server, is placed closer to the devices. Edge servers or devices can process and summarize some data, so not all details are transmitted to a central server, improving the latency. Reducing latency is critical for applications that require quick response times, such as self-driving automobiles.
- **Bandwidth.** Bandwidth is the capacity or how much data is transmitted over a network. Since edge computing limits data transmission to a central server over the internet, it reduces bandwidth constraints. Devices may collect large volumes of data; however, not all data can be transmitted to a server in real time. Therefore, allocating some computation away from central servers can help avoid bandwidth constraints.
- **Availability.** The increased number of devices connecting to the internet has increased the demand for more cloud services. Since users rely heavily on these devices for daily tasks, many users are impacted when cloud services are interrupted. Given the increased number of devices accessing these services at a given time, it is becoming a greater

challenge for cloud services to maintain system availability. Edge computing can offload some of the demand on cloud servers and help increase system availability for users.

- **Security.** Since data is most vulnerable to cyber hacks while it is in transit, reducing the volume of data can reduce some of the security risks. However, edge computing cannot mitigate the inherent risk if the individual devices are not adequately protected.

Edge Computing Use Cases

Healthcare

The healthcare industry collects medical data from a wide variety of sources, such as wearable devices that patients use at home, implanted medical devices, or devices in hospitals or medical offices. Rather than transferring all of the data to a central server for analysis, some critical monitoring can be done at the device level.[14] Processing data at the device level can speed up alerts during a medical emergency, such as a heart attack. After analyzing incoming data, the device can determine which data should be stored on the main server and which should be discarded. The device can also summarize data for more permanent storage. Further, edge computing can be helpful during robot-assisted surgery where real-time data is needed.

Manufacturing

With the evolution of industrial IoT, factories can incorporate various devices on production lines to collect data.[13] The devices can capture everything from temperature readings to the number of operations and the number of items produced and notify supervisors of potential problems. Since not every measurement, such as temperature reading every minute, has to be recorded on centralized servers, edge computing can help summarize the data for long-term storage. On the other hand, edge computing can alert of a possible malfunction because of faster data processing closer to the device rather than on a central server.

Edge Computing Management and Governance

Edge computing can be one of the more complex technologies for an organization to manage for various reasons, such as the following.

- Significant increases in the type and number of devices used in the organization will require various managers to inventory the devices periodically and monitor their performance. If managers are unaware of any device malfunction, they may depend on incorrect computations.

- The localized hardware used for edge computing increases the need for securing the additional hardware. Each connection point and device creates vulnerabilities for the network. One of the advantages of a centralized data center or server is that you have better control over the physical security of the hardware. However, edge computing increases the organization's technology and cyber risk exposure by placing some hardware closer to devices that collect data. Since edge devices and hardware are on the perimeter of the network, defining the boundaries of the protection zone may be challenging. With many devices, tracking and ensuring that all security measures are in place is more difficult. Further, if third parties provide edge nodes/hardware, the organization may not have any control over security protocols. Therefore, managers should carefully consider third-party service provider contracts for adequate security protocols.
- Significant increases in the volume of data being collected require a complex data management strategy. Managers must consider what data to keep, for how long, and how to summarize, anonymize, and store it.
- Since each device collecting data may have a different format of data, sharing data among devices and calculating various measures may require standardizing data across devices. Managers should be aware of these issues and do their due diligence to ensure that calculations do not have any errors.
- Given the variety of data collection devices, consider whether the specialized hardware used to process data can handle computation for all potential devices. If managers fail to have a long-term plan for investing in edge computing, they may over- or underinvest, causing operational delays.
- Data in transit is always vulnerable to cyberattacks. Therefore, managers should pay close attention to the controls around the connectivity of devices to edge hardware and evaluate security protocols.
- Managers should consider the ownership of data collected by devices when processing and storing data. If managers fail to consider what type of data and how the data is used, the organization may be at risk of violating data privacy regulations. Further, user data collected by devices may raise ethical concerns. Therefore, managers should evaluate whether the organization's data management policies are adequate and implement new procedures and policies to deal with edge computing.

Edge computing increases the number of managed devices in an organization. Therefore, managers will have to work with and depend on various vendors for devices, edge hardware, network, and other services. To manage edge computing, organizations will also need a variety of experts in programming, networking, security, and data management. If an organization is considering edge computing, managers should develop a strategy aligned with its business strategy. A long-term plan can enable managers to start small and expand without incurring unnecessary costs for switching devices, service providers, networks, or hardware.

As more devices are being developed, a common framework or standards for edge computing will enable faster adoption of these devices by organizations and the general public.

Notes

1. Tempus Public Foundation. (2022) The Future of Quantum Computing – An Interview with Prof. Sándor Imre. Study in Hungary (11 July). https://studyinhungary.hu/blog/the-future-of-quantum-computing-an-interview-with-prof-sandor-imre.

2. Salz, B., Watson, R., and Ciepiela, P. (2022). Quantum Computing: 5 Steps to Take Now. EY (21 November). https://www.ey.com/en_gl/consulting/quantum-computing-5-steps-to-take-now.

3. IBM. (n.d.). What Is Quantum Computing? https://www.ibm.com/topics/quantum-computing.

4. Giles, M. (2019). Explainer: What Is a Quantum Computer? *MIT Technology Review* (19 January). https://www.technologyreview.com/2019/01/29/66141/what-is-quantum-computing.

5. Yawar, S. (2022). How Much Does a Quantum Computer Cost? PureVPN (19 July). https://www.purevpn.com/blog/quantum-computer-cost.

6. Sodhi, B., and R. Kapur. (2021). Quantum Computing Platforms: Assessing the Impact on Quality Attributes and SDLC Activities. 2021 IEEE 18th International Conference on Software Architecture. https://ieeexplore.ieee.org/stamp/stamp.jsp?arnumber=9426783.

7. Yarkoni, S., Neukart, F., Tagle, E., et al. (2020). Quantum Shuffle: Traffic Navigation with Quantum Computing. Proceedings of the 1st ACM SIGSOFT International Workshop on Architectures and Paradigms for Engineering Quantum Software (November), pp. 22–30. https://doi.org/10.1145/3412451.3428500.

8. Biondi, M. Heid, A., Henke, N., et al. (2021). Quantum Computing Use Cases Are Getting Real – What You Need to Know. *McKinsey Digital* (14 December). https://www.mckinsey.com/capabilities/mckinsey-digital/our-insights/quantum-computing-use-cases-are-getting-real-what-you-need-to-know#/.

9. Future Business Tech. (2022). The Future of Quantum Computing: 9 Powerful Use Cases (8 January). https://www.futurebusinesstech.com/blog/future-of-quantum-computing-9-powerful-use-cases.

10. World Economic Forum. (2022). Quantum Computing Governance Principles. Insight Report (January). https://www3.weforum.org/docs/WEF_Quantum_Computing_2022.pdf.

11. Nash, K. (2022). Edge Computing Helps Feed Taco Bell's Digital Business. *Wall Street Journal* (20 October). https://www.wsj.com/articles/edge-computing-helps-feed-taco-bells-digital-business-11666302278.

12. Oracle. (n.d.). What Is IOT? https://www.oracle.com/ph/internet-of-things/what-is-iot/.

13. Shi, W., Pallis, G., and Xu, Z. (2019). Edge Computing. *Proceedings of the IEEE* 107 (8): 1474–4781.

14. Pratt, M. (2021). Top 10 Edge Computing Use Cases and Example. *TechTarget* (23 November). https://www.techtarget.com/searchcio/feature/4-edge-computing-use-cases-delivering-value-in-the-enterprise.

CHAPTER 13

Augmented Reality

Here are a few examples of how augmented reality is currently used in various industries a part from entertainment and training.

Arcadia Earth, New York City, using augmented reality, spread awareness about the impact of climate change.[1]

Nreal, a Chinese augmented reality start-up, is launching its Nreal air glasses in the U.K.[2]

Snap, the company behind Snapchat, has launched three generations of smart glasses since 2016. Snap expects everyone to be wearing augmented reality spectacles by 2032.[3]

New World Inc., an augmented reality art NFT company, recently partnered with Pure Spirits, a distillery specializing in craft products, such as white-label vodka and tequila. Together they provide an augmented reality Formula 1 race car experience that users activate through the artwork on the label.[4]

IKEA – the IKEA Place app lets you place digital furniture anywhere. The app lets you change wall color, place shelving systems and decorations, export the design in 3D or 2D, and send it to others for approval.[5]

Virtual Versus Augmented Reality

Two similar yet different technologies that have changed how we view the real world are virtual and augmented reality. Virtual reality immerses the user in an entirely virtual world, while augmented reality places virtual items in the real world. These two technologies have been popular in the entertainment industry for a while. However, organizations are recognizing how these technologies add value and create competitive advantage by changing how products are designed, improving the customer experience, and training employees.

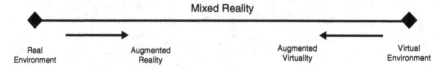

Figure 13.1   Milgram's Reality–Virtuality Continuum

Paul Milgram and Fumio Kishino introduced a popular depiction of reality and virtuality as a continuum used today.[6] As shown in Figure 13.1, the two endpoints in the continuum are:

- The real environment
- The virtual environment

Augmented reality is closer to the real environment, whereas augmented virtuality is closer to the virtual environment. According to the continuum, a virtual environment or virtual reality completely immerses an individual in a synthetic world without seeing the real world. On the other hand, AR technology augments the user's experience in the real world by superimposing virtual objects on the real world in real time.

Virtual reality (VR) uses computer technology to place a user in a three-dimensional simulated environment. Instead of looking at a computer screen, most commonly, you would use a virtual reality headset to immerse yourself in an experience. Virtual reality headsets can be used with other handheld devices to give users a fully immersive experience. For example, you could wear virtual reality headsets and use a handheld device to play tennis in your living room. The three types of VR headsets are as follows.[7]

1. **PC-based VR headsets.** These headsets offer high-quality sound, image, and head tracking for a more realistic experience. These headsets usually use cables to connect to a PC and are powered by external hardware.
2. **Standalone VR headsets.** These headsets do not require a PC or smartphone to deliver a VR experience. These headsets have a built-in processor, sensors, battery, memory, displays, and graphic processing units (GPU). As a result, they are less powerful than PC-based headsets.
3. **Mobile headsets.** These are shell devices used with a smartphone. The lenses in these devices separate the screen to create a stereoscopic image, giving an illusion of depth.

Users can combine VR headsets with various accessories such as a 3D mouse, optical trackers, wired gloves, motion controllers, body suits, treadmills, and smelling devices to enhance their experience.

Table 13.1   Comparison Between Virtual Reality and Augmented Reality

Virtual Reality	Augmented Reality
The user is immersed in a simulated environment.	The user is immersed in the real or physical environment.
Creates a new experience.	Adds to the current experience.
The digital environment may reflect a real place. However, it exists apart from the current physical reality.	The current real physical world is enhanced with digital objects in real time.
Users are controlled by the system.	Users can control their presence in the real world.
Users can interact with the digital environment. However, it does not have an impact on the real environment.	Users interact with the real environment, thus impacting the real environment.
Needs a headset.	Accessible with a smartphone.
Virtual reality headsets take over your vision to give you the impression you are somewhere else.	Augmented reality headsets add to your vision with additional objects or information over the real objects.

On the other hand, augmented reality (AR) is a mixed reality between the digital or virtual world and the real world. AR is defined as a real-time direct or indirect view of a physical, real-world environment that "has been enhanced or augmented by adding virtual computer-generated information."[8] Characteristics of an AR system are:

1. The ability to combine real objects with virtual objects in a real environment.
2. The ability to align real and virtual objects with each other.
3. The ability to maintain a three-dimensional environment.
4. The ability to interact with both the virtual and the physical world.
5. The ability to run in real time.

AR is not limited to a particular technology or a particular device. Even though current AR products primarily use sight, AR can integrate all senses, including hearing, touch, and smell.

Although there are many similarities between virtual reality and augmented reality, there are several differences between them. Table 13.1 compares various characteristics of virtual reality with augmented reality.

History

Various technical advances over the years have contributed to the development of virtual and augmented reality technology. The 1960s marked one of the first achievements in the field. Ivan Sutherland and his students created the first 3D graphics, which changed images as the user moved. In the 1970s and 1980s, many devices, such as the Walkman, digital watches, and organizers, started to become mobile, opening the door for wearable devices. In the 1990s, devices like the PalmPilot were small portable computers. These technologies provided the foundation for augmented reality. In the late 1990s Boeing scientists Caudell and Mizell first used the term augmented reality after they developed an AR prototype. The progress we see today can be attributed to AR becoming a distinct field of research during the late 1990s, leading to greater collaboration among researchers. Virtual and augmented reality technology is not a single software or hardware. It is a combination of various software and hardware devices. VR and AR continues to depend on the advances in multiple fields of study to provide users with a fully immersive experience.[9]

Augmented Reality Equipment

A variety of technologies make AR possible. AR uses a combination of hardware devices, such as displays, and software, which enables image processing, tracking, overlaying, and displaying.

Types of Displays

Unlike VR, AR integrates the real world; therefore, the displays need to be mobile. AR displays can be categorized into the following three categories based on the positioning of the display.[9]

1. **Head-worn.** These displays are attached to the user's head. Some head-worn displays have limited mobility because they must be connected to computers, such as a laptop. Some displays move computation to the cloud and connect using Bluetooth, lengthening the battery life.
2. **Handheld.** These displays can be bulkier than head-worn displays. However, handheld displays have the greatest potential to introduce AR to the mass market.
3. **Spatial.** These displays are placed within the environment and provide limited interactions. Spatial displays are helpful for large exhibitions or presentations. For example, television commentators, using a camera feed, can overlay visuals highlighting a route or player during a play of sporting events. A drawback of spatial displays is that when individuals move around, the objects may appear misaligned.

The most common AR devices integrate sight and sound into their applications. Other senses require further development before widespread use. AR displays can also be categorized based on which human sensory input is used or enhanced.[9]

1. **Visual.** There are three types of visual displays. The first type of display uses a digitized video feed of the real world and overlays other digital images on the video feed. For example, the game *Pokémon Go* uses the video from the camera and overlays images of the creatures onto the mobile screen. The second option uses a wearable headset with a see-through front, such as eyewear, where the virtual feed overlays reality. The third option uses projective displays, which do not require any eyewear. Virtual images are projected on real images in a room for a large audience.
2. **Aural (sound).** Sound is an increasingly important part of virtual and augmented reality. Currently, aural displays are used more in virtual environments and are in development for augmented environments. Another concept in development is to make the user feel sound waves.
3. **Haptic (touch).** These interfaces are bidirectional, programmable communication that uses touch. Haptic devices use kinesthetic senses, such as force and motion, and the tactile sense.
4. **Olfactory (smell) and gustatory (taste).** These displays are still in the very early stages of development.

Interactions with Users

AR systems have to determine the orientation of a user, track the user's movement, and sense the environment to combine reality with virtual objects. Interactions with users can be broadly categorized into positional tracking and interactions with users.

Positional Tracking

An AR system must track the user's movement with six degrees of freedom: three variables for positioning and three angles for orientation. There are several ways to track user movement. Each method has its benefits and limitations.[9]

1. **Mechanical, ultrasound, and magnetic.** These techniques measure distance using static devices that send and receive sound waves or electromagnetic fields around the user. This method is limited to indoor use.

2. **Global positioning systems.** GPS uses the satellite positioning techniques used by other navigation devices.
3. **Radio.** This method places active radio frequency identification chips inside structures to track and position.
4. **Inertial.** This method uses a computer, motion sensors, and rotation sensors to continuously calculate an object's position, orientation, and velocity.
5. **Optical.** This method uses one or two tiny cameras to recognize landmarks or determine movement.
6. **Hybrid.** The hybrid tracking methods use a combination of the methods and provide the most promising way to deal with limitations posed by indoor or outdoor mobile AR environments.

User Interfaces

Another important component of AR is the user interface (UI). Users need a way to interact with both virtual and real-world objects. AR systems should enable users to select, annotate, or manipulate physical objects. Also, AR interfaces need to support selecting, positioning, and rotating virtual objects, drawing trajectories, assigning quantitative values, and enabling text input. Several user interfaces used in AR are discussed briefly below.[9]

- **Tangible UI and 3D pointing.** The most basic tangible unidirectional device is the mouse. The mouse communicates from the user to the AR system. Paddles and wands are 3D equivalents of a mouse.
- **Haptic UI and gesture recognition.** Devices that provide communication through touch is called haptic UIs. There are two types of haptic devices, namely kinesthetic and tactile. Joysticks and steering wheels that suggest force, motion, or resistance are kinesthetic sense-based devices. Tactile devices communicate temperature, roughness, or rigidity. The most common form of a tactile device is data gloves. A drawback of data gloves is that they inhibit the use of hands in doing real-world activities.
- **Visual UI and gesture recognition.** These devices track hand movement using a camera directed at the user's hands.
- **Gaze tracking.** This method uses tiny cameras to track the user's pupils.
- **Aural UI and speech recognition.** These UIs use microphones and earphones to record and recognize speech and interact human-to-human.
- **Text input.** The basic form of text input is by using a keyboard. However, using even a small, foldable keyboard in an AR system can be cumbersome. Another option is to use soft keyboards such as

laser-projected virtual keyboards. However, these can also take up valuable screen space. AR systems using smartphones and mobile devices can use built-in keypads or pen-based handwriting recognition. Speech recognition software can also be used for text input.

■ **Hybrid UI.** Using a combination of UI devices may provide the user with a more natural experience. Since each modality has its drawbacks and benefits, AR systems will most likely benefit from a multimodal UI.

AR Use Cases

Augmented reality is used in various industries to not only enhance customer experience but also to enhance employee experience and effectiveness. Here we discuss how several industries plan to adopt or currently use AR.

Medical applications. Surgeons can benefit from overlaying images obtained from ultrasounds, CT scans, and MRI scans over other images to get a better visual of the organs. Further, AR can simulate the view obtained from laparoscopic images. These tools can help teach medical students, help surgeons prepare for surgeries, calibrate tools used during surgery, and assist the surgeon.

Entertainment. AR can allow live users to have the added experience of augmented reality during sporting events. For example, seeing the hockey puck in a live game is sometimes very difficult. AR can enhance the real world, highlighting where the puck is during the game and enabling hockey fans to experience the game fully. Further, AR can provide an enhanced gaming experience.

Manufacturing. AR can help workers design, assemble, and maintain products and systems. Designers can use AR to combine specifications while developing the product. Assembly workers can use AR for training and assembly. Detailed schematic diagrams and other documentation can be overlaid on components to help assemble them or diagnose problems.

Education. AR is being explored in math, art, and engineering education. AR enables students to immerse themselves in learning, apply concepts to real-world problems, and test the proposed solutions in a simulated environment.

Business management. AR can enhance customer experience and help back-office functions such as planning, management, marketing, and advertising. For example, AR can improve collaboration by allowing multiple people to view, discuss, and interact with 3D data models.

Personal applications. AR can be used to gather information about people at networking events and help you remember details from your past meetings. AR systems can help you get additional historical information as you tour historical sites, for example. AR systems can help you navigate by overlaying data or virtual objects on your camera screen. For instance, as you walk around the city, your smartphone can display virtual data, such as restaurant reviews and discounts, to help you choose where to eat.

Challenges and Limitations of AR

Devices, such as the Oculus, are currently available to the mass market. However, most of these devices offer virtual reality gaming experiences. On the other hand, the availability of AR devices is still limited for the mass market. The following three main general requirements should be developed in order for AR to be available for the mass market.

1. **Framework.** A significant challenge the AR industry should overcome is the lack of development standards. Creating standards will accelerate the development of AR software applications and devices because they will help increase compatibility with devices and other software applications. For example, if technologies to track, sense, display, and interact are developed independently of the device, these technologies could be easily integrated with various wearable devices and applications. Having a standard will enable quick development and easy adoption by various user interfaces facilitating the adoption of AR.

2. **Wireless network, data storage, and access technology.** When using an AR system, users need to be able to retrieve data, interact with other users over large distances, and input information to the system to manipulate virtual objects. These activities need large amounts of data to be accessed and processed. AR systems can streamline the user interface by moving computation load to remote servers. However, this introduces a challenge: users need to be able to access the data. Therefore, good wireless networks, data storage, and secure access technologies are important components of successful adoption of AR by the mass market.

3. **Content.** AR is currently used in specific industries such as the military and manufacturing, to do specific tasks. However, the adoption of AR by the mass market will depend on the availability of content that is not specific to a task or context.

AR has several technical, social, ethical, and legal challenges. A brief discussion of these challenges follows.

Technical Challenges

As with many new technologies, technical challenges may affect the outcome of any adoption. Managers should consider these when implementing augmented reality in the organization.

- **Software application design.** AR uses several technologies. Therefore, managers must decide how the AR system will be used when designing AR software applications. These decisions will influence the technical specifications of software development. For example, will the AR device need to be mobile? Will it be used indoors or outdoors? If outdoors, how will the device track movement in new environments and calibrate the device? If you develop software applications for a mobile device, consider where you plan to process the data and how much memory and processing power is required. Other technical challenges revolve around how to accurately register depth, how to make the user interface intuitive, and how to separate the software applications from the hardware devices. Since the user experience depends on various software applications working together, creating a standard and integrating software can be challenging.
- **Hardware.** Hardware design remains a challenge in AR. The hardware devices for mobile AR have to address how to increase the device's battery life, reduce the device's weight, and handle various weather conditions and shock from movement. Also, if AR is to be widely accepted, the device's aesthetic features must be appealing to a variety of users. Another challenge is making the devices ergonomic. Users should not feel uncomfortable wearing the device; the device should not negatively impact the body from prolonged use or hinder the user's natural movement. Further, the device market needs to address issues related to connecting the device to a local server and handling the processing and storage of data.

Since there is a need for collaboration between various fields, AR development can be very costly. The high development price of AR applications, software, and hardware is a major AR development challenge.

Social Challenges

Managers need to be aware of potential social or personal issues when developing AR applications, such as the following.

- **Acceptance of technology.** Getting public acceptance of AR for a business can be challenging. The public may not yet know the benefits of AR and may be skeptical about using it. Lack of awareness may lead to concerns about security, privacy, digital fatigue, information overload, or personal safety.

- **Physical safety.** Users engrossed in the AR experience may suffer from immersion distraction, which is being so engrossed in the AR experience that they are fully unaware of the surroundings. Users may lack spatial awareness and walk into objects while trying to avoid virtual objects. Some users can experience physical damage, such as hearing loss, damage to eyesight, and behavioral changes. For example, users of the popular AR-based game *Pokémon Go* have reported several incidents where users have suffered physical injury by walking off a cliff or into traffic while using the game.[10] Therefore, AR systems should prevent users from over-relying on AR systems, so they don't miss important cues from the real environment.

- **Updated content.** Currently, the content available for AR is limited to specific tasks, training, or situations. Therefore, users may not see the benefit of adopting AR. Further, updating AR content to keep abreast of changes in the real world can be challenging. If content is not updated, the AR system may lead the user to see and hear things different from the real environment and misalign virtual objects.

- **The right context for AR.** AR may not be suitable for every situation for the organization. The user experience will depend on selecting the suitable device, application, and software for the right purpose. AR should significantly contribute to the user by either assisting in performing a specific task or providing additional information in a timely, convenient manner. Therefore, if AR is adopted without considering the suitability of AR given the context, user experience may be impeded. For example, flight simulation applications on a smartphone do not provide the user with an immersive experience of learning to fly. Creating content promoting businesses is still challenging and can be expensive and complicated.

Ethical Challenges

Given the immersive nature of AR, users may forget their physical environment and behave inappropriately, such as trespassing. AR users may hijack public spaces and upset the general public. Allowing AR users to access information about people around them is an invasion of privacy. Gathering data and annotating details on people in real time is an ethical concern with AR systems. The immersive nature may lead users to believe that virtual situations are real. Therefore, if a user is insulted or harassed in AR and VR, it may influence the user's well-being in real life.

Legal Issues

The lack of regulation in AR can create security and privacy issues because there is no clear guidance on what is allowed. Inconsistencies in AR programming and lack of oversight can increase the risk of harm for the user, increasing the risk of litigation for the firm. Ensuring the security and privacy of the users remains a challenge. If the AR system is hacked, hackers can overlay objects and cause bodily harm to the user, and use data stored to damage the reputation of the user and the firm. The law has yet to address the following issues related to AR: How will the courts deal with street crimes, such as indecent exposure or virtual groping, in the augmented/virtual worlds? If an individual inflicts harm on another, such as sharing personal information or private pictures, will organizations be held liable?

Management and Governance of AR

Like any other technology, AR needs the involvement of the board of directors and executive management. The board of directors and management should perform due diligence to ensure that the correct use case is identified for AR. When selecting the use case, the board and management should consider whether the AR use case and its adoption is aligned with the firm's strategy, adds value to its users, and enhances customer satisfaction. Apart from ensuring that the correct use case is identified, the management and the board of directors should consider the risks associated with AR. AR will introduce and increase the firm's risk exposure; therefore, you should pay close attention to additional risks arising from AR solutions. AR-related risks can stem from the following.

- **Lack of ownership.** Lack of ownership can increase AR-related risks to the company. Management should establish clear roles and responsibilities specifying the following.
  - Who is the AR sponsor or owner?
  - Who is responsible for all AR-related decisions?
  - How are AR related risks managed?
  - How are AR risks incorporated into the enterprise risk portfolio?

- **Theft of assets.** AR mobile devices can be very expensive and easily stolen. Therefore, management should ensure that they have policies and procedures to track devices and ensure their security of the device.
- **Lack of training.** Management should ensure that users are trained to use mobile AR devices. Lack of training can lead to physical harm and increase a firm's liability. Therefore, additional training materials may need to be developed to ensure the users' safety.
- **Increased litigation.** Management should have a risk response to the increased litigation risks that may occur from enduring physical harm to the user. Therefore, they should consider possible insurance plans and the adequacy of these plans' terms.
- **Lack of performance measures.** Management should also consider documenting the business case for AR and the tangible business goals for the AR solution. In addition, establish performance evaluations related to AR. For example, how would success be determined if the adoption of AR were to increase customer satisfaction in a retail store? Management will need to collect and analyze data about the use of AR and customer satisfaction. When creating performance measures, management should carefully consider whether the performance measure directly identifies the use of AR. The inability to evaluate the effectiveness of AR can increase the firm's risk.
- **AR vendor risks.** AR risks can arise from various AR vendors. Management should consider integrating AR vendor management practices into existing processes or creating new standalone AR vendor management practices to mitigate risks related to AR vendors. Carefully evaluating terms of use contracts and monitoring vendor performance can reduce some risks related to AR vendors.
- **Data risk.** Data risks related to AR arise from constant monitoring of the real environment. Management should consider how to classify data collected by AR devices, such as sensitive public data. Other considerations include how to store the data, whether sensitive data is stored in compliance with laws, how long to retain the data, and what events are monitored and stored. Improper use and data storage can increase the company's litigation risks and harm the company's brand or reputation.
- **Cyberattacks.** Vulnerabilities in devices and malicious actors can create cybersecurity issues that impact AR use and users, and the entire firm. Therefore, management should develop policies, procedures, and processes to monitor, manage, respond to, and remediate any cybersecurity threats that can be targeted toward AR devices and users.

- **Risk of discrimination.** Management should also consider whether there are equity and inclusion issues related to AR adoption in the firm. Is the firm penalizing a specific group of users, such as people with disabilities and underserved communities, because of the immersive experience? Neglecting certain user groups may negatively impact the company's reputation and financial performance. Therefore, management should review and evaluate accessibility, anti-discrimination, and privacy laws for immersive technologies.[11]

AR governance and management should consider policies and practices to mitigate these risks. Management should safeguard the software application, devices, and content design, from intentional and unintentional harm.

Notes

1. Reuters. (2022). Augmented Reality Exhibit in New York Looks at Impact of Climate Change (29 April). https://www.reuters.com/world/us/augmented-reality-exhibit-new-york-looks-impact-climate-change-2022-04-29/.
2. Browne, R. (2022). Chinese Start-up Nreal Is Launching Its Augmented Reality Glasses in the UK This Spring. CNBC (25 April). https://www.cnbc.com/2022/04/25/chinese-ar-start-up-nreal-to-launch-smart-glasses-in-the-uk.html.
3. Best, S. (2022). The Smart Glasses of the Future? *Daily Mail* (18 April). https://www.dailymail.co.uk/sciencetech/article-10727901/MailOnline-tests-Snaps-augmented-reality-Spectacles-expects-wearing-2032.html.
4. Newsfile Corp. (2022). New World Partners with Pure Spirits to Create Augmented Reality Experience at Formula 1 Miami. News release (3 May). https://finance.yahoo.com/news/world-partners-pure-spirits-create-060000009.html.
5. White, J. (2021). IKEA's Revamped AR App Lets You Design Entire Rooms. *Wired UK* (20 April). https://www.wired.com/story/ikea-revamped-ar-app-design-entire-rooms/.
6. Milgram, P., and Kishino, F. (1994). A Taxonomy of Mixed Reality Visual Displays. *IEICE Transactions on Information and Systems* E77-D (12):1321–1329.
7. Aniwaa team. (2021). Types of VR Headsets: PC VR, Standalone VR, Smartphone VR. Aniwaa (updated 6 August). https://www.aniwaa.com/guide/vr-ar/types-of-vr-headsets/.
8. Carmigniani, J., Furht, B., Anisetti, M., et al. (2011). Augmented Reality Technologies, Systems and Applications. *Multimedia Tools and Applications* 51 (1): 341–377.
9. Van Krevelen, D., and Poelman, R. (2010). A Survey of Augmented Reality Technologies, Applications and Limitations. *The International Journal of Virtual Reality* 9 (2): 1–20.
10. Gupta, K. (2021). Nintendo's Best-Selling Game, Pokémon Go, Has Caused Numerous Fatalities and Accidents. ESGN Asia (19 July). https://esgn.asia/nintendos-best-selling-game-pokemon-go-has-caused-numerous-fatalities-and-accidents/.
11. Dick, E. (2021). Principles and Policies to Unlock the Potential of AR/VR for Equity and Inclusion. Information Technology & Innovation Foundation (1 June). https://itif.org/publications/2021/06/01/principles-and-policies-unlock-potential-arvr-equity-and-inclusion/.

CHAPTER 14

Introduction
to Cybersecurity

Major Cybersecurity Incidents in the News

February 2022. The UK government revealed the existence of a "serious cyber security incident" affecting the Foreign, Commonwealth, and Development Office (FCDO).[1]

February 2022. Avita Health System in the UK detected unauthorized activity and prevented a security incident. The company was able to secure the network and restore operations before a breach of private information could occur.[2]

November 2021. The hacking group Belarusian Cyber-Partisans attacked the state-run railway's computer system. The group managed to encrypt or destroy internal databases, causing delays to trains and affecting the movement of Russian troops.[3]

October 2021. Ecuador's largest private bank, Banco Pichincha, confirmed that it suffered a cyberattack. The bank had to shut down portions of its network, which disrupted operations and took its ATM and online banking portal offline.[4]

August 2021. Poly Network is a platform that connects different blockchains. On August 10, 2021, Poly Network suffered an anonymous attack in which over $610 million in cryptocurrencies was stolen. However, the attacker started to return half the funds several days later.[5]

May 2021. Colonial Pipeline, America's largest refined products pipeline, suffered a ransomware attack that took their systems offline, which led to fuel shortages across the East Coast. The hackers were able to breach the company's network using a compromised password.[6]

March 2021. Microsoft experienced several zero-day attacks on their internal Exchange email servers, providing access to email accounts. Based on the characteristics of the attack, the Microsoft

(*Continued*)

(*Continued*)

> Threat Intelligence Center attributed the attack to a state-sponsored organization.[7]
>
> **March 2021.** SITA Passenger Service System (US) Inc., which serves multiple airlines, including Star Alliance members, reported a systems breach affecting hundreds of thousands of passengers' frequent flyer data.[8]
>
> **March 2021.** Volkswagen USA learned of a data breach affecting over 3.3 million customers from the United States and Canada. The breach took place between August 2019 and May 2021. The breach was enabled by a third-party vendor leaving one of its systems unsecured online.[9]

What Is Cybersecurity?

News reports of data breaches have made cybersecurity a part of everyday language. Cybersecurity breach incidents are pertinent not only to government agencies, publicly traded companies, celebrities, or public figures but also to small companies and individuals. Cybersecurity is not a specific emerging technology. However, managers need to be aware of cybersecurity when adopting new technology or using technology in general.

What is cybersecurity? It is the protection of computer systems and networks from unauthorized information disclosure, theft of or damage to hardware, software, or electronic data, intentional disruption to business operations, and misdirection of services provided by the company. Before the widespread use of the internet, company information systems had limited connectivity outside the organization. Therefore, companies focused on securing their information systems from unauthorized access, use, and changes to data from within the company.

With the increased use of the internet and the World Wide Web, e-commerce has become a significant part of business operations today, leading to highly interconnected information systems. With this increased connectivity, companies have to protect the organization's information systems from inside stakeholders and various outsiders. Consequently, cybersecurity measures should protect critical systems and sensitive information from unauthorized access and use. Therefore, organizations should design cybersecurity measures to combat threats against networked systems and applications regardless of where the threats originate.

What do cybercriminals want? One reason cybercriminals attack a company is to obtain sensitive information. Cybercriminals target customers' personally identifiable information (PII), such as names, addresses, national identification numbers such as Social Security numbers, and credit card information. Cybercriminals sell these records in underground digital marketplaces or demand a ransom to release the data. Most often, management feels that their company does not maintain PII of any significance. Most managers fail to understand that cybercriminals do not collect data from only one company. Cybercriminals collect pieces from various sources and assemble them like a puzzle before selling the data in an underground digital marketplace. Even if a company's data is not entirely compromised, cybercriminals collect small pieces of data and combine them with other data stolen from different companies to create profiles that are representative of reality.

Other than PII, cybercriminals may also target company proprietary data such as product designs and strategic plans, such as a move to a new market or potential mergers with another company. Cybercriminals may use such data to influence the market and disrupt company plans. Further, cyberattacks can be carried out solely to disrupt operations or intentionally inflict harm on individuals such as employees, customers, or suppliers.

According to a recent PwC survey, CEOs are concerned that disruption due to a cyberattack will affect their company's financial goals.[10] Cyberattacks have become so common today that the most pressing question for management is not whether the company will be attacked but rather when it will be attacked.

According to IBM, the average data breach cost in 2022 was USD 4.35 million globally and USD 9.44 million in the United States.[11]Calculating the exact cost of a data breach can be very challenging. When a thief walks into a building and steals a piece of art from a wall, we can assess the value of the stolen asset based on how much we paid for it. However, calculating the cost of a data breach is difficult. A company might not know whether criminals stole data after a cyberattack. Most often, cybercriminals copy the data. Even though we may still have the data in the database, hackers can sell the duplicated data, compromising the safety and well-being of the company and the associated individuals. To calculate the total loss, a company must consider all the costs incurred to detect, respond, and recover from the attack. Although reputational damage is more difficult to quantify, the cost cannot be ignored when evaluating the total loss.

Cybersecurity Challenges

Cybersecurity is challenging because many components must work together to secure information systems and data. Anything we do in a company can either increase or decrease the vulnerability of the information systems. The following are several factors contributing to increasing information system vulnerability.

- **Increasing connectivity.** Today, information systems are highly connected to each other. With Internet-of-Things (IoT) technologies, more devices are connected to information systems to track and collect data at various points. Information systems connect to multiple devices within the organization, and third-party applications, allowing access to internal and external stakeholders. The increased connectivity creates the need to increase access points and secure them. With increased access to the network and applications, organizations find it challenging to track and secure all access points.

- **Mobile devices.** Today, every employee has a mobile device. Most employees bring their mobile devices and connect to the company's Wi-Fi network. The vulnerabilities in mobile devices that are not managed by the company can create access points for cybercriminals. In addition, company-owned devices can connect to unsecured networks. The flexibility of mobile devices reduces how much control an organization can have over these company assets. Connecting these devices to outside networks increases the risk of downloading malware that can harm the organization's network. For example, malware downloaded to a mobile device while connected to an external network can infect the company information systems when the employee connects the device to the company's Wi-Fi network. Mobile devices can also be easily misplaced, increasing vulnerability for the organization.

- **Technology advances.** Every day, organizations build new devices, applications, and procedures to address various business problems. With these advances, technology introduces vulnerabilities because of a lack of adequate testing or knowledge, inexperience, or sometimes oblivion. Advances in technology can be challenging for firms to keep up with. When an organization implements a new technology, new tools, or features, it can create more opportunities for hackers to exploit the system.

- **Fragmented complex regulations.** Organizations must navigate a growing number and increasingly complex system of regulations and rules. There are many regulations, such as the General Data Protection Regulation, the California Consumer Privacy Act, and the Cybersecurity Law of the People's Republic of China. These compliance requirements can be a burden and drain the resources from actual preventive and detective cybersecurity measures, leaving the company more vulnerable to an attack. When organizations are pressed for resources, compliance requirements can take precedence. Sometimes conflicting priorities can weaken the defense mechanisms of the company.

- **Third-party providers.** With the advent of cloud computing, third parties maintain many IT services, applications, and platforms for the company. Therefore, storing data on the cloud increases the dependence on third parties. If the service providers lack cybersecurity measures, the company will face negative consequences through data loss and breaches. If the systems maintained by third-party providers are not secure, these vulnerabilities create opportunities for cybercriminals to access company data through third-party providers.
- **Cybersecurity expertise.** Security expertise is becoming difficult to source and retain; therefore, organizations should consider cultivating this talent organically. Organizations must also recognize that employee tenure is short in the current technology workforce. Therefore, it is essential to plan for employee turnover of experienced professionals and recognize the long-term benefits of cultivating expertise transmitted from veterans to newcomers.
- **Social engineering.** Using various tools, criminals can create elaborate stories to trick people into giving out information on their own. These techniques continue to develop, and it can be difficult to gauge whether a story or explanation is accurate, increasing the vulnerability of individuals.
- **Difficulty tracking cyber criminals.** Cybercrime as a business model is growing. Cybercriminals can hide their tracks using the dark web, multiple networks, and hijacking other people's computers. Because of a lack of adequate evidence, the likelihood of prosecution of cybercrime is low. Lack of accountability and legal consequences encourage more cybercrime, causing an influx of attacks that organizations cannot keep up with.

Cybersecurity Domains

A strong cybersecurity strategy should not be focused on one area but rather should address every aspect of computing in a company. Therefore, when management considers security measures, they should ensure that all of the following areas have been considered.

Computer Networks

A computer network is made up of connected computers sharing resources, such as data storage, printers, and communication devices. There are many different types of computer networks. Some popular network types used by companies are as follows.

- **PAN** (personal area network). A PAN is the smallest and the most basic type of network, typically for one person in a single location. A PAN is designed to handle a few devices, including a wireless modem, one or two computers, printers, and phones.
- **LAN** (local area network). LANs connect devices in close proximity to each other, typically a building or a couple of nearby locations. This type of network is the most common and simplest type of network used in companies, allowing for the sharing of resources by those in the organization.
- **WLAN** (wireless local area network). WLANs function the same as a LAN but rely on wireless network technology, such as Wi-Fi, eliminating physical cables.
- **CAN** (computer area network). These networks can be spread across several buildings that are fairly close to each other so users can share resources.

Software

Software is a set of computer instructions written to carry out a task or an operation. Software is broadly categorized into application software and system software.

- **Application software** is a program that performs a specific function. These software packages are designed to help end-users carry out tasks with minimal computing knowledge. A company may use different applications for various functions, such as customer relationship management (CRM) software, accounting applications, spreadsheet applications, or document creation applications. Enterprise resource planning (ERP) applications such as Oracle and SAP are software programs with many modules that span the whole organization. Application software can be a standalone application installed on a desktop or a cloud application accessed via a web browser.
- **System software** is a program that manages hardware resources. System software enables application software to run on a given hardware. Operating systems like Windows, macOS, Linux, and UNIX are examples of system software.

Data

To create information, an organization should collect, record, store, and analyze various pieces of data. Information is defined here as organized and formatted data that is useful for management decision-making. The procedures used to collect, record, store, and analyze data are called data management practices. Understanding what data is critical to the company, such as data that provides a competitive advantage, is an important first step to ensuring the integrity of the data. Good data management procedures will protect the company's sensitive information from cyberattacks and mitigate damage to its reputation, assure its stakeholders' privacy, and lessen the likelihood of litigation. For more information about data and data management, see Chapter 3.

End-Users

An end-user is anyone with access to the company's information systems. An end-user can be an internal end-user, such as an employee, or an external end-user, such as a vendor or a payroll service provider.

Storage

Data is stored in various formats. Some data is stored physically, such as in a filing cabinet, and most is stored in digital forms, such as a database. The company can own and maintain databases, or it could use a third-party service such as a cloud service provider. The cloud is a term used to describe the on-demand availability of computer system resources accessible over the internet. Managers should have a good understanding of what cloud services the organization uses. For more information, see Chapters 3 and 12.

Hardware

An organization will use various computer hardware devices such as servers, desktops, various mobile devices, printers, and copy machines. Management should consider all devices connected to the network to establish a sound cybersecurity strategy.

Security Concepts

One common misconception among people is that cybersecurity is all about technology and technical capability. Most managers shy away from discussing cybersecurity, fearing they will not understand all the technical details. Table 14.1 presents several myths and realities of cybersecurity.

Table 14.1   Cybersecurity Myths Versus Reality

Myth		Reality
1	The IT department is responsible for cybersecurity.	The responsibility lies with every employee.
2	You will immediately know when your computer system is compromised.	It can take months and sometimes years to realize that your system has been compromised.
3	We can achieve complete cybersecurity.	Cybersecurity strategy should be continuously updated, and new strategies adopted as new threats emerge.
4	Compliance is the same as a robust cybersecurity strategy.	Compliance with regulations is a checking-the-box activity and does not translate to a robust security strategy.
5	We haven't experienced a breach, so our security should be strong.	New and sophisticated cyberattacks evolve daily.
6	Criminals don't target small businesses.	The lack of sophisticated security solutions in small businesses makes these businesses a softer target for cybercriminals.
7	We are unlikely to experience a cyberattack because we don't have any interesting data, such as consumer information.	Any business is highly likely to witness a cyberattack at some stage.
8	Cyberthreats are only external.	Insider threats are equally perilous and need the same level of attention as external threats.
9	Bring your own device (BYOD) is safe and secure.	Any personal devices connected to the company's network can put the company at risk.
10	Anti-virus/ anti-malware software is enough for a good cybersecurity strategy.	Software solutions are only a part of a good cybersecurity strategy. Software alone cannot detect and prevent all types of cyber attacks.

Management Oversight of Security

A big part of cybersecurity involves people, most importantly senior management. Cybersecurity is not a technology issue but a management one. Even though a company needs IT experts to assess cyber threats and implement software solutions for cybersecurity, senior management involvement is necessary for the following areas.

- **Select a risk response.** Senior managers are responsible for choosing a risk response appropriate for the company. Whether the response is to reduce, accept, share, or avoid risk will depend on the resources invested, management's risk tolerance level, and management's risk appetite.

- **Develop and communicate cybersecurity policy.** Senior management should decide which sanctions they are willing to impose on noncompliant employees. Additionally, the active support and involvement of senior management can communicate and encourage employees to follow protocols, policies, and procedures implemented in the company.
- **Approve investment to acquire cybersecurity solutions.** Senior management is responsible for investment decisions and resource allocation. Even with enough expertise, the company would be vulnerable to cyberattacks if senior management does not understand the importance of cybersecurity and allocate enough resources to safeguard the company's digital assets.
- **Monitor and evaluate the performance.** Like every other area of performance, management should take responsibility for assessing the performance of the cybersecurity strategy and hold all employees accountable.

Another security concept relevant to cybersecurity is defense in depth. Defense in depth employs multiple layers of controls to avoid a single point of failure. Imagine having a door with one lock. A thief trying to get in will only have one lock to pick. What if you have a chain lock and a deadbolt lock in addition to the doorknob lock? Multiple locks make breaking entry a lot more difficult for the thief. What if you also have a security alarm that detects when the lock is tampered with? This not only prevents a break-in but also alerts the owner and the authorities of the attempt. Defense in depth uses overlapping, complementary, and redundant controls to increase effectiveness. If one control fails or is circumvented, another control will stop or slow down the attack.

Time-Based Model

When implementing defense in depth, management should consider a combination of preventive, detective, and corrective controls.

- **Preventive controls.** Deter or prohibit the threat from occurring.
- **Detective controls.** Identify the threat while it is taking place or after the fact.
- **Corrective controls.** Remediate the outcome of a threat event.

Imagine that you are fast asleep and a thief breaks into your home. You have implemented a preventive control if you have locked your doors and windows. This may slow down the intruder; however, it may not completely prevent the intruder from using a lock pick to gain entry. Not only do you want to lock the doors and windows, but you also want to have a security system that will alert you to an attempted break-in. The sound of the security system is a detective control indicating an intrusion. The security system calling the local authorities and the police arresting the intruder is a corrective activity.

If the thief is getting away with some valuables when you realize there has been a break-in, it is too late. The thief bypassed all preventive security measures before the alarm notified law enforcement and they arrived. The time-based model considers whether the combination of controls we implement is adequate. The goal of the time-based model is to employ a combination of preventive, detective, and corrective controls to protect the information system long enough to recognize that an attack is occurring and take the necessary steps to stop it. In this example, if the time-based model is applied, the time it takes for the intruder to break into the home and find the valuables (or you) should be greater than the time it takes to alert you and the authorities, and for the police to arrive at your home and arrest the intruder.

Therefore, the objective of the time-based model can be expressed as follows.[12]

$$P > D + C$$

where

P = the time it takes an attacker to break through the organization's preventive controls

D = the time it takes an attacker to break through the organization's detective controls

C = the time it takes an attacker to break through the organization's corrective controls

If $P > D + C$, the organization's security strategy is effective.

How Hackers Attack

Cybercriminals methodically plan their attacks. Generally, we see a combination of social engineering techniques, hacking, and malware being used to carry out an attack. Cybercriminals use the following three steps to carry out an attack: plan, execute, and cover their tracks.

Plan

The first step is to conduct reconnaissance. Here, the attacker will gather information about the target and vulnerabilities in the target's firm, network, applications, and internal controls. Reconnaissance activities can be categorized as physical or logical, depending on whether there is human involvement. Logical reconnaissance attacks will use techniques such as ping sweeps and port scans to scan for network, applications, and systems vulnerabilities.

- **Ping sweep.** Every device has a unique identifier called an IP address. The objective is to identify which hosts are active in a network. An attacker pings or calls each device and waits for a response. If the device responds, the attacker knows it is an active host.
- **Port scans.** A port scan can be carried out after a ping sweep. Once the attacker identifies active devices using a ping sweep, they attempt to identify which ports (locations in the network where communication packets are sent) are open to sending and receiving data. Like a ping sweep, the attacker sends a communication to a port and waits for a response. If the attacker receives a response, they identify the port as valid.

Physical attacks start with human involvement. Most often, attackers will use social engineering techniques to gather information. Social engineering is tricking or deceiving an individual to voluntarily provide personal or company information. A popular social engineering technique is phishing, where an elaborate pretext is created to pretend to be a legitimate company or person. For example, during the COVID-19 pandemic, when people were working from home, an attacker could send an e-mail requesting information about access to specific data or assistance to log in to a system.

Another method for reconnaissance is dumpster diving, which is looking through someone else's trash. An attacker can obtain e-mail addresses from discarded printed e-mails, common expenses using a discarded expense report, or current employee names from memos. The data collected from dumpster diving can create the pretext to deceive company employees.

Eavesdropping is another way to collect information about the target. Eavesdropping can be physical or digital. Physical eavesdropping can be as simple as listening to two employees talk about a work problem at the coffee cart in front of the building. Digital eavesdropping uses a man-in-the-middle technique to listen to phone calls, e-mails, text messages, and other forms of communication. The attacker will place themselves in the middle of the conversation and silently observe the communication using various electronic devices.

Execute

After careful reconnaissance, a hacker carries out the attack. The hacker would use a combination of hacking techniques, social engineering techniques, and malware to conduct the attack. Table 14.2 briefly describes several common methods used to carry out cyberattacks.

Table 14.2 Common Cyberattack Strategies

Hacking Techniques

Botnet	A botnet is a powerful network of hijacked computers controlled by a hacker. The hijacked computers are called zombie computers. The bot header, controlled by the hacker, installs software that responds to the hacker's instructions without the suspicion of the owners of the zombie computers.
Brute force attack	A brute force attack is conducted by using a trial-and-error method to guess login information. The attacker systematically checks all possible passwords, phrases, and usernames until the correct login is found.
A denial-of-service (DoS) attack	A DoS attack aims to shut down a network or a machine, making it inaccessible to its intended users. There are two general approaches to a DoS attack. (1) Flooding occurs when a network or machine receives too much traffic causing it to slow down and eventually shut down. (2) When a hacker sends input to a network or device that takes advantage of bugs or vulnerabilities in the target, causing the system to crash or destabilize, it is called a cashing service. The most common flooding DoS attack is a buffer overflow attack. The hacker sends more traffic to the network or machine than it is designed to handle, causing a system to slow down and eventually shut down. Recently, there have been distributed denial-of-fervice (DDoS) attacks, where a single system is attacked from multiple locations at once.
Spoofing	Spoofing is when the hacker masquerades as a trusted device to gain access to the system. Spoofing attacks come in various forms, such as e-mail, website, caller ID, text messaging, GPS, IP (internet protocol) address, webpage, DNS (domain name system), or ARP (address resolution protocol). For example, when the hacker uses IP address spoofing, they are concealing the identity of the packet-sending device by impersonating a computer in another computer system.

Social Engineering

Tailgating/piggybacking	The hacker gains unauthorized access/entry by closely following an authorized user. Sometimes the authorized user will be unaware of the other person, yet other times the authorized user may hold the door open out of common courtesy.
Phishing	Phishing is where a hacker sends an elaborate but fraudulent message designed to trick the person receiving the message into voluntarily providing confidential information. There are four types of phishing: 1. Spear phishing – targeting a specific group or type of individual. 2. Whaling – a more targeted attack than spear phishing. These attacks target top-level executives. 3. Smishing – using short message services. Usually, the message contains a clickable link or a return phone number. 4. Vishing – the hacker uses voice calls to get personal information. An example would be receiving a call seemingly from Microsoft or the electric company, or a sweepstakes to get information.

Table 14.2   (Continued)

Hacking Techniques

	Malware
Ransomware	Malware (malicious software) is a file, program, or code designed to infect, steal, or exploit a computer or network. Ransomware is a type of malware. The purpose of ransomware is to hold a victim's information hostage by encrypting the information until a ransom is paid to the hacker. Ransomware attacks are evolving and becoming popular because of the increase in the number of vendors who provide ransomware as a service.
Viruses/worms	A virus, like a living organism, needs a host to replicate itself. A computer virus is malware that attaches to another program, such as a file or document. A virus will replicate only when a user executes the original file. On the other hand, a worm is a self-replicating malware. A worm can infect other computers on a network while remaining active on the infected system.
Logic bombs	A logic bomb is a piece of malware that is triggered when a specified condition is met. They are generally embedded in functioning programs. When the trigger is a date, the bomb is called a time bomb. Some logic bombs have valid uses. For example, a free trial version may count the number of logins and limit the trial version when a specified number of attempts are finished. However, logic bombs can be used for malicious activities, such as deleting files when an employee is terminated.
Trojan horses	A Trojan horse disguises itself as a legitimate program. A Trojan horse may be hidden in an attachment or document. Once the file is downloaded, or an attachment is opened, the malicious code will execute. There are many types of Trojan horses designed for specific purposes. For example, a backdoor Trojan enables the hacker to gain remote access to a computer using a back door. A banker Trojan targets a user's banking accounts in an attempt to steal credit and debit card information. Spy Trojans sit and spy on a user's activity.

Cover the Tracks

Once a hacker gains access to a computer and administrator rights, the next step is to cover their tracks. A hacker would want to destroy evidence of their presence to maintain access and evade detection. If the hacker plans to maintain long-term access, they may make the system look like it did before. Routinely, a system administrator may check the system log files to see whether there has been an intrusion. Erasing the evidence of a compromise generally starts by erasing the contaminated logins and any possible error messages generated during the attack process and flagged data in system logs. A hacker may modify the system logs to hide the attack.

The hacker may use a rootkit, automated tools designed to hide the attacker's presence. They can disable the logging of activity and discard all existing logs. Then the attacker configures the system so that it does not log the future activities of the hacker. Further, a hacker may gain access to auditing modules and disable the system auditing tools. An attacker may use track-covering tools such as Privacy Eraser, Wipe, BleachBit, or ClearProg to free cache space, delete cookies, clear internet history, or delete logs, and remain undetected. Further, a hacker may create backdoors providing access to the system in the future in case the organization detects the hacker's presence and disables the current access rights.

Cybersecurity Trends

The following are several trends in cybersecurity threats.[13]

- **Supply chain and Internet of Things attacks.** With the increased use of 5G networks and the Internet of Things, the increased connectivity between devices creates vulnerabilities for the organization and its supply chain partners. An attack on one device can quickly provide access to other devices and partner networks. Therefore, device manufacturers should consider building sophisticated 5G hardware and software to control potential attacks.
- **Ransomware-as-a-service.** The latest business model to offer ransomware as-a-service makes malware readily available to anyone. The availability of such services can increase cyberattacks in the future.
- **Availability of cybersecurity toolsets.** Experts expect an increase in the number of bad actors creating a business by providing custom toolsets for cyberattacks.
- **Increased attacks on cloud services.** As organizations use more cloud services, not establishing strong security measures will increase the company's vulnerability to cyberattacks.
- **Increased attacks on automobiles and consumer devices.** Hackers may eavesdrop on conversations of individuals and use data readily available on the internet to perform reconnaissance and carry out more targeted attacks.
- **Artificial intelligence.** AI technology has helped develop cybersecurity software using machine learning to detect suspicious activity on a company's network. However, AI is now being used to develop smart malware and attacks that will bypass the latest security protocols.

- **State-sponsored cyber warfare.** As the tension between countries increases in the future, states will turn to cyber warfare. These attacks will be targeted toward not only governments but also public and private companies.
- **Insider threats.** Insider threats will continue to be a challenge for cybersecurity. Unintentional human error will continue to be a major reason for data breaches.

In Chapter 15, we discuss cybersecurity governance and management.

Notes

1. Jowitt, T. (2022). Foreign Office Suffered "Serious Cyber Security Incident." *Silicon* (9 February). https://www.silicon.co.uk/e-regulation/governance/foreign-office-suffered-serious-cyber-security-incident-441010.

2. Avita Health System. (2022). Avita Health System Issues Statement on Cybersecurity Incident. *Richland Source* (10 February). https://www.richlandsource.com/news/avita-health-system-issues-statement-on-cybersecurity-incident/article_9940d6ec-8ac1-11ec-b61a-d7e2b47c3f14.html.

3. Roth, A. (2022). Cyberpartisans Hack Belarusion Railway to Disrupt Russian Buildup. *The Guardian* (25 January). https://www.theguardian.com/world/2022/jan/25/cyberpartisans-hack-belarusian-railway-to-disrupt-russian-buildup.

4. Chakraborti, S. (2021). Cyberattack Shuts Down Ecuador's Largest Bank, Banco Pichincha. *AppViewX* (26 October). https://www.appviewx.com/blogs/cyberattack-shuts-down-ecuadors-largest-bank-banco-pichincha/.

5. Kharpal, A., and Brown, R. (2021). Hackers Return Nearly Half of the $600 Million They Stole in One of the Biggest Crypto Heists. *CNBC* (11 August). https://www.cnbc.com/2021/08/11/cryptocurrency-theft-hackers-steal-600-million-in-poly-network-hack.html.

6. Turton, W., and Mehrotra, K. (2021). Hackers Breached Colonial Pipeline Using Compromised Password. *Bloomberg* (4 June). https://www.bloomberg.com/news/articles/2021-06-04/hackers-breached-colonial-pipeline-using-compromised-password.

7. Microsoft Security. (2021). HAFNIUM Targeting Exchange Servers with 0-Day Exploits. Microsoft Blog (2 March). https://www.microsoft.com/en-us/security/blog/2021/03/02/hafnium-targeting-exchange-servers.

8. Farrer, M. (2021). Airline Data Hack: Hundreds of Thousands of Star Alliance Passengers' Details Stolen. *The Guardian* (5 March). https://www.theguardian.com/world/2021/mar/05/airline-data-hack-hundreds-of-thousands-of-star-alliance-passengers-details-stolen.

9. Cimpanu, C. (2021). Volkswagen Discloses Data Breach Impacting 3.3 Million Audi Drivers (10 June). *The Record*. https://therecord.media/volkswagen-discloses-data-breach-impacting-3-3-million-audi-drivers.

10. PwC. (2023). PwC's 26th Annual Global CEO Survey. https://www.pwc.com/gx/en/issues/c-suite-insights/ceo-survey-2023.html.

11. IBM. (2022). IBM Report: Cost of a Data Breach 2022 – A Million-Dollar Race to Detect and Respond https://www.ibm.com/reports/data-breach.

12. Schwartau, W. (1998). Time-based security explained: Provable security models and formulas for the practitioner and vendor. *Computers & Security* 17 (8): 693–714.

13. Lim, M. (2021). The New Normal of Cybersecurity: Examining the Top Three 2021 Trends and 2022 Predictions. *CPO Magazine* (29 December). https://www.cpomagazine.com/cyber-security/the-new-normal-of-cybersecurity-examining-the-top-three-2021-trends-and-2022-predictions/.

CHAPTER 15

Cybersecurity Management

An excerpt from the FACT SHEET: Biden-Harris Administration Announces National Cybersecurity Strategy:[1]

Today, the Biden-Harris Administration released the National Cybersecurity Strategy to secure the full benefits of a safe and secure digital ecosystem for all Americans. In this decisive decade, the United States will reimagine cyberspace as a tool to achieve our goals in a way that reflects our values: economic security and prosperity; respect for human rights and fundamental freedoms; trust in our democracy and democratic institutions; and an equitable and diverse society. To realize this vision, we must make fundamental shifts in how the United States allocates roles, responsibilities, and resources in cyberspace.

- We must rebalance the responsibility to defend cyberspace by shifting the burden for cybersecurity away from individuals, small businesses, and local governments, and onto the organizations that are most capable and best-positioned to reduce risks for all of us.
- We must realign incentives to favor long-term investments by striking a careful balance between defending ourselves against urgent threats today and simultaneously strategically planning for and investing in a resilient future.

The Strategy recognizes that government must use all tools of national power in a coordinated manner to protect our national security, public safety, and economic prosperity.

Cybersecurity Strategy

Cyberattacks are a common threat facing every organization. To mitigate these threats, companies are taking steps such as the following.

- **Creating new organizational positions.** As with anything, when it comes to cybersecurity, organizations need an expert to guide them through cybersecurity measures. Therefore, companies are creating new positions such as chief information security officer (CISO) and chief risk officer (CRO). The CISO is responsible for an organization's information and data security. The CRO assesses risks or threats that might compromise the organization's financial stability. The need for CISO and CRO positions has increased over the past years, and companies are continuing to redefine the responsibilities of these positions focusing on information system security.
- **Introduce cybersecurity training programs.** Cybersecurity is the responsibility of every employee in the organization, not just IT. Many cybercriminals get access to systems using unsuspecting employees. For example, circulating a cat video among colleagues can spread spyware on the company network. Every employee needs to recognize potential threats and know how to mitigate those threats. Therefore, organizations are developing and requiring employees to take annual cybersecurity training.
- **Increase compliance with cybersecurity regulations.** Organizations are increasing monitoring and reporting activities to comply with the increased regulation around cybersecurity.

Even though these measures are positive activities, not taking a holistic approach to cybersecurity may cost the organization in the long run. Therefore, managers should consider developing a cybersecurity strategy and incorporating cybersecurity activities into the organization's business and IT strategy.

A strategy is a high-level plan; hence, a cybersecurity strategy is a high-level plan for how the organization plans to secure its assets and minimize cyber risk. Generally, a cybersecurity strategy is created for the next three to five years. Creating a cybersecurity strategy is critical today because of the increase in cybersecurity attacks, integration, the complexity of system architecture, and the dependence on technology for business operations. There is no indication that cyberattacks are decreasing; therefore, organizations need to have a plan in place to respond and take a more proactive approach in avoiding them. The steps to create a cybersecurity plan can be summarized as follows.[2]

1. **Understand the cybersecurity threat landscape.** Evaluate the threats the company faces and understand the impact of these threats on the business operations. For example, if a denial-of-service attack takes web servers offline, what is the effect on operations, customer experience, and lost revenue? Assess the level of risk the company is willing to undertake and identify the key areas in which investment in cybersecurity is needed. Determine which systems are most at risk or impact the organization most.
2. **Assess your cybersecurity maturity.** Use an established framework, such as the NIST cybersecurity framework, to evaluate the organization's cybersecurity maturity. Determine where the organization should be in three to five years.
3. **Determine how to improve your cybersecurity program.** Brainstorm options for bridging the gap between the current and desired level of cybersecurity. Present the options with pros and cons to top management for review, feedback, and support.
4. **Document the cybersecurity strategy.** Create or update existing documents with plans, policies, guidelines, and procedures. Make sure to include key personnel and their responsibilities to carry out the cybersecurity strategy. Finally, update cybersecurity awareness training initiatives.

Cybersecurity Governance and Management

In Chapter 14, we provided several examples of cyberattacks on high-profile organizations. Given the dire consequences on business operations, cybersecurity has gained the attention of boards of directors. Creating a cybersecurity strategy is the preliminary step in providing oversight over cybersecurity. To develop a strategy and manage cybersecurity, managers should continuously assess the company's policies, processes, and procedures. Managers can use a framework such as COBIT 2019 to oversee IT management and governance in general. If managers want to focus on cybersecurity, the NIST framework for cybersecurity is a good framework. We provide more information about these frameworks in the Appendix.

NIST Framework

The NIST framework provides a common taxonomy for organizations to:[3]

1. Describe the company's current cybersecurity posture.
2. Describe the company's target state of cybersecurity.

3. Identify and prioritize opportunities for improvement within the context of a continuous and repeatable process.
4. Assess progress toward the target state.
5. Communicate among internal and external stakeholders about cybersecurity risk.

The NIST framework is a risk-based approach to managing cybersecurity. It consists of three parts: the framework core, the implementation tiers, and the framework profiles. The framework guides management through the following key functions of cybersecurity management.

- **Identify.** The first step in addressing cybersecurity is to create an inventory of assets such as physical devices, internal and external systems, software, stakeholders, and their responsibilities, data, and data flow within the organization. Further, managers should also identify key issues that impact the business environment, such as the company's role in the supply chain and the national infrastructure, technological dependence, and its vision, mission, and strategy. Other issues managers should identify are legal and regulatory requirements, risk exposure concerning the supply chain, the processes to manage risks in the organization, and the potential impact and likelihood of given risk events.
- **Protect.** This step guides managers in assessing whether specific controls have been established to protect the organization's assets and data from a cyberattack. Possible controls to manage access, increase awareness of cybersecurity, secure data and information, and maintain the security of assets are discussed in detail in the next section.
- **Detect.** This function guides management in thinking about how to detect an attack that is currently taking place. Managers should evaluate whether they can identify anomalies in network traffic or events in real time. Managers should establish roles and responsibilities for detecting anomalies and processes to monitor the organization's network for malicious activities. Specific detective controls are discussed later in this chapter.
- **Respond.** This function guides management in creating a plan to respond to any cyberattacks. Managers should consider whether they have a plan on how to respond to an incident, contain an incident, and provide feedback. Management should assess whether employees understand their roles and responsibilities for addressing an incident.
- **Recover.** Here managers consider how to communicate about the attack incident to external stakeholders and incorporate lessons learned.

Cybersecurity Controls

Controls are policies, procedures, processes, and activities a company implements to ensure that all stakeholders and electronic devices/processes achieve a set objective. A company can define control objectives to safeguard assets, comply with laws and regulations, communicate financial performance using reliable financial statements, reduce fraud, and ensure efficient and effective operations and use of resources. Based on the function of the control activity, we can categorize controls as preventive, detective, or corrective. Preventive controls ensure that data gathered and recorded is accurate and complete. Even with many preventive controls, there may be times when inaccurate or incomplete data may be gathered. Therefore, we cannot completely depend on preventive controls. We also need detective controls to identify whether there is missing or inaccurate data. Detective controls enable the detection of errors. Once errors have been identified, corrective controls address these errors and rectify them.

Managers should implement various policies, procedures, and processes to protect an organization from cyberattacks.

Preventive Controls

Preventive controls are proactive measures that safeguard assets and enable efficient business operations. These measures reduce or delay the ability of a hacker to break through the defenses. We discuss preventive controls related to cybersecurity based on two major components: people and information systems.

People

Cybersecurity is the responsibility of every employee, not just the managers in the IT department. Preventive cybersecurity controls should be enabled by the executive management and followed by all employees.

Develop a Security-Aware Culture   Executive management should set the tone at the top and the company culture. Management should communicate the importance of security throughout the company and lead by example by following security policies diligently. Management should clearly demonstrate that they value and support employees who follow prescribed security policies and enforce sanctions for violating the security policy.

Training   Cybercriminals often get access to critical information during reconnaissance through unsuspecting employees. These employees do not necessarily work in the IT department of a company. Cybersecurity is every employee's responsibility because anyone can unintentionally grant access to company information. Therefore, all employees should be trained on why security measures are essential, how to follow safe computing practices, and how to recognize and avoid social engineering attacks geared toward them. Companies should continuously train employees to keep up with the latest schemes hackers use. Therefore, managers should consider educating themselves and their employees about the following:

- **Access controls.** Educate employees on the importance of restricting access to buildings and information systems so that employees are not frustrated or demotivated. A better understanding of why these controls exist would motivate employees to be proactive and not circumvent them. For example, understanding why it is essential not to let anyone follow you into a building makes employees more aware.
- **Safeguarding documents.** Educate employees on document usage practices. Train employees not to discard company documents in trash cans but to shred documents. Invest in shredders that shred paper into small bits rather than strips for further protection.
- **Downloading practices.** Train employees to be critical about downloads. Educate them about why they should not download files, pictures, and MP3s from unknown sources. Train employees to be suspicious of e-mails they receive with strange requests or poor grammar asking for sensitive information. Inform employees why it is crucial to verify the e-mail by calling the sender using a known phone number rather than a number stated on the e-mail.

Information Systems

Additional systems controls will provide increased security from internal and external threats. The following are some of the information systems controls that employees should adhere to.

User Access Controls Granting and monitoring user access to information systems is challenging for many organizations. Controlling access is made more difficult due to the number of users requiring access to the system, employee turnover, third-party access points, and seamless integration of systems. There are two different layers of access controls.

Physical access controls These control who can physically access the company's system. If a company's server rooms or computer devices are easily accessible, perpetrators can enter a building. Attackers frequently use disguises such as an IT help desk employee or janitorial staff to gain entrance to the building. Then the hacker uses various devices to download company information or upload malware. Therefore, having physical access controls such as key cards and locks and maintaining point-of-sale devices behind counters are essential preventive controls.

Logical access controls Cybercriminals do not necessarily have to be physically present to penetrate an information system. Therefore, companies should be careful about who is allowed to log into a system. Logical access controls are tools used to validate and authorize users and devices that access a system or network so that there is accountability. Logical access is a two-step process involving authentication and authorization.

Authentication When a user or a device accesses the system, the first step is to validate or authenticate the identity of the user. Authentication technologies check whether the user's credentials match those in a database. For example, when an employee enters a username and password, the authentication technology checks whether the username and password match the username and password in an existing database. If there is a match, the employee is given access to the system. There are various authentication types.

Authentication may be categorized as *single-factor* or *multifactor authentication* based on the number of factors checked. Since usernames and passwords can be easily guessed or stolen, strong validation uses multifactor authentication, requiring users to provide two or more identifiers. These identifiers are a combination of something you know, such as a username and password, something you have, such as a key card or a USB key, and something you are, such as a fingerprint or facial recognition.

Today, most companies use two-step authentication. For example, a user first enters a username and password. Then the user is prompted to enter a personal identification number (PIN) sent using text messaging, for example. Multifactor authentication can also have several drawbacks. Just like employees can forget usernames and passwords or write them down, employees may lose key cards or USB keys. There are several drawbacks to using biometric data for authentication as well. For example, biometric data has to be stored, and there is no guarantee that the database will not be compromised. Unlike usernames and passwords, biometric data cannot be replaced if compromised. Biometric data might not work efficiently all of the time. For example, the system might not recognize a voice if an employee has a cold or a fingerprint if the employee has a paper cut.

Another way to provide strong authentication is to use multimodal authentication. *Multimodal authentication* combines several elements of the same factor to authenticate a user or device. For example, a user may be required to do a facial scan, provide a fingerprint, and say a command for voice recognition. The results are combined using a fusion algorithm to provide a single yes/no decision. Banks require users to enter a username and password and request a PIN sent using a text or e-mail. The advantages of multimodal biometric authentication are that it provides a higher level of accuracy and resists fraud by making it harder to fake multiple traits. It also provides the flexibility to address temporary changes, such as having a cold, and increases user acceptance because the user has more choices.

Authorization This addresses what a user or device can access in the system once they have been authenticated. Users' job responsibilities should determine what they can see in the system. Therefore, before creating authorization, you should have a good understanding of the various job responsibilities and the database elements that are related to those responsibilities. Using an access control matrix, a table showing the users in one column and various database elements in the top row, you can match the user to various database elements. The access control matrix should be periodically evaluated to ensure that the right employees have the correct authorizations. Sometimes, when employees move to a different role, get promoted, or leave the company, they may have access to unnecessary database elements. This may create vulnerabilities in the system that cybercriminals can exploit.

Network Security

A computer network is an interconnection of devices, also called hosts, for the purpose of sending and receiving data. A computer network also includes network devices, such as routers, switches, hubs, and bridges that help two different hosts to communicate. Effective and efficient network access controls are vital to achieving network security. Network security should support confidentiality, integrity, and availability of data. To ensure network security, companies should use hardware, software, and cloud security components. Hardware components include servers and various other devices. Security software components should be installed on devices across the network as a precaution. Several network security concepts are presented next.

Perimeter Defense Perimeter defense is analogous to building a wall around a house to keep intruders out. With cybersecurity, perimeter defense involves filtering incoming data using firewalls and secure gateways. Firewalls are special-purpose hardware devices or software that help protect information systems. Border routers are devices connecting the company's information system to the internet. Firewalls and border routers use a set of if-then rules, also called access control lists, to determine the validity of the arriving data packets. Packet filtering is an examination of various fields in the packet's header to determine what to do with the packets. Perimeter defense mechanisms act as the first-order defense against an attack.

Layered Security and Defense in Depth   Layered security uses multiple layers of security controls to increase the protection of an information system. This form of security is to provide more protection if one layer fails. Imagine visiting a famous museum. You will approach the main gate to enter, then walk through metal detectors, and finally, get your bags inspected. Layered security is like this process.

A border router can quickly filter good packets and pass them to the main firewall, where a more detailed check is performed. Then other firewalls can be used to perform a deep packet inspection where the actual data is examined. Layered security is a component of defense in depth. Defense in depth uses multiple security measures, sometimes intentionally designed to be redundant so that when one line of defense is compromised, additional measures are in place to combat an attack. In this example, defense in depth will require you to walk through metal detectors and submit to a pat down. Your bags will be scanned before a guard physically inspects the items.

Network Segmentation   Network segmentation divides a network into similar sections by placing barriers between the parts so the individual parts cannot interact. A network can be segmented either physically or virtually. If hackers pass the perimeter defense and enter a network without segmentation, nothing will prevent them from accessing critical systems and databases. Apart from creating an additional barrier, segmenting can lead to better performance due to less congestion. Also, segmentation can help with compliance requirements. Splitting the network into zones makes it easier to implement compliance rules for a specific network zone. Other advantages of network segmentation are stronger data protection, threat containment, protection from insider attacks, improved monitoring, and increased threat detection.

Zero-Trust Framework   The zero-trust framework emphasizes that companies should not trust any traffic unless properly verified. This concept enables companies to protect against insider threats. When companies allow employees to connect their own devices to the network, even though the device might be known to the network, its vulnerabilities can be used to gain access to the company network. Therefore, the zero-trust approach protects networks against insider threats and compromised credentials of known users/ devices within the internal perimeter.

Additional Network Considerations   A major part of network security depends on the proper authentication and authorization of users and devices.

Apart from authentication and authorization, organizations should also pay attention to the following.

- **Endpoint security.** An endpoint device is any hardware connected to a local area (LAN) or wide area networks (WAN), such as workstations, laptops, smartphones, printers, and mobile devices. Every endpoint comes with certain default settings for easy installation. However, the default setting can have many unnecessary options. Therefore, to minimize any vulnerabilities, endpoints should be hardened. Hardening is the process of configuring the endpoints to eliminate unnecessary default settings.
- **Anti-virus/anti-malware software.** Anti-virus software prevents networks by stopping endpoint devices from being infected. Anti-malware software detects and destroys malicious programs that have infiltrated the network. Companies should install anti-virus/malware tools, update periodically, and review malware threats.
- **Application security.** Managers should ensure that the software used throughout the network is secure. To achieve application security, you can limit the software used, keep up to date with the latest security patches, and harden applications.
- **Change management controls.** Change management ensures that modifications to hardware, software, or processes are authorized, accurate, and implemented properly. All changes should be identified, documented, approved by management, tested adequately, converted and implemented correctly, and reviewed for any errors on a timely basis.

Detective Controls

Detective controls help determine whether there is an intruder. Even with multiple preventive controls, it is extremely difficult to stop hackers from infiltrating the company's information system because of the system's complexity. Therefore, it is important to determine quickly whether there is an intrusion. Penetration testing, intrusion detection systems, and continuous monitoring are several detective controls used to monitor whether an attack is in progress.

Penetration Testing

A penetration test, also known as a pen test or ethical hacking, is an authorized simulated attempt by either an internal audit or an external security team to break into the company's information system. Even though penetration testing almost always succeeds in breaking into a system, periodically testing the system enables the company to recognize any additional protections needed to increase the time and effort required to compromise the system.

There are several types of penetration testing. An open-box pen test is where a hacker is provided some information regarding the target company's security information. A closed-box pen test, also known as a "single-blind" test, the hacker is provided only the company's name. In a covert pen test, also known as the "double-blind" pen test, the hacker is aware of the scope of the test and has other details of the test; however, the IT security professionals in the company are unaware of the attack. The goal is to see how the IT team reacts and responds to the attack. In an external penetration test, the hacker attempts to penetrate the company's website or external network servers in an attempt to access other systems. In an internal pen test, the hacker attacks the company's internal network to determine how much damage an insider, such as a disgruntled employee, can cause from behind the main firewall of the company's network. A hacker may use brute-force attacks or other methods described in Chapter 14 to carry out the attack. After completing an attack, the hacker will share their findings with the company's security team. This information is then used for planning necessary upgrades and patch management.

Intrusion Detection Systems

An intrusion detection system (IDS) is a device or software application that monitors network traffic. The IDS alerts system administrators if there is suspicious network activity or policy violations. Even though the primary function of an IDS is anomaly detection and reporting, some detection systems can block traffic sent from suspicious IP addresses. There are two types of IDSs:

1. A network intrusion detection system monitors inbound/outbound traffic from all the devices on the network.
2. A host intrusion detection system runs on all computers or devices and can detect any malicious traffic that originates from the host.

There are two main methods of IDS deployment. (1) A signature-based IDS monitors all packets traversing the network and compares them to a database of known attack signatures. (2) An anomaly-based IDS monitors network traffic and compares it to an established baseline to determine whether the traffic pattern is typical for the network or device. IDSs are prone to false positives, especially after the initial implementation. Therefore, companies need to configure the IDS products to recognize normal traffic on the network. A more serious mistake is when IDSs return a false negative or miss a threat. False negatives are becoming a massive threat because malware is evolving and becoming more sophisticated. Intrusion prevention systems

(IPSs) are similar to IDSs, but they can be configured to stop threats without the involvement of a system administrator.

Continuous Monitoring

Business environments, hacking techniques, and malware continue to evolve. Therefore, it is important to continuously monitor the threat landscape, assess the risks and risk responses, and modify policies and procedures as necessary.

Corrective Controls

Corrective controls help rectify problems once they have been identified. After an intrusion is detected, it is essential to take corrective action to contain the problem, reduce the damage, recover and restore any data, and safeguard the information assets from future attacks. Some corrective controls companies will need to implement are:

- **Reboot the system.** Sometimes the best option to contain and stop an attack is to take the system offline. Rebooting may interrupt business operations because the system will be offline. Therefore, the IT security team needs to consult business managers to weigh in on the consequences and determine whether it is an option. For example, in a hospital, rebooting a system can interrupt an ongoing surgery, causing harm to a patient. Business managers must be involved in decisions on responding to cyberattacks.
- **Repair and replace.** Repair and replace any devices and cables that have any physical damage. Reissue access cards if they were compromised.
- **Manage patches.** A patch is code released by software developers to fix a particular vulnerability. Complex operating systems and applications have many vulnerabilities. Software developers periodically release code to fix these vulnerabilities. Patch management regularly monitors, applies, and tests patches and updates to all software the company uses. Since patches modify complex software, applying patches is not a straightforward process. Sometimes, patches can create new problems. Therefore, companies must test the patch carefully to avoid crashing the application.
- **Quarantine a virus.** When anti-virus software finds a suspicious file, it quarantines it. Like a person with a contagious ailment, quarantining a file separates it from the rest of the files by placing it in a specific storage device area. The original file is then deleted and cannot be accessed. Once the file is transferred to a hidden folder that other programs cannot access, you can decide whether you want to delete it.

- **Business continuity, disaster recovery, and incident response plans.** A business continuity plan outlines procedures and instructions an organization must follow in the face of a significant disruption, such as a malicious attack by cybercriminals, to maintain or quickly resume all business functions. A disaster recovery plan outlines how the IT function can get back up and running in the face of a disaster. An incident response plan is a set of tools and procedures your security team can use to identify, eliminate, and recover from cybersecurity threats.

Cybersecurity Reporting and Disclosure

Most often, a cybersecurity incident can also impact the company's external stakeholders, such as supply chain partners and investors. For example, a security incident can disrupt business operations, causing delays, denial of service, or loss of personal information. A system crash can impact manufacturing and distribution delays in subsequent supply chain partners. Given the connectivity in a global marketplace, other organizations, investors, customers, and regulators need to know whether their data has been compromised through your company.

Since a cybersecurity incident shows an inefficient process and costs the company millions of dollars for remediation actions, some companies may decide to hide the details of cybersecurity incidents. Therefore, it is necessary to have specific regulations in place to ensure that companies are acting ethically and responsibly about cybersecurity. Further, one necessity for an efficient capital market is transparency, reducing information asymmetry between internal and external stakeholders. Therefore, regulators of the capital market system have also taken an interest in cybersecurity governance, disclosures, and reporting. We discuss recent developments in disclosure and reporting requirements next.

AICPA Cybersecurity Risk Management Examination

The American Institute of Certified Public Accountants (AICPA) cybersecurity risk management examination enables external audit practitioners to provide a general-purpose report on the effectiveness of an organization's cybersecurity risk management program. The risk management examination has two distinct but complementary subject matters, namely:[4]

1. A description of the entity's cybersecurity risk management program
2. The effectiveness of controls within that program

The cybersecurity risk management examination report contains three main components. They are:

1. **Management's description.** Management provides a description of the entity's cybersecurity risk management program, including how the company identifies its information assets, manages the cybersecurity risks, and monitors the key security policies implemented.
2. **Management's assertion.** Management provides assertions that the description in the report was presented in accordance with set description criteria and that the controls, either at a point in time or for a specific period, were effective in achieving cybersecurity objectives.
3. **Practitioner's opinion.** The opinion addresses:
   - Whether the description of the entity's cybersecurity risk management program is presented in accordance with the description criteria, and
   - Whether the controls within that program were effective to achieve the entity's cybersecurity objectives based on the control criteria.[4]

   Even though this is a general-purpose report, the practitioner can restrict the use of the report to specific users.

SOC for Cybersecurity

System and organization controls (SOC) reports mainly deal with third-party service providers. The objective of the SOC for cybersecurity is to communicate useful information about cybersecurity risk management programs to relevant stakeholders. SOC for cybersecurity is intended to:[5]

1. Provide common criteria for disclosures about a company's cybersecurity risk management program.
2. Provide common criteria for assessing program effectiveness.
3. Provide comparability.
4. Permit management flexibility.

Even though SOC for cybersecurity and AICPA cybersecurity risk management examination have the same three main components, the SOC for cybersecurity is performed for a third-party service provider rather than your own company. The AICPA cybersecurity risk management program implies that managers should consider risks delegated to third parties. (See the Appendix for more details on SOC.)

SEC Reporting and Disclosure Requirements

The SEC requires companies to disclose any material incident in a Form 8-K and provide information about significant risks in the risk factors Item 1A section in Form 10-K.[6] However, in March 2022, the SEC proposed new cybersecurity reporting requirements. These changes were proposed to increase comparability, consistency, and decision usefulness. The proposed disclosures would require companies to:

1. Disclose the incident in a Form 8-K within four business days of determining the materiality of a cybersecurity incident.
2. Disclose on an annual basis its cybersecurity risk management policies and procedures, governance practices, and to what extent the board members pose cybersecurity expertise.

These proposed rules will burden the company's cybersecurity response team, management and the board of directors, business operations, and the reporting process.

Notes

1. The White House. (2023). FACT SHEET: Biden-Harris Administration Announces National Cybersecurity Strategy. White House Briefing Room (2 March). https://www.whitehouse.gov/briefing-room/statements-releases/2023/03/02/fact-sheet-biden-harris-administration-announces-national-cybersecurity-strategy/.
2. Scarfone, K. (n.d.). How to Develop a Cybersecurity Strategy: Step-by-Step Guide. *TechTarget*. https://www.techtarget.com/searchsecurity/tip/How-to-develop-a-cybersecurity-strategy-Step-by-step-guide.
3. NIST. (2018). Framework for Improving Critical Infrastructure Cybersecurity. Version 1.1 (16 April). https://nvlpubs.nist.gov/nistpubs/CSWP/NIST.CSWP.04162018.pdf.
4. AICPA. (2017). *Reporting on an Entity's Cybersecurity Risk Management Program and Controls: Attestation Guide*. Hoboken, NJ: Wiley.
5. AICPA. (n.d.). System and Organization Controls: SOC Suite of Services. https://www.aicpa.org/resources/landing/system-and-organization-controls-soc-suite-of-services.
6. SEC. (2022). SEC Proposes Rules on Cybersecurity Risk Management, Strategy, Governance, and Incident Disclosure by Public Companies. Press release, U.S. Securities and Exchange Commission (9 March). https://www.sec.gov/news/press-release/2022-39.

APPENDIX

Governance Frameworks

Given the proliferation of technology in a company, business professionals throughout an organization are interested in the governance and management of information technology (IT). For example, executive management and accounting professionals need to attest to the functioning of internal controls over financial reporting. Given the dependence on IT for recording, analyzing, and communicating financial information, these individuals need to understand the controls over IT. Every employee must be aware of and follow the internal controls for IT. Circumventing any controls can create system vulnerability and put the organization at risk. Therefore, every business employee should have a foundational understanding of the purpose and objectives of the governance frameworks to take responsibility for the efficient and mindful use of technology. This appendix presents several frameworks that business users, especially management, should understand.

COSO Internal Control Framework

The Committee of Sponsoring Organizations of the Treadway Committee (COSO) developed the original internal control framework in 1992 to guide organizations in creating internal control policies. In 2013, COSO revised the framework to reflect the changing business ecosystem, such as the greater dependence on technology. To be more flexible, the overall goal of the framework is to provide principles rather than strict rules. This flexibility allows judgment in designing and implementing controls in a changing environment. Even though the principles are not specific to a technology, the overall control environment is necessary for proper IT governance and control. By following the principles, a company can establish an effective system of controls that can reduce the overall risk while meeting the organization's objectives or goals. The objectives defined by the COSO internal control framework are:[1]

- **Operations.** The ability to use resources effectively and efficiently.
- **Reporting.** The ability to reliably report accurate information internally and externally.
- **Compliance.** The ability to comply with appropriate laws and regulations.

The framework comprises five components working together to provide a system of overall organizational control. Each of these areas has several key principles that can be used to establish appropriate control processes in the organization. Table A.1 lists the components and the associated principles.

1. Control Environment

The control environment is the foundation of the control system within the company. The control environment sets the tone at the top by ensuring that management is engaged and the control systems have proper oversight. For

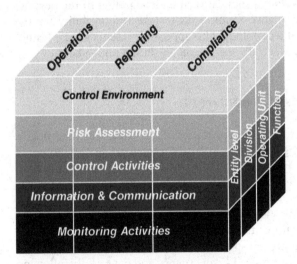

Figure A.1   COSO Integrated Framework

Source: COSO. (2013). Internal Control – Integrated Framework. Executive Summary. Committee of Sponsoring Organizations of the Treadway Committee (May). https://www.coso.org/Shared%20 Documents/Framework-Executive-Summary.pdf.

Table A.1   COSO Integrated Framework Components and Principles

Component	Principles
Control Environment	The organization demonstrates a commitment to integrity and ethical values.
	The board of directors demonstrates independence from management and exercises oversight of the development and performance of internal control.
	Management establishes, with board oversight, structures, reporting lines, and appropriate authorities and responsibilities in the pursuit of objectives.
	The organization demonstrates a commitment to attract, develop, and retain competent individuals in alignment with objectives.
	The organization holds individuals accountable for their internal control responsibilities in the pursuit of objectives.
Risk Assessment	The organization specifies objectives with sufficient clarity to enable the identification and assessment of risk relating to objectives.
	The organization identifies risks to the achievement of its objectives across the entity and analyzes the risks as a basis for determining how the risks should be managed.
	The organization considers the potential for fraud in assessing risks to the achievement of objectives.
	The organization identifies and assesses changes that could significantly affect the system of internal control.
Control Activities	The organization selects and develops control activities that contribute to the mitigation of risks to the achievement of objectives to acceptable levels.
	The organization selects and develops general control activities over technology to support the achievement of objectives.
	The organization deploys control activities through policies that establish what is expected and procedures that put policies into action.
Information and Communication	The organization obtains or generates and uses relevant, quality information to support the functioning of internal control.
	The organization internally communicates information, including objectives and responsibilities for internal control, necessary to support the functioning of internal control.
	The organization communicates with external parties regarding matters affecting the functioning of internal control.
Monitoring	The organization selects, develops, and performs ongoing and/ or separate evaluations to ascertain whether the components of internal control are present and functioning.
	The organization evaluates and communicates internal control deficiencies in a timely manner to those parties responsible for taking corrective action, including senior management and the board of directors, as appropriate.

Source: COSO. (2013). Internal Control – Integrated Framework. Executive Summary. Committee of Sponsoring Organizations of the Treadway Committee (May). https://www.coso.org/Shared%20 Documents/Framework-Executive-Summary.pdf.

example, the board of directors should evaluate whether the benefits of adopting an emerging technology align with the business strategy and assess the potential risk exposure. The board should evaluate and prioritize IT projects and monitor their progress. Therefore, the board of directors should have sufficient knowledge of IT processes and controls to provide high-level oversight. Senior management should also understand the unique challenges of implementing innovative technologies and providing support through training, communicating changes to employees, and establishing appropriate controls as needed.

2. Risk Assessment

The primary purpose of this component is to identify all potential events that can hinder the achievement of the organization's objectives. Adopting any technology can create additional risks to consider. For example, the risk of data loss can come from either equipment failure or external threats, such as hackers. The interconnectivity of organizations with their business partners increases the risk of threats and data loss. A weak link in third-party partners can increase the possible threats to systems. When using newer technology, consider the potential risk of not having sufficient technical knowledge within your teams, especially if there is a turnover of key personnel.

3. Control Activities

Control activities for IT protect the data and keep mission-critical systems operating. Each technology added to the IT architecture will require additional controls specific to the risks associated with that technology. Some key control activities mentioned under the COSO framework include:

- **Safeguarding assets.** Implementing logical and physical access controls to protect the technical infrastructure. These controls include proper authentication of users, the configuration of the network, software, hardware endpoints, and networks, data encryption, and restriction of access to data and systems.
- **Segregation of duties.** Ensuring that there is segregation of duties within the responsibilities of the system.
- **Development and acquisition controls.** Establish relevant technology acquisition, development, and maintenance process control activities.
- **Change management.** System change management procedures to ensure continuous operations.

4. Information and Communication

Management should obtain and evaluate the information needed to support their internal control responsibilities. This component addresses the importance of identifying information requirements, capturing internal and external data, processing relevant data into information, maintaining quality throughout processing data, considering the costs and benefits of acquiring and disseminating information, and communicating the information pertinent to the right person. Since data is collected, stored, processed, and communicated using various systems, managers should consider whether technology enables the effective creation and communication of information. An effective control system can only be maintained with clear communication in both top-down and bottom-up directions.

5. Monitoring Activities

Management, along with the board of directors, should continuously monitor the effectiveness of the control system. The review should cover each of the five components of the framework. Management should determine whether the implemented controls are adequate and functioning as expected. If deficiencies are found, managers should consider whether compensating rules exist and communicate them to the appropriate parties to take further action. In addition, management should review the environment for new risks that may require additional controls. The continuous monitoring of the performance of control activities enables management to promptly detect and correct any arising issues.

COSO Enterprise Risk Management

The enterprise risk management (ERM) framework, initially developed in 2004, was updated in 2017 to emphasize the importance of considering risks in setting the strategy and driving performance.[2] ERM evaluates risks from the perspective of the entire organization rather than individual departments or functions. This framework enables organizations to build on existing risk management practices and helps management to understand how risk management can accelerate growth and enhance performance. Concerning IT, for example, when managers decide to implement new technology, they should consider the following questions.

- What risks are derived from using the technology?
- Does the technology selected enable the organization to align its strategy with its mission?

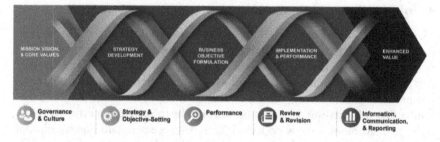

Figure A.2 COSO Enterprise Risk Management

Source: COSO. (2017). Enterprise Risk Management – Integrating with Strategy and Performance: Executive Summary. Committee of Sponsoring Organizations of the Treadway Committee. https://www.coso.org/Shared%20Documents/2017-COSO-ERM-Integrating-with-Strategy-and-Performance-Executive-Summary.pdf

This framework guides organizations to consider the proliferation of data, increased automation, and artificial intelligence in their risk management practices. The framework's focus helps to optimize risks with positive outcomes and minimize threats or adverse outcomes.

The components of the COSO enterprise risk management framework move an organization from developing its mission and core values to implementing and performing them. The five main components are:[2]

1. **Governance.** Describes the overall tone of the organization, well-established oversight responsibilities, ethical values, and culture.
2. **Strategy and objective-setting.** Describes how to establish a risk appetite, align risk with the overall strategy, and prioritize the risks based on risk appetite.
3. **Performance.** Identifies risks that may impact the achievement of strategy and business objectives.
4. **Review and revision.** Explains how reviewing the entity's performance evaluates how well risk management is functioning overtime.
5. **Information, communication, and reporting.** Describes how information flows from internal and external stakeholders throughout the organization.

Table A.2 shows the principles and practices organizations can apply regardless of size, type, or sector.

Table A.2   The Five Main Components of COSO ERM

Component	Set of Principles
Governance and Culture	Exercises board risk oversight
	Establishes operating structures
	Defines desired culture
	Demonstrates commitment to core values
	Attracts, develops, and retains capable individuals
Strategy and Objective-Setting	Analyzes business context
	Defines risk appetite
	Evaluates alternative strategies
	Formulates business objectives
Performance	Identifies risk
	Assesses severity of risk
	Prioritizes risks
	Implements risk responses
	Develops portfolio view
Review and Revision	Assesses substantial change
	Reviews risk and performance
	Pursues improvement in enterprise risk management
Information, Communication, and Reporting	Leverages information and technology
	Communicates risk information
	Reports on risk, culture, and performance

Source: COSO. (2017). Enterprise Risk Management – Integrating with Strategy and Performance: Executive Summary. Committee of Sponsoring Organizations of the Treadway Committee. https://www.coso.org/Shared%20Documents/2017-COSO-ERM-Integrating-with-Strategy-and-Performance-Executive-Summary.pdf

COBIT

ISACA developed the Control Objectives for Information and Related Technologies (COBIT) framework for information technology management and governance in 1996. In 2012, ISACA integrated several frameworks and established COBIT 5 as a single, principles-based framework that covers every aspect of IT management and governance from project initiation, development, and implementation through to the final disposition of the technology. The framework was updated again in 2019 to reflect the integration of IT within organizations. COBIT 2019 addresses the need for flexibility and introduces focus areas.[3] A focus area is a specific domain or issue, such as cloud computing, cybersecurity, DevOps, or digital transformation, that can be addressed by a collection of governance and management objectives and their components.

The framework takes a risk-based approach to assist managers in assessing risks from both the technology and business operations perspectives.[3] COBIT 2019 is based on the following six principles that guide IT management and governance practices.

1. **Meeting stakeholder value.** The enterprise information technology environment should provide value to its organization and stakeholders.
2. **Enabling a holistic approach.** The framework identifies that enterprise IT is comprised of several components that must work together holistically to achieve the set objectives.
3. **Dynamic governance system.** The framework enables evaluating the impact of changes in design factors, such as the organization's strategy, goals, size, and compliance requirements, on enterprise governance of IT systems.
4. **Separating governance from management.** The framework makes a clear distinction between governance and management, recognizing that the two disciplines encompass distinct types of activities, require different organizational structures, and serve different purposes.
5. **Tailored to enterprise needs.** The governance system considers the design factors when customizing and prioritizing the governance system components.
6. **End-to-end governance system.** The framework integrates governance of IT into enterprise governance, which covers not only the IT function but also all technology and information processing within the enterprise.

COBIT aims to achieve greater value creation through the enterprise governance of IT by aligning IT practices with business practices and policies. COBIT provides three specific benefits of enterprise governance of IT (EGIT), which are:

1. **Benefits realization.** EGIT creates value from investments in technology and eliminates projects that will not provide such value to the business.
2. **Risk optimization.** EGIT systematically addresses the risks that are inherent in implementing new technology or the use of current technology. COBIT recognizes that governance principles can also help to preserve value in the organization by reducing risk.

3. Resource optimization. EGIT enables planning and coordinating changes to the infrastructure to use the technology resources, personnel, and end-users.

Since COBIT focuses on the governance and management of enterprise information technology, distinguishing between the two is essential. The governance of an organization sets the overall objectives of the organization based on stakeholder needs. They also prioritize the objectives and set the overall direction of the company. Finally, governance is responsible for monitoring the organization's actions against the agreed-upon objectives. On the other hand, management is responsible for the execution of the overall objectives set forth by the governance bodies. The activities for management include planning, building, running, and monitoring the activities. COBIT requires the separation of governance and management to oversee the IT environment.

Following the principles outlined in the framework can help an organization improve the quality and control over its IT environment. With the continuing expansion of newer technologies, the ability to manage risks is of increasing importance. The framework recognizes the importance of aligning IT with enterprise goals to manage IT investment, operations, and risks. The framework as shown in Figure A.3 provides a common set of goals and objectives for IT professionals and business managers.

The framework provides three governance objectives: evaluate, direct, and monitor (EDM). There are also four management objectives:[3]

1. Align, plan, and organize (APO)
2. Build, acquire, and implement (BAI)
3. Deliver, service, and support (DSS)
4. Monitor, evaluate, and assess (MEA)

The governance system comprises seven components that individually and collectively work together to operate a good enterprise governance system. The seven components are:

1. Processes
2. Organizational structures
3. Principles, policies, and frameworks
4. Information
5. Culture, ethics, and behavior
6. People, skills, and competencies
7. Services, infrastructure, and applications

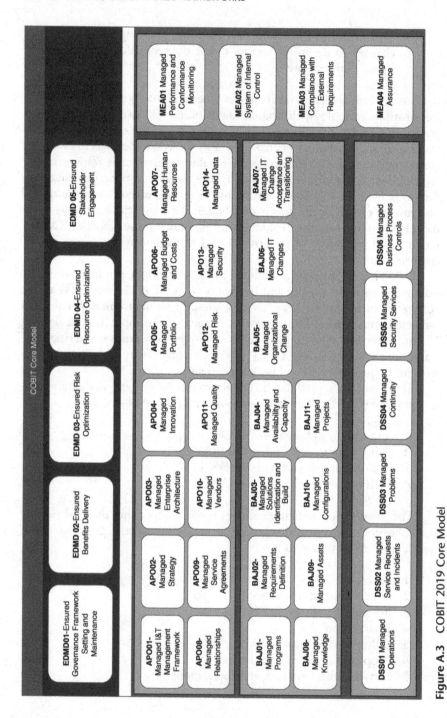

Figure A.3 COBIT 2019 Core Model

Source: ISACA. (2019). *COBIT 2019 Framework: Introduction and Methodology.* https://store.isaca.org/s/store/browse/detail/a2S4w000004Ko9cEAC.

NIST

Cybersecurity threatens a nation's security, economy, and public safety by exploiting critical infrastructure. Therefore, the National Institute of Standards and Technology (NIST) was tasked with "identifying and developing cybersecurity risk frameworks for voluntary use by critical infrastructure owners and operators."[6] The framework uses business drivers to guide cybersecurity activities. It considers cybersecurity risks as a component of the organization's risk management processes. Even though the focus of the framework is critical infrastructure, the framework can be used by any organization.

Organizations have different threats, vulnerabilities, and risk tolerance levels. Therefore, the framework allows organizations to customize practices based on the company's critical processes and prioritize investment based on the organization's needs. Given the flexibility in how an organization implements the framework, "compliance with the framework" can be confusing and may mean different things to different organizations. Consequently, an important aspect is that "compliance" should express compliance with an organization's cybersecurity requirements and not with the framework.

The NIST framework provides a common taxonomy for organizations to:[4]

1. Describe the company's current cybersecurity posture.
2. Describe the company's target state of cybersecurity.
3. Identify and prioritize opportunities for improvement within the context of a continuous and repeatable process.
4. Assess progress toward the target state.
5. Communicate among internal and external stakeholders about cybersecurity risk.

The NIST framework is a risk-based approach to managing cybersecurity with three parts.

1. **The framework core.** The core is a "set of cybersecurity activities, outcomes, and informative references common across sectors and critical infrastructure."[6] The framework is clear that the core is not a checklist of actions to perform but a set of outcomes identified by stakeholders that will help manage cybersecurity risk. The core consists of the following:
   - Functions: identify, protect, detect, respond, and recover
   - Categories: subdivisions of functions

- Subcategories: subdivisions of categories
- Informative references (specific sections of standards, guidelines, and practices)

    Table 13.4 in the cybersecurity chapter (Chapter 13) shows the complete framework core functions, categories, and subcategory listing.

2. **The implementation tiers.** These "provide a mechanism for organizations to view and understand the characteristics of their approach to managing cybersecurity risk, which will help in prioritizing and achieving cybersecurity objectives."[4] Implementation tiers range from "partial" (Tier 1) to "adaptive" (Tier 4) and describe the rigor in cybersecurity risk management practices.

    - **Tier 1, partial.** The organization's risk management practices are not formalized and have limited cybersecurity awareness. The organization does not understand its dependencies.
    - **Tier 2, risk-informed.** The organization has approved risk management practices, some awareness of cybersecurity risks, and an understanding of the dependencies. However, it may not have proper policies established to manage risk.
    - **Tier 3, repeatable.** The organization's risk management practices are formalized. It has cybersecurity awareness, established practices to manage risk, and understands its dependencies.
    - **Tier 4, adaptive.** The organization continuously adapts its cybersecurity practices based on changing risks and activities. It takes an organization-wide approach to manage risks.

        An organization will determine the tier based on its current risk management practices, legal and regulatory environment, business strategy/objectives, and other organizational constraints. Progression to higher tiers is recommended only after evaluating a cost-benefit analysis.

3. **The framework profiles.** An organization can use the profiles to align its cybersecurity practices with its mission, risk tolerance, and resources. For example, an organization can create a current profile indicating the state of current practices. A target profile, on the other hand, will indicate an aspirational state. Organizations may decide to have multiple profiles that are aligned with different components or needs. Creating profiles and comparing the current versus the desired state may reveal gaps in cybersecurity risk management objectives.

System and Organization Controls (SOC)

Many organizations outsource non-value-added business processes, such as payroll, to third-party companies. Entrusting another organization with your critical data and business processes can increase your company's risk exposure. The risk is greater if the third-party organization does not follow appropriate internal controls and governance practices in its IT procedures. Any vulnerabilities and system failures at third-party organizations can also result in significant system downtime, loss of data, or security risk for your company.

Early on, the accounting profession realized that dependence on third parties for various services could impact the assurance of a company's financial performance. The American Institute of Certified Public Accountants (AICPA) recognized the importance of evaluating the IT environment at third-party service providers as part of assuring financial statements. Consequently, AICPA has developed audit and reporting protocols, called system and organization controls (SOC) reports, that help instill trust in the third-party services.[5] An independent public accounting firm prepares this report at the request of service organizations for distribution to its customers. There are three main types of SOC reports:

- **SOC 1.** A review of the internal controls of a service organization for financial reporting.
- **SOC 2.** A report on controls at a service organization relevant to trust services principles (TSP) of security, availability, processing integrity, confidentiality, or privacy.
- **SOC 3.** These are general-use reports that can be freely distributed to users who need assurance about the controls at a service organization but do not need the detailed SOC 2 report.

The SOC 2 report is the most relevant SOC report for technology. The SOC 2 report is based on trust services criteria, listed in Table A.3.

If your organization uses a third party to host data/applications or software, blockchain, cloud services, or credit card processing, consider obtaining a SOC 2 report.[6] However, when reviewing a SOC 2 report as a manager, remember that SOC 2 reports are based on management assertions. In other words, the service organization's management is responsible for selecting the trust services category or categories to be included in the report and setting the scope of the examination. The determination is based on the understanding of the user entities' needs. Consequently, SOC 2 reports do not specify

Table A.3   Trust Services Principles

Criteria	Description
Security	Controls to protect systems from unauthorized access, use, or damage. Protects the system through multiple logical and physical access controls.
Availability	Systems and data are available according to the objectives.
Processing Integrity	System processing is complete, valid, accurate, timely, and authorized to meet objectives.
Confidentiality	System protection is provided for confidential information. Typically, this is the organization's proprietary information, such as trade secrets, production plans, and so on.
Privacy	The system protects information deemed as private or personal to an individual or group. Examples include employee Social Security numbers or customer credit cards.

Source: AICPA. (n.d.). Trust Services and Information Integrity. https://us.aicpa.org/interestareas/frc/assuranceadvisoryservices/trustdataintegritytaskforce (accessed 31 March 2023).

a set of minimum controls suitable for a specific organization or industry sector. SOC examinations can address additional subject matters, such as HIPAA security measures. Other special SOC reports you may see are SOC for supply chain and SOC for cybersecurity.

SOC for cybersecurity differs from general SOC 2 reports in the following areas:

- **Scope.** SOC 2 reports' scope is limited to a defined service, whereas SOC for cybersecurity provides information about the organization's cybersecurity risk management program.
- **Intended audience.** SOC 2 reports are detailed audit reports. Generally, this report is an auditor-to-auditor (service organization's auditor to your company auditor) report. SOC for cybersecurity is appropriate for executive management as well as general stakeholders who have an interest in your cybersecurity risk management program.
- **Controls.** SOC 2 reports are based on one or more trust services principles, whereas SOC for cybersecurity may use other frameworks such as COBIT, NIST, or TSP.
- **Third-party risk.** SOC 2 reports can include or not include subservices of the third parties. SOC for cybersecurity does not allow for this flexibility.
- **Sensitive information.** SOC 2 reports contain detailed results of auditor's tests and controls, whereas SOC for cybersecurity does not.

Conclusion

As business professionals, it is important to be aware of these frameworks to appreciate the established IT controls and be responsible users of an organization's resources. Using one or more of these governance frameworks will help management properly oversee the implementation and long-term maintenance of the systems. The frameworks will help guide and align the organization's goals and objectives with the utilization of technologies. They can help better protect the organization from external and internal threats, which can compromise the security of the organization.

Additional Resources

AICPA System and Organization Controls: SOC Suite of Services, https://www.aicpa.org/resources/landing/system-and-organization-controls-soc-suite-of-services

COSO internal control integrated framework guidance, https://www.coso.org/sitepages/internal-control.aspx?web=1

COSO enterprise risk management guidance, https://www.coso.org/SitePages/Guidance-on-Enterprise-Risk-Management.aspx?web=1

COBIT 2019 Framework: Introduction and Methodology, available at: https://www.isaca.org/resources/cobit

National Institute of Standards and Technology Cybersecurity Framework, https://www.nist.gov/cyberframework

Notes

1. COSO. (2013). Internal Control – Integrated Framework. Executive Summary. Committee of Sponsoring Organizations of the Treadway Committee (May). https://www.coso.org/Shared%20Documents/Framework-Executive-Summary.pdf.
2. COSO. (2017). Enterprise Risk Management – Integrating with Strategy and Performance: Executive Summary. Committee of Sponsoring Organizations of the Treadway Committee. https://www.coso.org/Shared%20Documents/2017-COSO-ERM-Integrating-with-Strategy-and-Performance-Executive-Summary.pdf
3. ISACA. (2019). *COBIT 2019 Framework: Introduction and Methodology*. https://store.isaca.org/s/store#/store/browse/detail/a2S4w000004Ko9cEAC.
4. NIST. (2018). Framework for Improving Critical Infrastructure Cybersecurity. Version 1.1 (16 April). https://nvlpubs.nist.gov/nistpubs/CSWP/NIST.CSWP.04162018.pdf.
5. AICPA. (n.d.). System and Organization Controls: SOC Suite of Services. https://www.aicpa.org/resources/landing/system-and-organization-controls-soc-suite-of-services.
6. Halterman, C., and Houtekamer, D. (2021). Are You Measuring Everything You Need to Build Trust? System and Organization Controls (SOC). SOC 2 – SOC for Service Organization: Trust Services Criteria. EY (March). https://assets.ey.com/content/dam/ey-sites/ey-com/en_gl/topics/consulting/ey-soc-thought-leadership-client-brouchure.pdf.

ABOUT THE AUTHORS

Nishani Vincent, PhD, CGMA, ACMA, is the Joseph F. Decosimo and UC Foundation Associate Professor of Accounting at the University of Tennessee at Chattanooga. Prior to her academic career, she worked as an information systems consultant. Her research interests in IT governance and risk management stem from her professional experience in system implementations in a variety of industries. At UTC, she teaches undergraduate and graduate Accounting Information Systems classes. She has published in the *Journal of Information Systems*, the *International Journal of Accounting Information Systems*, *Issues in Accounting Education*, *Current Issues in Auditing*, the *International Journal of Accounting and Information Management*, and *Strategic Finance*, among other publications. She is a member of the American Accounting Association, the Chartered Institute of Management Accountants U.K., and ISACA.

Amy Igou, PhD, CMA, is the Halverson Associate Professor at the University of Northern Iowa and the director of the Master of Accounting program. Before her academic career, she worked at a manufacturing corporation for 19 years, mostly in financial systems. At UNI, she teaches Accounting Information Systems, Business Analytics for Accountants, and Fraud Analytics. Her research interests include using emerging technologies in the classroom and the profession. She has published in the *Journal of Emerging Technologies in Accounting*, the *Journal of Accounting Education*, the *Strategic Finance Journal*, the *CPA Journal*, and the *Business Process Management Journal*. She is a Certified Management Accountant and a long-time member of the Institute of Management Accountants, where she has received the Platinum Service Award.

ABOUT THE WEBSITE

The companion website with instructional material for *Emerging Technologies for Business Professionals* can be found at www.wiley.com\go\vincent\emerging technologies. The companion website provides the following resources for individual chapters.

- Chapter Learning Objectives
- Powerpoint Slides
- Multiple Choice Questions
- Discussion Questions

In addition to the chapter resources, the companion website includes a sample syllabus containing course learning objectives, a schedule, and a course grading rubric.

INDEX

Page numbers followed by *f* and *t* refer to figures and tables, respectively.

A

AARI, 169
Accessibility:
  of AR with smartphone, 221*t*
  of Automation Anywhere
    software, 118
  of computer system resources, 239
  of data, 22, 54
  in data lakes, 38
  of DLT, 169
  evaluating, 231
  of quantum computers, 201–202, 208
  of user access controls, 254–255
Accounting, 173–174, 238, 265, 277
  AI use in, 82
  blockchain-based, 137
  data analytics for, 47
Accuracy:
  of AI models, 73, 75, 90I, 92,
    96–98, 100
  of biometric authentication, 256
  of bots, 164, 187
  of data, 22, 30, 56, 133
  evaluating, 173
  as performance measure, 75, 195*t*
  in smart contracts, 131, 144
Active World, 148
Address resolution protocol (ARP), 244*t*
Advanced Computing, 11
Airbnb, 3
AIRS, 99
Alantra, 168
Alexa, 10, 72, 81*t*
Alibaba, 3
Align, plan, and organize
  (APO), 273, 274*t*
Alternative Airlines, 107
Alteryx, 45

Amazon, 78, 101, 103, 144
Amazon Braket, 206–207
Amazon Web Services (AWS), 207
American Institute of Certified Public
  Accountants (AICPA),
  261–262, 277, 279
Amoral computing, 16–17
ANNs (artificial neural
  networks), 79, 79*f*
Anonymity, 110–111, 121
Anti-money laundering (AML) laws, 174
Apache Foundation, 46
Apache Spark, 46–47
Apartheid law, 16
Apple, 66, 87
Application security, 258
Application software, 238
Arcadia Earth, 219
ARP (address resolution protocol), 244*t*
Artificial intelligence (AI):
  benefits of, 90–91
  biases in, 102–103
  building, 73–74
  as cybersecurity trend, 246
  definition of, 10, 72–73
  ethical considerations for, 101–104
  factors in failure of, 90*t*
  governance and management
    of, 98–101
  implementation framework for,
    88–92
  implementation lifecycle of, 92–98
  legal implications of, 103–104
  platforms for, 81
  risks of, 91–92, 102*f*
  RPA vs, 164–165
  types of, 74–81
  use cases for, 82–84

Artificial neural networks
  (ANNs), 79, 79*f*
Asymmetric encryption, 114, 115*f.*
  See also Encryption; Public-key
  encryption
Augmented intelligence, 73, 88
Augmented reality (AR):
  challenges of, 226–229
  characteristics of, 221
  definition of, 12–13
  equipment for, 222–223
  history of, 221–222
  management of, 229–231
  use cases for, 225–226
  user interactions with, 223–225
  virtual reality vs, 221*t*
Aural UI, 224
Australian Financial Review, 15
Authentication:
  biometric, 225
  in blockchains, 129*t*
  as control activity, 268
  encryption as, 120
  in information systems, 255
  multifactor, 225
  multimodal, 225–226
  in network layer, 142, 257–258
  security threats to, 154
Authorization, 112, 256–258
Automated processes, 64, 179–180, 184,
  192, 194. *See also* Bots; Robots
Automation, *see* Robotic Process
  Automation (RPA)
Automation 360, 169
Automation Anywhere, 165,
  169–170, 172
Automation Anywhere University,
  169–170, 177
Automation bias, *see* Bias
Availability:
  of AR devices, 226
  in bot creation, 187
  in cloud computing, 139
  cybersecurity and, 209, 246
  of data in network security, 256
  in distributed ledger technology, 119

in edge computing, 213–214
in RPA performance, 195
in smart contracts, 131
system and organization
  controls and, 277
Avalanche (AVX), 110*f*
Aviatrade, 107
Avita Health Systems, 233
Axie Infinity Marketplace, 157

B

BAI (build, acquire, and implement), 273
BakerySwap, 157
Balanced Scorecard Method, 195*t*
Banco Pichincha, 233
Bandwidth, 120, 151, 213
Banksy, 107
Bias:
  in AI applications, 102–103
  in AI failure, 90*t*
  automation, 103
  confirmation, 103
  data, 24, 67–68, 91, 94–96, 101, 103
  of managers, 18
  sampling, 103
  stereotype, 24
  types of, 103
Bieber, Justin, 159
Big data, 29–32, 30*f*, 32*f*
Binance, 135–136, 156–157
Binance (BNB), 110*f*
Binance USD (BUSD), 110*f*
Biometrics, 151, 255–256
BitCars, 107
Bitcoin (BTC), 110*f*
  acceptance of, 107, 156
  decentralized nature of, 10, 118
  history of, 108–109
  mining of, 113
  as permissionless blockchain, 129
  popularity of, 110
  proof of work and, 121
  use of, 124–125
  wallets, 112
Bitcoin Cash, 156
Bitgild, 107

Black-box effect, 20
Blbajari, Marcelo, 179
BleachBit, 246
Blockbuster, 1–2
Blockchain(s):
  coalitions of, 136, 136f, 139–141, 143
  companies invested in, 137f
  consortiums, 130, 136, 136f, 139–141
  cryptocurrency and, 108, 111
  definition of, 10, 113–114
  federated, 130
  future trends of, 144–145
  in gaming, 128
  governance and management
    of, 139–144
  history of, 108–109, 109t
  hybrid, 129–130, 136
  layers of, 128
  permissioned, 129–130, 129t, 136, 145
  permissionless, 129–130, 129t, 136
  properties of, 114–124
  in quantum computing, 11
  top platforms of, 138t
  types of, 129–132
  use cases of, 137–139
Blockchain 2.0, 109t
Block-creation interval, 120
Block hashes, 123–124
BlueMail, 87
Blue Prism, see SS&C Blue Prism
Blue Prism University, 177
Boeing, 222
Boston College, 51
Bots, 87, 165–168. See also Automated
    processes; Robots
  attended, 168
  creating, 187
  design and building of, 11, 172–173,
    185–186
  developers of, 170
  as document processors, 173
  sample flowchart of, 186f
  as tracking devices, 177
  unattended, 168
Bot Insight, 169
Botnets, 244t

Bot Store, 169
Brute force attacks, 244t, 259
Build, acquire, and implement
    (BAI), 273, 274t
Buterin, Vitalik, 109t
Buy-in, 9, 89–90, 181–182, 197

C
California Consumer Privacy Act
    (CCPA), 65, 236
CAN (computer area network), 238
Cardano (ADA), 110f
Cashing services, 244t
Caudell, Thomas, 222
CCPA (California Consumer Privacy
    Act), 65, 236
Center of excellence (COE), 193
Centralized networks, see Networks,
    centralized
Chacko, Mathew, 51
Chainlink (LINK), 110f
Change management:
  controls, 258, 268
  in failed AI projects, 90t
  in failed RPA projects, 182t
  risks of, 7t, 196–197
  in RPA development, 190, 192
Chatbots, 3, 72, 80, 83, 87
ChatGPT, 87
Chia, Stan, 27
Chief information security officers
    (CISOs), 250
Chief risk officers (CROs), 250
Classification models, 42, 76
ClearProg, 246
Cloud computing, 153, 169–171,
    212–214, 213f, 230, 237–238, 272
Cloudera, 46
Cloud services, 210, 212–214,
    239, 246, 277
Clustering, 41, 47, 77
CNN, 87
COBIT framework, 6, 192, 251,
    271–273, 274t, 278–279
Coca-Cola, 51
Coding-Required Tools, 45–46

COE (center of excellence), 193
Coinbase Wallet, 157. *See also* Crypto
  wallets; Digital wallets
CoinMarketCap, 134
Cointelegraph, 127
Colonial Pipeline, 233
Computer area network (CAN), 238
Computer-enabled oracles, *see* Oracles
Computer vision, 80–82
Computing, conventional, 202–204
Confirmation bias, *see* Bias
Confusion matrix, 97
Consensus Algorithms, 125, 129*t*
  in blockchains, 108, 114
  in hybrid blockchains, 130
  proof-of- stake, 135
  in protocol layer, 141
  in quantum computing, 207
  types of, 121–123
Control activities, 267*t*, 268–269
Control environments, 265–266, 267*t*
The Conversation, 15
Co-occurrence groups, 41
Corrective controls, 241–242,
  253, 260–261
Cosmos (ATOM), 110*f*, 157
COSO ERM framework, 265–271, 266*f*,
  267*t*, 270*f*, 271*t*, 279
COVID-19 pandemic, 72, 243
CRM, *see* Customer relationship
  management
CROs (chief risk officers), 250
Cross-chain oracles, *see* Oracles
Crossing the Chasm (Moore), 28
Cryptocurrency:
  acceptance of, 107, 145
  characteristics of, 110–111
  definition of, 109–110
  developments in, 202
  example of, 124–125
  in gaming, 128
  governance and management of, 144
  history of, 108–109, 109*t*
  marketplaces, 156–157
  NFTs and, 158
  popular, 110*f*

  proof of stake and, 121
  staking, 135–136
  transactions, 112–113
  wallets, 134–135, 157–158
Cryptocurrency exchanges,
  see Exchanges
Cryptokitties, 127
CryptoPunks, 107, 157
Crypto wallets, 134–135, 157–158. *See
  also* Coinbase wallet; Digital wallets
Customer analysis, 47
Customer relationship management
  (CRM), 175, 184, 238
Cyberattacks:
  in augmented reality, 230
  corrective controls for, 260
  data management and, 239
  disruptive nature of, 235
  in Ecuador, 233
  execution of, 243
  management of, 241, 253
  myths around, 240*t*
  from quantum computing, 209
  risk management of, 91
  strategies against, 250–252
  strategies used for, 244*t*
  toolsets for, 246
  vulnerability to, 4, 215
Cybercriminals, 234–237, 240*t*, 242, 250,
  253, 255–256, 261
Cyber-Partisans, 233
Cybersecurity:
  in advanced computing, 12
  in augmented reality, 229
  challenges of, 235–237
  COBIT framework and, 272
  controls, 253–261
  definition of, 234–235
  domains, 237–239
  governance and management
    of, 251–252
  incidences of, 233
  management over, 240–241
  myths about, 240*t*
  NIST framework and, 275
  quantum computing use in, 207–209

reporting of, 261–262
resources for, 279
strategy, 249, 250–251
system and organization
    controls, 277–278
trends, 246–247
Cybersecurity Law (People's Republic of
    China), 236

D
DAI, 110*f,* 156
Dashboards, 41, 41*f,* 56, 164
Data analytics:
    best practices for, 52–53
    descriptive, 39–40, 58
    diagnostic, 40–42
    ethical considerations for, 67–68
    implementation of, 53–56
    predictive, 42–43
    prescriptive, 43
    process of, 56–59
    quality of, 43, 53, 58–61, 60*f,* 94, 98
    tools for, 44–47
    types of, 39–43
    use cases for, 47–48
Data and Analytics Big Idea
    Initiative, 51
Data bias, *see* Bias
Data breaches, 65, 234–235, 247
Data collection:
    by bots, 164
    in edge computing, 202
    ethical considerations for, 66–68
    governance of, 61
    hardware for, 215
    in metaverse, 151
    preparing for, 96
    with RPA, 57
Data distribution, 40, 77, 201
Data Governance Institute, 61
Data lakes, 37–38, 55
Data layer of blockchain, 128,
    132, 142–143
Data marts, 38
Data privacy, 21, 64–65, 210, 215
Data queries, 40
Data reductions, *see* Filtering

Data storage:
    in AR, 226
    in blockchains, 113–114
    comparisons of, 38*t*
    in computer networks, 237
    costs of, 64
    in data warehouses, 37, 54
    in flat files, 32
    improper use of, 230
    in in-memory databases, 35–36
    maintainance of, 56
    in quantum computing, 202
    in relational databases, 33–34
Data swamps, 38
Data visualization, 31, 41, 44–46
Data warehouses, 36–38, 36*f,* 53–56, 58,
    61, 63, 94
Davos, Switzerland, 71, 91
DDoS (distributed denial-of-service)
    attacks, 244*t*
Decentralized networks, *see* Networks,
    decentralized
Decision support systems (DSSs), 43, 273
Decision trees, 42
Decoherence, 205
Defense in depth, 241, 257
Delayed proof of work (dPoW), 122
Delegated proof of stake (DPoS), 122.
    See also Proof of stake (PoS)
Deliver, service, and support
    (DSS), 273, 274*t*
Deloitte, 165
Denial-of-service (DoS) attacks, 244*t*
Denison Yachting, 107
Department of Health and Human
    Services, 164
Detective controls, 241–242, 252–253, 258
Development flexibility, 120
DevOps, 272
Diagnosis, 84
Digital disruption:
    cybersecurity and, 234–235
    examples of, 1–2, 233
    impact of, 2–4
    planning for, 261
    in quantum computing, 203, 205
    risks of, 7*t*

Digital divide, 68
Digital wallets, 109–114, 124, 144. *See also* Coinbase Wallet; Crypto wallets
Dimension reduction, 77–78
Dines, Daniel, 170
Distributed denial-of-service (DDoS) attacks, 244*t*
Distributed ledger technology (DLT), 118–121, 119*f*
DNS (domain name system), 244*t*
Dogecoin (DOGE), 110*f*
DoS (denial-of-service) attacks, 244*t*
DPoS (delegated proof of stake), 122
dPoW (delayed proof of work), 122
Drilling down, 40–41
DSSs (decision support systems), 43, 273
Dumpster diving, 243
Dungeons and Dragons, 48
D-Wave, 205

E
Eavesdropping, 243
Edge computing:
   cloud computing vs, 212–214, 213*f*
   conventional computing vs, 202–203
   definition of, 202
   example of, 210–211
   explanation of, 211
   in IoT, 11, 212
   use cases of, 214–216
EDM (evaluate, direct, and monitor), 273
EGIT (enterprise governance of IT), 272–273
Emerging technology, impact of, 2–4
Encryption:
   asymmetric, 115*f*
   in blockchains, 108, 114–116, 138
   as control activity, 268
   as property of DLT, 120
   public-key, 116, 116*f*
   in quantum computing, 207–208
   in RPA lifecycle, 197*f*
   in smart contracts, 131
Endpoint security, 258
End-users:

analytic tools for, 28, 44–45, 53–56
COBIT framework and, 42
cybersecurity for, 239
data analytic tools for, 10
in data lakes, 37
in data marts, 38
diagnostic tools for, 2
expectations of, 9
interface for, 93
oversight for, 179
in RPA projects, 11, 164–166, 182*t*, 191
software tools for, 42, 238
training for, 94
Enterprise governance of IT (EGIT), 272–273
Enterprise resource planning (ERP) systems:
   blockchain relation to, 141
   data analytics and, 28, 30
   data quality and, 59
   risks of, 7–8
   RPA and, 11, 164–165, 173
   software, 238
Equal Credit Opportunity Act, 103–104
Ethereum (ETH), 107, 109, 110*f*, 127, 156–158
Ethics (ethical issues):
   in AI, 88, 94–95, 100–102
   in AR, 228–229
   of artificial intelligence (AI), 101–104
   blockchain governance and, 140
   in COBIT framework, 270
   in COSO framework, 267*t*, 270
   of cybersecurity reporting, 261
   of data analytics, 67–68
   of data government, 64–68
   data-related factors of, 19
   in edge computing, 215
   framework for IT, 23–24
   in hacking, 258
   IT-related, 21–23
   of metaverse, 154, 159–160
   of non-fungible tokens (NFTs), 159–160
   people-related factors of, 20–21

in RPAs, 191, 198–199
systems-related factors of, 20
ETL (extract, transform, load), 36–37, 45
European Mint, 107
Evaluate, direct, and monitor
    (EDM), 273, 274*t*
Eve Online, 128
Exchanges, 124, 128, 133–136, 134*t*,
    151, 156, 158
EY, 56, 203

F

Facebook, 147
Facial recognition technology (FRT), 15
Fair Credit Reporting Act, 66
Fair Housing Act, 103–104
Family Educational Rights and Privacy
    Act (FERPA), 66
FASB (Financial Accounting Standards
    Board), 60
FCDO (Foreign, Commonwealth, and
    Development Office), 233
FDA (Food and Drug
    Administration), 163–164
Federal Trade Commission, 65
Feedback loops, 67
File Management, 166
Filtering, 30, 40, 256–257
Financial Accounting Standards Board
    (FASB), 60
Finney, Harold Thomas, II, 109*t*
5G networks, 151, 207, 211, 246
Flat files, 32, 32*f*, 34, 63
Food and Drug Administration
    (FDA), 163–164
Forecast generation, 82
Foreign, Commonwealth, and
    Development Office (FCDO), 233
Fortnite, 148
Foundation (NFT marketplace), 157
FRT (facial recognition technology), 15

G

Gartner, 2, 52
Gates, Bill, 170
Gaze tracking, 224

"The Gender Divide" (PYMNTS
    study), 87
General Data Protection Regulation
    (GDPR), 21, 62, 65, 236
General Electric Co., 211
Gesture recognition, 224
Golden State Warriors, 27
Google, 15
Google Cloud AI, 81*t*
Governance and management. *See also*
    IT governance
    of AI, 98–101
    of blockchain, 139–144
    of cryptocurrency, 144
    of cybersecurity, 251–252
    of smart contracts, 143–144
Gramm Leach Bliley Act, 66
Grande, Ariana, 159
Graph databases, 34, 63
Graphical user interface (GUI),
    165–166, 168
GSM, 201
Gucci, 107

H

Haber, Stuart, 109*t*
Habitat (gaming platform), 148
Hacking:
    of AR systems, 229
    block hashes and, 124
    cryptocurrency and, 113
    edge computing and, 214
    ethical, 258
    opportunities for, 236
    preventive controls against,
        253–255, 257–260
    quantum computing and, 202
    reports of, 233
    risk assessment of, 268
    techniques of, 242–246,
        244*t*–245*t*
    of wallets, 135
Hadoop, 46–47
Hadoop Distributed File System
    (HDFS), 46
Haptic UI, 224

Hardware wallets, 135. *See also*
    Crypto wallets
Harvard Business Review, 64
Hash functions, 116
HDFS (Hadoop Distributed File
    System), 46
Healthcare, 84
Health Insurance Portability and
    Accounting Act (HIPAA), 66
Hershey's, 8
Hess, Nicolas, 168
Hidden structures, 17
Hortonworks, 46
Host intrusion detection systems, 259
Human resources, 48, 83

I
IBM, 71–72, 144, 203, 235
IBM Quantum Experience, 206
IBM Watson Studio, 81*t*
IDS (intrusion detection
    systems), 259–260
IKEA, 219
Image analysis, 84
Immutability, 123–124, 137
Inc., 21
Information Technology (IT):
    ethical framework for, 23–24
    risks of, 7*t*
In-memory databases, 34–36
Input oracles, *see* Oracles
Instacart, 87
Institutionalization, 121
Integration:
    in AI, 73, 88
    of bias, 103
    of bots, 87, 197*t*
    of COBIT framework, 271–272
    of complex systems, 20
    of COSO framework, 266*f*, 267*t*, 279
    of data, 36–37, 82, 151
    deep-learning, 81*t*
    in end-user analytics tools, 44, 46
    of reality in metaverse, 148
    of RPA tools, 169, 172,
        175–176, 193, 196
    in smart contracts, 131

via AR, 221–223, 226–227, 230
Intellectual property, 21–22, 140. *See also*
    Property rights
Internet of Things (IoT):
    connectivity of, 236, 246
    data collection from, 19
    definition of, 211–212
    edge computing use in, 11, 207, 211
    latency in, 211–212
    in manufacturing, 214
    in metaverse, 151
    in protocol layer, 141
    quantum computing use in, 202
Internet Protocol (IP), 243, 244*t*, 259
Interoperable networks, 149
Intrusion detection systems
    (IDS), 259–260
Inventory counting, 82
IonQ, 206
IoT, *see* Internet of Things
IP, *see* Internet Protocol
ISACA, 271
IT, *see* Information Technology
IT Convergence, 179
IT governance, 5. *See also* Governance
    and management
    in COBIT framework, 265–266
    in COSO framework, 265–266
    definition of, 5

J
James, LeBron, 156
Jeopardy (TV show), 72
Joyce, Thomas, 5
JPMorgan Chase, 87

K
Karma Automotive, 107
Kernel PCA, 78
Keyes, Jim, 2
Kim, Y.-G., 151–152
Kishino, Fumio, 220
Knight Capital Americas LLC, 5
KnownOrigin, 157
Know Your Customer (KYC)
    laws, 174
Konst, Stefan, 109*t*

L

LANs (local area networks), 238, 258
Larva Labs, 157
Latency, 35, 120, 213
Layered security, 257
Lead generation, 82, 175.
    See also Marketing
Learning:
    deep, 71, 74, 78–80
    reinforcement, 78
    semi-supervised, 78
    supervised, 75–76, 76*f*
    unsupervised, 77–78, 77*f*
Learning RPA, 177
Ledger Nano X, 135, 157
Lidl, 8
Linux, 238
Litecoin (LTC), 110*f*
Local area networks (LANs), 238
Logical access controls, 255
Logic bombs, 245*t*
Los Angeles Lakers, 27
Lucerne University, 107

M

Machine learning (ML), 99
    in advanced computing, 11
    AI and, 71–72, 81*t*, 145, 246
    Apache Spark and, 46–47
    in complex systems, 20
    deep learning vs, 78–79
    in IoT, 212
    in prescriptive analytics, 43
    Qlik Sense and, 44
    in quantum computing, 207
    RPA and, 173
    SPA and, 172
    types of, 74–78, 75*f*
McKinsey, 164
macOS, 238
Malware:
    anti-virus software for, 240*t*, 258
    development by AI, 246
    evolution of, 259–260
    in mobile devices, 236
    use of, by hackers, 242–243, 245*t*, 255

Manutiu, Sven, 168
MapR, 46
MapReduce, 46
Marketing. *See also* Lead generation
    personalized, 47
    strategies of, 27
    use of advanced analytics in, 4
    viral, 27
Masking, 67
Massively multiplayer online games
    (MMOs), 127–128
Matplotlib (library), 46
MEA (monitor, evaluate, and assess), 273
"The Merge" (NFT by Pak), 157
Merkel root, 123–124
Merkel trees, 109*t*, 116–117
Meta, 147
MetaMask, 157
Metaverse:
    architecture of, 152*f*
    building blocks of, 150–153
    challenges of, 154
    definition of, 148
    ethical Issues of, 159–160
    major elements of, 149
    NFT economy and, 158–160
    three phases of, 148–150
Microsoft, 144, 171, 233–234
Microsoft Azure AI, 81*t*
Microsoft Excel, 11, 45, 99, 123,
    164–166, 187–188
Microsoft Flow, 156–157, 171
Microsoft Learn, 177
Microsoft Power Automate, 171–172
Microsoft PowerBI, 41, 44
Microsoft Powertools, 171
Microsoft Threat Intelligence
    Center, 234
Milgram, Paul, 220
Milgram's Reality–Virtuality
    Continuum, 220*f*
Minecraft, 148
Mintable, 157
MIT Sloan Management Review, 51
Mizell, David, 222
ML, *see* Machine learning

MML Capital, 168
MMOs (massively multiplayer online games), 127–128
Model fit, 97–98, 98f
Modularizing, 18
Monitor, evaluate, and assess (MEA), 273, 274t
Monitoring, continuous, 258, 260, 269
Monte Carlo simulations, 207
Moore, Geoffrey, 28
Mow, Samson, 128
Mundie, Craig, 28
Myth Market, 157

N

Nakamoto, Satoshi, 108, 109t
Natural language processing (NLP), 74, 80, 83, 172
NBA Top Shot, 156
Netflix, 1–2, 78
Network intrusion detection systems, 259
Network layer of blockchain, 79, 128, 142
Networks, centralized:
  crypto exchanges and, 133
  data analysis of, 53–54
  decentralized networks vs, 117–119, 118f
  digital currencies as, 111
  DPoS as, 122
  in manufacturing, 214–215
  PoA as, 123
  in RPA projects, 191
  vulnerability of, 7
Networks, decentralized, 117–118
  blockchain as, 10, 114
  centralized networks vs, 117–119, 118f
  consortium blockchains as, 130
  crypto exchanges and, 133
  data analysis of, 53–54
  in DLT design, 120
  example of, 124
  metaverse and, 153
  of oracles, 133
  peer-to-peer, 111

  in permissionless versus permissioned blockchains, 129t
  in RPA projects, 191
Network security, 256–258
Network segmentation, 257
New World Inc., 219
NFTs, see Non-fungible tokens
Nifty Gateway, 157, 159
NIST cybersecurity framework, 251–252, 275–276, 278
NLP, see Natural language processing
Non-fungible tokens (NFTs):
  advantages of, 155–156
  creating, 157–158
  definition of, 154–155
  economy of, 158–160
  ethical Issues of, 159–160
  marketplaces, 156–157
  types of, 155
Nreal, 219
NumPy (library), 45–46

O

OCR (optical character recognition), 173, 177
Oculus, 11, 226
Off-White, 107
Online wallets, 134. See also Crypto wallets
OpenAI, 87
OpenSea, 127, 156
Optical character recognition (OCR), 173, 177
Optimization models, 43
Oracles, 10, 132–133, 141–142, 144, 238
Outliers, detecting, 41, 47, 56, 58, 82
Output oracles, see Oracles
Oxford Quantum Circuits, 206

P

Packet filtering, see Filtering
Pak (digital artist), 157
PalmPilot, 222
PAN (personal area network), 238
Pandas (library), 45–46
Paper wallets, 135. See also Crypto wallets

Parent hashes, 124
Parizher, Vadim, 210–211
Park, S.-M., 151–151
Pavilions Hotels, 107
Penetration testing, 258–259
Perimeter defense, 256–257
Personal identification number
 (PINs), 255–156
Personally identifiable information
 (PII), 234–235
Phillips auction house, 107
Phishing, 244*t*
Piggybacking, 244*t*
PINs (personal identification
 number), 255–156
Ping sweeps, 243
Pixelmatic, 128
Pokémon Go, 223, 228
Polkadot (DOT), 110*f*, 157
Polygon (MATIC), 110*f*
Poly Network, 233
Port scans, 243
PowerQuery, 45
Predictive maintenance, 47–48
Preventive controls, 241–242,
 253–255, 258
Preventive maintenance, 83
Principal component analysis (PCA), 78
Privacy:
 in AI, 100
 in AR, 228–229
 in bots, 187
 cryptocurrency and, 113
 of data, 64–65, 68
 data regulation of, 215
 ethics and, 21–22
 in immersive technologies, 231
 laws, 66
 in metaverse, 153–154, 160
 quantum computing and, 202, 210
 of stakeholders, 239
 in trust services principles,
 277–278, 278*t*
Privacy Eraser, 246
Private-key encryption, 115–116, 115*f*,
 116*f*, 124, 134–135, 157. *See also*
 Encryption

Process discovery, 169
Production optimization, 48
Proof of authority (PoA), 123
Proof of elapsed time (PoET), 122
Proof of stake (PoS), 109, 121–122, 135
Proof of work (PoW), 109, 121–122
Proof of work mining (PoW),
 113, 121–122
Propagation delay, 120
Property rights, 22, 137. *See also*
 Intellectual property
Protocol layer of blockchain,
 128, 141–142
Public-key encryption, 114–116, 115*f*,
 116*f*, 124, 134–134, 144. *See also*
 Asymmetric encryption; Encryption
Pure Spirits, 219
PwC, 72, 235
PYMNTS, 87
Python, 44, 45–46, 206

Q
Qiskit, 206–207
Qlik Sense, 44
Quality checks, 83
Quantum computing, 11, 151
 about, 204
 architecture of, 205–206
 definition of, 202
 governance and management
 of, 208–210
 history of, 203–204
 limitations of, 204–205
 service providers, 206–207
 used cases of, 207–208
Quantum Informatics National Lab, 201
Quantum key distribution, 201
Quarantining, 260
Qubits, 204–206, 208

R
Random-access memory
 (RAM), 34–35, 46
Ransbotham, Sam, 51
Ransomware, 233, 245*t*
Ransomware-as-a-service, 246
Rarible, 156

Real-time rendering, 149
Real-time strategy (RTS), 127–128
Recruiting, 83
Redbox, 2
REEDS Jewellers, 107
Regression, 42, 76–77
Relational databases, 10, 32–35, 33*f*, 63, 123
Resume scanning, 83
Return on investment (ROI), 174, 195
Rigetti processor, 206
Risk Assessment, 267*t*, 268
Roberts, Simon, 168
Roblox, 148
Robots. *See also* Automated processes; Bots
  as automated processes, 179
  employee tracking by, 177
  ethical issues with, 198
  in healthcare, 214
  personal, 170
  security and, 172
  use of UiPath platform in, 170
Robotics, 163, 211
Robotic process automation (RPA):
  bots in, 167–168
  creation of, 165–166
  definition of, 11
  development of, 192–193
  effect of, on business, 164–165
  ethics and, 198–199
  example of, 163–164
  failure of, 182*t*
  framework of, 180–182
  future trends of, 172–173
  governance and management of, 191–199
  impact of, 2
  life cycle of, 182–190
  objectives of, 191–192
  performance of, 194–195, 195*t*
  resources for, 177
  risks and controls of, 196–198, 197*t*
  software applications of, 169–172
  as type of AI, 74
  use cases of, 173–177

Roboyo, 168
Rometty, Ginni, 71–72
Rootkits, 246
RPA, *see* Robotic process automation
RPA Workspace, 169
R programming language, 44, 46
Rstudio, 46
RTS (real-time strategy), 127–128

S
Salesforce Einstein, 81*t*
Sampling bias, *see* Bias
SAP, 238
SAS (Statistical Analysis System), 45
Scott, Travis, 159
Scrapy (library), 46
Second Life, 148
Securities and Exchange Commission (SEC), 5, 263
Security, *see* Cybersecurity
Service operations, 48, 174–175
Service providers:
  for edge computing, 215–216
  as end-users, 239
  ethical issues and, 20
  for oracles, 144
  for quantum computing, 206
  security measures of, 237
  SOC reports on, 262, 277
Shiba Inu (SHIB), 110
Shor, Peter, 203
Siemens AG, 211
Silver bullet, 9
Singapore Model AI Governance Framework, 91
Siri, 10, 73
SITs (system integration tests), 189
SITA Passenger Service System (US) Inc., 234
Smart contracts, 108, 120
  advantages of, 131–133
  as blockchain development, 10
  in data layer, 141–142
  definition of, 130–131
  developments in, 132–133
  future trends of, 144–145

in gaming, 127
governance and management
of, 143–144
in NFTs, 155–156
in protocol layer, 141
uses of, 137, 139
Smart process automation (SPA), 172
Smishing, 244*t*
Snapchat, 219
Snow Crash (Stephenson), 147
SOC, *see* System and
organization controls
Social Engineering, 237, 242–244,
254
Solana (SOL), 110*f*
Spear phishing, 244*t*
Speech recognition, 224
Spiewak, Stephen, 28
Spoofing, 244*t*
SS&C Blue Prism, 170–172
Stadtmueller, Lynda, 210
Stakeholders, 4, 6–9, 12
AI effect on, 88, 94, 99
of blockchain, 122, 130
buy-in from, 89, 90*t*, 197, 197*t*
communicating to, 53, 270, 275
cybersecurity and, 234, 236,
252–253, 261–262
data collection of, 22, 239
ethics and, 16–17, 198
input from, 63
involvement of, 184
needs of, 52, 57, 62, 274
providing value to, 272
quantum computing and, 209
in RPA projects, 190, 194
Staking, 135–136
Star Alliance members, 234
Statista, 107
Statistical Analysis System (SAS), 45
Stephen Silver Fine Jewelry, 107
Stephenson, Neal, 147
Stornetta, W. Scott, 109*t*
Summary statistics, 40
SuperRare, 157
Sutherland, Ivan, 222

Symmetric encryption, 115*f. See also*
Encryption
System and organization controls
(SOC), 101, 277–280
System integration, 20
System integration tests (SITs), 189
System software, 238
Szabo, Nick, 109*t*

T
Taabo Imports, 107
Tableau, 41, 44, 54
Taco Bell, 210
Tailgating, 244*t*
Tangible UI, 224
Technological imperative, 17
Technological inertia, 17
TensorFlow, 81*t*
Tether (USDT), 110*f*
Tethys Solutions, 169
Tezos, 156–157
Theta Drop, 157
3D pointing, 224
Throughput, 120, 195*f*
Time series modeling, 42
Tokens, *See* Non-fungible tokens (NFTs)
Torres-Rivera, Sahra, 163–164
Transaction hashing, 123
Transaction validation speed, 120
Travala.com, 107
Trojan horses, 245*t*
TRON (TRX), 110*f*
Trust services principles (TSP),
277–278, 278*t*
Turing, Alan, 72
Tyler, Jay, 164

U
Uber, 3
Ubisoft, 128
UiPath, 170–171
UiPath Academic Alliance, 177
UiPath Studio, 167*f*
UiPath StudioX, 167*f*
Uniswap (UNI), 110*f*
University of Nicosia, 107

Usability, 120, 138
USB keys, 255
USD Coin (USDC), 110*f*, 156
User access, 34, 254
Utah Jazz, 27

V
Viacom, 1
Virtual reality (VR), 11–12, 151, 158,
    219–222, 221*t*, 226, 229
Virtual reality headsets, 151, 220–221,
    221*t*, 223
Viruses, 245*t*, 260
Vishing, 244*t*
Visual UI, 224
Vivid Seats, 27
VLOOKUP, 187
Voigt, Christian, 168
Volkswagen USA, 234
VR, *see* Virtual reality

W
Walkman, 222
Wall Street Journal, 87, 163, 210
WANs (wide area networks), 258
Watson supercomputer, 72
Whaling, 244*t*

Wide area networks (WANs), 258
Windows, 238
Wipe, 246
Wireless local area networks
    (WLANs), 238
"With Big Data Comes Big
    Responsibility" (*Harvard Business
    Review* article), 64
WLANs (wireless local area
    networks), 238
WorkFusion, 172
World Economic Conference (2017),
    71
World Economic Forum, 91, 209
Worms, 245*t*

X
XRP, 110*f*

Y
Yacht Break, 107
Yum Brands Inc., 210

Z
Zero-trust frameworks, 257
Zombie computers, 244*t*
Zuckerberg, Mark, 147